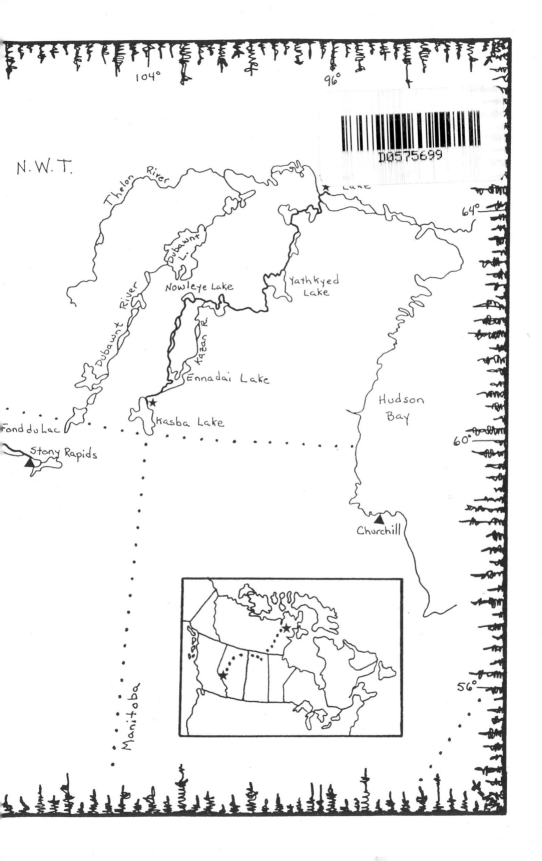

N.W.T.

Thelon River

Dubawnt L.

Nowleye Lake

Dubawnt River

Yathkyed Lake

Kazan R.

Ennadai Lake

Fond du Lac

Kasba Lake

Stony Rapids

Hudson Bay

Lake

64°

60°

56°

Churchill

Manitoba

104°   96°

GOING INSIDE

GOING INSIDE

*A Couple's Journey of Renewal
into the North*

ALAN S. KESSELHEIM

M&S

Canadian Cataloguing in Publication Data
Kesselheim, Alan S.
Going inside: a couple's journey of renewal into the north

ISBN 0-7710-4450-X

1. Kesselheim, Alan S., 1952-   – Journeys – Canada, Northern.   2. Zitzer, Marypat – Journeys – Canada, Northern.   3. Canoes and canoeing – Canada, Northern. 4. Canada, Northern – Description and travel.   I. Title.

FC3963.K47 1995   917.1904'3   C95-930728-1
FI090.5.K47 1995

Typesetting by M&S

Endpaper map by Marypat Zitzer

Lines on page 160 by Robert Service are from "The Spell of the Yukon" in *The Complete Poems of Robert Service*, New York, Dodd, Mead, 1940 (reprint of 1907 ed.).

Excerpts on pages 224-5 and 258-9 by Thierry Mallet are from Farley Mowat, *Tundra*, Toronto, McClelland & Stewart, 1973, and were originally published in Thierry Mallet, *Glimpses of the Barren Lands*, New York, privately published, 1930.

Printed and bound in Canada on acid-free paper

McClelland & Stewart Inc.
The Canadian Publishers
481 University Avenue
Toronto, Ontario
M5G 2E9

1 2 3 4 5   99 98 97 96 95

To The Stowaway

When people who have been swallowed up in northern wilderness talk of returning to civilization, they say that they are going "Outside." It seems, at first, an ironic convolution of speech. After all, the boreal wilds are about as outside as you can get. Yet, the longer one is in the North, the more enfolded by the womb of wilderness one becomes, the more right and true it seems to think of yourself as inside in some primordial sense. All the hubbub and politicking and frantic activity of society, even your own existence there, appears increasingly strange, unruly, outside the boundaries of sane living.

Introduction

When we left our home in Montana for the headwaters of the Smoky River in Alberta, beginning a wild, watery journey that would last more than a year, Marypat and I were both in dire need. For the previous year we had accepted the drudgery and strain of preparing for the journey. We had dried mountains of food on our dehydrator, used up reams of paper in search of route descriptions, maps, and equipment sponsorship, and drawn our bank accounts down to nothing.

But trip logistics were the least of it. We had handled those dozens of times. Even the length of this journey wasn't unprecedented; five years earlier we had navigated a parallel route, spent a similar span of time in the northern wilds.

Far more troubling than that, our relationship was under severe strain. For years our lives together had been an emotional roller-coaster and our interaction fraught with tension and uncertainty.

But the wilderness had always been our bond, our emotional sustenance, the place to find our shared balance. And, in the

wilds, we had always undergone a profoundly healthy trans-
formation.

The first time it occurred to me that I might be leading a double
life, I paid little attention. I was near Boot Springs, in the Chisos
Mountains of Big Bend, Texas, waiting for a friend in the shade
of some scrub oak. I had been in the desert for weeks, held there
by its oceanic spell. An acorn woodpecker worked its way up a
nearby tree, some Mexican jays flew past through a shaft of
sunlight.

Then my friend came down the trail toward me. She saw me,
we made eye contact, but she kept walking right on by, hunting
around. Only when I called out did she turn back, startled. "I
didn't even recognize you," she said. "Isn't that strange? But you
look so different."

We had seen each other within the last month, knew each
other well, yet she had taken me to be a stranger. And it wasn't
that I was bearded and dishevelled from weeks of outdoor living.
Someone other than the friend she expected was sitting there
near Boot Springs.

Since that time I've realized that her reaction wasn't unique.
Similar wilderness meetings have occurred, and when I give
slide shows of our trips and a close-up of me appears on the
screen, often someone will say, "Geez, who's that?"

Something does happen in the wilderness that has a profound
and transforming effect. It shouldn't be a surprise. One's appearance can change radically, even in a short time, because of stress
or sickness or depression. Why wouldn't isolation in the wilderness have as dramatic an impact?

I know that this is true. In the wilderness my sense of humour
grows, I become less compulsive. My self-absorption and tunnel
vision — encouraged by civilized life — diminish, and I observe
my surroundings more keenly. I dream vividly, I listen better,
I am thoughtful for long, quiet periods. That this should be

reflected in my features, the look in my eyes, seems absolutely reasonable.

"It is our best time together," Marypat tells me, and she's right. We are more loving, more attentive to each other, more spontaneous and relaxed, more joyful.

We go to the wilds not so much to seek an adventure, a burst of excitement and thrills, but to live there. We like to go alone, to feel immersed in, surrounded by, and finally accepted into the embrace of wild and sublime places. We go out of a need to find that person in each of us who is obscured in the day-to-day of crowded, hectic living: the quiet, changed person I became in the desert that a friend didn't recognize.

This time, though, neither of us was confident of the restorative powers of an adventure together. We couldn't leave behind the emotional knots in our partnership the way we could our belongings, the bills, the rest of civilization. They came along for the ride, as real as the canoe that would carry us down the many miles.

As our departure loomed close, I would catch myself studying Marypat, or gazing in the mirror, wondering whom I would find looking back at me in the wilderness.

I

FOLLOWING THE FLOODS

I

THE ATMOSPHERE IN the van is quiet, subdued. Marypat and I sit in the back amongst the packs and gear that, in a few hours, will be stuffed inside our red canoe. We exchange glances now and then, little smiles.

Outside, the landscape I have studied on maps for months flashes by. We drive over little rivers, the blue lines that I find so evocative on sheets of paper. They are clear and small, swiftly flowing, winding through marshes where I expect to see moose, disappearing into dark stands of trees. The Little Smoky, the Simonette, each one part of the watery pattern woven through the north – rivers that will join the flow of the Smoky, that we will paddle by again in a few days or a week. Mount Robson and the other high peaks of the Rockies hover just out of view over the horizon, screened off by the dense conifer forests. White wooden cutouts of caribou periodically adorn the roadside, like cattle-crossing signs in ranch country. We stop at one of them and snap pictures of each other riding bareback.

As we draw closer to Grande Cache and the Smoky River, to the start of our journey, I remember Marypat's words of a few

nights earlier. We had stood together in the evening, overlooking a shallow valley south of Calgary. Prairie grassland swept
away in all directions, swallows caught insects in the cooling
twilight.

"Do you think we'll be all right?" she asked. "Sometimes I
think we've drifted apart."

"Well, it hasn't been an easy couple of years." We stood side
by side, looking out, not touching. "But I think it will be good
for us."

I remember, too, how hollow the words had sounded, how it
had seemed, in a way, that I'd said nothing at all.

"Grande Cache," Matthew intones from the driver's seat, like
a tour guide. Corrugated-aluminum buildings, mud-spattered
logging trucks, trailer homes. All quickly gone by.

And then the van tips steeply into the valley, the trans-
mission straining against the vehicle's weight. I put my hand
against the seat in front of me, bracing against gravity, against
the inexorable pull of this beginning, try for a last glimpse of the
high peaks before the river valley swallows us, but see only the
foothill ranges.

Just before the bridge we turn off onto a muddy, rutted track.
A bikini-clad woman, skin tanned a melanomic brown, stands
by a canvas tent. A large log smoulders in a fire pit. We rumble
past, across the river cobbles, and stop, facing the big, hurrying
river.

Mud and water is everywhere, as if a deluge has just ended.
Marypat clambers out of the van and I follow her to the water's
edge. The river is high and swollen, muddier than we expected
for mid-July.

When we came across the border from Montana, the immi-
gration officer had mentioned heavy rains and flooding in the
north and helicopter evacuations of campgrounds. I hadn't paid
much attention then, but it looks as if the flood waters are only
just now receding.

Matthew and Sandy rummage around in the cooler for lunch,

start making pickle-and-cheese sandwiches with odds and ends of food. They are on their way to Alaska on vacation and have agreed to drop us off. Nothing to do now but unload, reorganize ourselves for the wilderness life that will be ours for more than a year.

A jet boat roars toward us from downriver, breasting the heavy current in slow motion, then pulls over to tie up in some willows. Our sunbathing neighbour goes to greet the three or four men who jump to shore.

They soon see our pile of gear and come charging over, still pumped up from their own river adventure.

"Better watch those rapids," one of them waves vaguely down the valley. "There's a big one just around the corner. Down farther, they get really big." They eye our little craft sceptically, wish us luck, then pound off toward their campsite.

Later, after we've changed into trip clothes and crammed the canoe full of gear, a small man in a green Forestry Department uniform comes over.

"Out for a little trip, eh?"

"A pretty big trip, actually," I say. "We'll be gone more than a year, spend the winter in northern Saskatchewan and end up next summer in the Northwest Territories."

"What'd you do? Win the Lotto or something?"

"No. Just saved up our money. It costs less to go on a trip than it does to stay home, unless you have big debts."

He's still grappling with the scope of it. "Wow. I've always wanted to do something like that. Just pack up and go off north on a river."

"Water seems high," Marypat interrupts.

"You should've seen it a week ago!" He points at the mud and scarred brush behind us. "This whole camp was under water. It's still pretty high, all right."

Preparing for departure takes less time than I'd expected. Pictures snapped, the van checked for forgotten essentials, the canoe waiting patiently in the shallows. Before I'm ready we're standing around with nothing to do; we need a bottle of champagne to make a toast and break across the bow, a ceremonial pipe to smoke. But these beginnings, instead of being portentous moments, are as mundane as a workaday morning.

We push the canoe into deeper water, feeling the ankle-numbing cold of glacial melt, step in, gather the spray skirt around our waists. The canoe grinds on a rock. I lean against my paddle to shove off, shrug at Matthew and Sandy.

Then I feel the river take hold. The canoe bumps again before we're in deep water. I aim for a V in a side channel. It's all so familiar; the surprising heft of a loaded boat, the gathering momentum as the current accepts and adopts us, the first quick steering strokes, my body reading the river through the paddle and hull.

I look back once to see the red van parked below the bridge, Matthew and Sandy watching us go, then I need to pay attention. When I turn for a final wave, they've already disappeared around the bend.

2

STEEP, DARK HILLS rise away from the Smoky, trees thick as fur on the slopes, broken up with blocks of clearcut, denuded and littered. We say nothing at all for a time, each coping with the abrupt transition from one life to another, each surprised by the velocity and unruly bulk of the river.

It pulls us along at a rate that makes me want to backpaddle, to slow the action. Willows along the banks are still under water, backwaters are more whirlpools than eddies, full of flood debris, roiling like huge, noisy drains as we slide by. My strokes need to be emphatic, committed, or they have no effect at all.

In what seems like no time, the first rapid appears ahead: humped-up waves, white froth, with no good place to stop and scout. I've read that this is considered a moderate rapid, but as we come near it looks bigger.

"Let's stay way right," I yell as we get sucked in. "See if we can skirt the biggest waves."

The murky water hides obstacles. We barely miss a dangerous obscured rock. A side-curler shoves us farther out than we want. We're in the centre of the waves, ploughing deeply into one after another. Marypat leans out to draw the bow straight, and just then a wash of water fills her spray skirt. There are more waves ahead. All we can do is ride them out, bracing and reacting as we go, feeling the boat twist heavily under our knees.

Even after the rapid, the river gives us no time to relax, keeps boisterously bearing us downhill. The banks whip past as though we're riding on a great watery train. Islands and gravel bars rush toward us, half submerged, trees bobbing and flailing under the onslaught of current. Route choices have to be made in seconds, one after another.

It's just as well we're keeping busy, I think. A more tranquil beginning would only have given us time to wallow in the difficult emotions of separation. As long as we don't blow it . . .

Marypat points ahead with her paddle. A large cow moose stands at the edge of an island, head up, watching us. Then she takes off, high-stepping through a chaos of brush, snapping branches. Two calves clamber after her. They are more rich red than brown, fuzzy-looking, spindly-legged. One charges into a channel and tries to cross to another island. Its little head is carried quickly downstream, but it swims steadily, finds its footing again, and wobbles to safety. I see it shake spray and look back for its mother, then we're past.

Downstream, a large coal mine comes into view. An imposing white structure, like a grain elevator, squats by the railway
tracks that border the river. The mine itself sits farther up the
hillside. Coal is only one in the battery of extractive industries
that supply Alberta's economy. Oil and gas, timber, coal, animal
fur – the province has a long history of sucking up and selling
products for which the rest of the world clamours.

In 1821 the Hudson's Bay Company sent Ignace Giasson up
the Smoky River in an effort to exploit new, fur-rich territory.
That they should have attempted such an arduous route is a
measure of how heated the competition was between the Hudson's Bay Company and its rival, the North West Company.

I imagine "Yellow Head," as his Iroquois companions nicknamed Giasson, struggling up this surging river, pushing into
the mountain fastness, tracking through impenetrable brush.
Beaver, I'm sure, were plentiful, but at what price? The Smoky
was abandoned by the HBC within a year, too difficult even for
its most intrepid men.

Grande Cache was one of Giasson's fur-storage points, and
his name for the spot stuck. The tradition of exploitation that
he began is also carried on, by the loggers and miners who live in
the trailers we drove by in town. The river is still as wild and
daunting as it was two hundred years ago, but the surrounding
wilderness has been infiltrated, stands of timber razed, hillsides
dug up for coal, wells punched down for oil.

We call an early end to our first day, already swept nearly twenty
miles downstream. Marypat has to leap out onto a gravel bar and
grab the bowline in order to stop our momentum. It's like stepping off a fast-moving escalator.

"We could make sixty miles a day on this river!" I guess. "Too
bad the best whitewater of the whole summer is crammed into
the first week."

As we set about making our first camp, the first night out in a string of four hundred, Marypat seems mopy, preoccupied. Where normally she would be quick with camp chores and busy with her beadwork and other projects, she paces fretfully along the shoreline, gazes off into the distance with her arms crossed, hugging herself.

"Why is it so hard?" she finally bursts out, close to tears. "Everyone tells us how much they envy us, but right now I envy them! Aren't you sad?" Her tone is almost accusing.

"Not the way you are, MP. But you always have a tougher time with these beginnings. Somehow I prepare for them, but I think you live too much in the present to do that."

She sighs and walks to me. We hold each other, there on the gravel bar, alone as we have come to love being alone, but anxious in a new and profound way.

For more than a decade we have taken remote northern water journeys, from Quebec to the Yukon. And this is our second year-long expedition. The challenges posed by water and weather are things we now take in stride. We already have friends here and there along our route, and will spend the winter in a cabin we helped build five years earlier. But the anxiety and turmoil at this beginning is internal, the challenges, to a large extent, inner ones. It is a wilderness without a map.

"It'll come," I say, with more conviction than I feel. My hand lies against her head. The cloudy river rushes by, fast and intimidating, just below our feet.

3

FOR TWO CANTERING days the railway tracks stay alongside the Smoky. No train traffic, but an orange pickup truck rides the rails, passing us several times. Men stare blankly at us from the cab, as if we're specimens behind glass. No one waves. Once, it is raining and we've eddied out just a few steps from the tracks to struggle into rain gear. Still no connection is made, no recognition.

I don't mind the estrangement from civilization, this time. I'm anxious to begin shedding those layers, to get free of possessions, the complications of making a living, endless maintenance chores, the extra pounds I carry on my out-of-shape body.

I'm eager to exchange it all for the routines of wilderness living. Finding dry wood and kindling fires, making the daily bannock bread, studying maps, trimming the boat so that we stay dry in waves. We're good at this, have spent years together getting better. Words are hardly necessary, even in the first days.

We camp, the second night, where the tracks cross the river. Again, an early stop after easy miles. We're reluctant to rush through the fast-water stretch of the Smoky. Only a few rapids punctuate our route later on, and we want to savour the excitement, ration the surges of adrenaline like a treat.

The next morning the river dives into a canyon. We lose the railway tracks and are enveloped by thick, wild foothills. The river drops twenty-five feet a mile in a visible ramp, and rapids come quickly, blending one into the next. The weather is cool and showery, a sky on the march. Light is constantly changing, altering the mood in the canyon abruptly, from cheerful to forbidding. We are in and out of rain gear half a dozen times.

Bend after bend the lessons of this river with its heady water level come to us, lessons that we'd best learn quickly. Marypat's in the bow, kneeling, eyes hunting downstream for the best route. I follow the language of her strokes, counter her moves to side-slip by a boulder, ferry away from waves, or punch through the big water. Sometimes she stands up briefly in the bow to see ahead, a move frowned upon by canoe schools.

"Looks good on the left, then toward the centre," she says, as she nestles into her stance again. Once there, unexpected obstacles require quick adjustments, a hurried shout, then we're on. Each pillow of water over a rock, each filament of river in contact with a paddle, tells us something, even if we couldn't articulate it exactly.

The big rapids before the Kakwa River confluence loom downstream. This morning is a warm-up, and we try to draw out our time in the pretty canyons, enjoy the ride, but the Smoky hurries us along.

A route description I've read cautions paddlers to stay well right and to land at the base of cliffs and scout the dangerous water. We are as far right as we can get, up against a sheer wall, backpaddling to slow our descent, but I see nowhere to land.

"I think the water's too high!"

A big ledge drops off ahead. It begins to rain again, the first few drops soft, then harder, pelting the river and blinding us. I claw at the wet cliff-face for a handhold, find nothing. The canoe glides closer to the roaring drop. Then my cold fingers find a flake of rock, cling to it, and we stop.

"You got us?" Marypat shouts.

"For now. Stand up and have a look, but don't take long."

I can tell by the way she leans, by her fidgety look, that she can't see far enough, that there is no clear shot.

"I think we can run the ledge out there." She points to the left. "I hope we can land below it, but I can't tell."

"We don't have much choice. We're too close to do anything but run it."

The rain is still coming hard, chilling us, obscuring the view, but I can't hold on any longer. Marypat settles in, tension in the set of her back. I let go and we immediately creep forward, then start to backpaddle hard.

"Farther out!"

Between strokes Marypat points to a slick tongue of muddy water.

We edge closer, dig in as hard as we can to get the angle right, then let the river have us. The canoe plunges smoothly over, twists once against a rock, then slams through the froth, taking on water. Down below, the next rapid waits: mammoth waves, a gravel-bar island, deep souse hole at the top. But a rocky beach is on the right, and we paddle in to the shallows to scout.

The rain tapers off, and I jump up and down on a rock, flapping my arms, trying to warm up. The roar of water is an insistent reminder of the next decision to be made, and I'm drawn toward it, stumbling over the rocks, then scrambling along steep, clayey banks. The earth is saturated, sucks me in to midcalf. Water weeps and slithers down the face. Clods of earth come away and topple down heavily. The river is the same grey colour, wild and thick with sediment.

Marypat and I stand together, looking, thinking our thoughts. We both know how alone we are, the dangers involved in making a mistake. And we can also imagine the brutal toil of the portage. Getting up the bank would be a nightmare, and at the top the vegetation is junglelike and dark. But we wouldn't drown, I remind myself, and the river looks menacing, its sound a threat, the waves huge.

Yet if we can get far enough out, ease ourselves down alongside the gravel-bar island, perhaps we can miss the worst of the hole and ride the edge of the waves. Around the bend the rapids are not as fierce, but continue out of sight. If we capsize, we're in for a long, cold ride. Still, the more I look, the more I think we can do it.

Then we're back in the canoe, spray skirt snug, life vests cinched up, our knees set against the hull. We run through our strategy again and again in our minds, then paddle hard to get mid-stream, face upriver for power, then pivot down. Our focus tightens – rain, the canyon, the dark woods, all disappear. The next stroke, the angle of the boat, the snarling hole of water coming toward us are all that matter. The current pulls us uncontrollably to the hole, no escape; hard as we paddle away, it pulls us harder.

"We're going in, MP! Paddle like hell and then brace."

It's always so much bigger, so much stronger, close up. At river level the hole is almost the size of the canoe. It gulps us down, smooth and greedy, and we battle through the high wave that then curls back against us, trying to keep us. The canoe takes on water, despite the decking. We wallow, but have no time to think about it.

"We're gonna hit the waves," MP says, backpaddling again.

The current, like a giant funnel, forces us into the steep, massive waves.

"Help me keep us straight!"

And we're in their midst, plunging, heavy with water, riding steadily up, then slamming hard into watery valleys. The noise engulfs us, the rapid an unharnessed, dangerous joyride. But the boat rides well, heavy as it is, and I concentrate on every stroke, take each wave carefully, reading it, feeling it.

At the bottom we spot an eddy and head for it. I realize how cold I am, how wooden my fingers are, clutching the paddle. Marypat climbs stiffly out and hauls us up enough to send the water back to where I'm bailing. I look up from the work and see her standing, hands tucked into her life vest, staring back up river with that same little smile she gets when she's dancing.

At the Kakwa River the sun breaks out. Soon our wet clothes are draped on rocks and we hop about naked in the warmth, eat lunch, then decide we can't leave this beautiful spot. The two mountain rivers, the Kakwa a third the size of the Smoky, join together with a sound like cheering mixed with all-out watery applause. Above the Kakwa rise sheer walls of river sediment topped with dense forest.

If we had portaged, how the hell would we have come down? We try to walk upstream, but are stopped by cliffs and thick, prickly undergrowth full of indistinct game trails, bits of animal scat, paw prints.

We are happy and unburdened in camp, sharing this team-work, basking in the competence we've already built up, infused by the joy of fast water. We haven't felt this way together for a long time. Even the shorter trips we've taken haven't been enough to get us over the sadness and frustration of these past few years. Somehow the prospect of this unbroken year out-doors is enough to relieve, at least momentarily, the oppressive weight we've carried.

Again the Smoky takes us on, at the same accelerated pace. Another day's light plays in the shadows of aspen groves. The trees look new, freshly painted. Their leaves in a breeze echo the chatter of river current. On straight stretches I can see the obvi-ous tilt of the valley, the broad descent of burgeoning water.

Old "Yellow Head" is on my mind again. In 1821 Lewis and Clark had been back from their exploration only some fifteen years. Almost nobody west of the Mississippi had white skin. I wonder if Giasson cursed his Hudson's Bay superiors on every fast bend; if he took the challenge of the ascent in stride, all in a day's work; whether he thought, as he passed the Kakwa River, that the route was insane, no matter what riches awaited the jaws of his traps.

I'm thankful to be heading downhill. At every bend huge waves rise up. We scout here and there, but mostly just run them, staying clear of the biggest, stopping to bail now and again. I'm in the bow, getting wet, facing the brunt of the waves, but quickly drying in the warm sunlight.

A cow elk and calf watch us pass a gravel bar. Golden-coated mule deer bound up the banks, then stand broadside to us in that majestic, vulnerable stance. At the base of a low cliff I notice a spot of red fur. We head that way, thinking a dead animal has washed up, and then the fur heaves a big, sleepy sigh. It's a beaver, obviously expecting no danger from the water, and protected from above by the cliff. We're within a paddle length before it wakes, startled, and dives under the canoe. Almost immediately it hauls back out, just downstream, grumpy as an old man wakened from his nap. Its fur is a sun-bleached red, almost blond, and it busies itself scratching an ear, haughtily ignoring us.

The last difficult rapids come where the Cutbank River joins the Smoky. We avoid the first dangerous stretch by ferrying well out into the river, then go for the waves mid-river for the final descent.

The canoe arrows up, momentarily out of the water, then crashes down. Water is in my face, dumped in my lap, drenching me to the armpits. I start to whoop in surprise and excitement, and find I can't stop. Marypat giggles, then yells for me to shut up and paddle. The waves keep coming. Big, cold mountains of water that we ride like bucking horses, knowing we can tame them.

4

THE SMOKY ABRUPTLY leaves the dense foothills and abandons its headlong drop, now only descending five feet in each mile. The current is still fresh and strong, but steady. We go miles without negotiating waves, sometimes floating lazily, other times paddling in our all-day rhythm.

Until now, the loud, inescapable noise of the river had kept me rivetted on the challenging water. Now that same water swirls and eddies sedately, and the valley opens to a stage full of sky and distant hills.

I am able to relax and return to my usual fascination with our maps, study the larger scale of land. Logging roads and gas fields, oil wells and fire towers punctuate the country. Pipelines and power lines, roads and railway tracks, bush airstrips and tiny settlements clutter the sheets of paper. Yet the river valley is lonely, unused, left out of the action. A condition that suits me fine.

Our camps are littered with huge pieces of driftwood, entire trees crammed up into stacks and jams, woody buttresses built by the force of the current. Many still have leaves on the branches. One night, collecting firewood, I follow the fresh tracks of a wolf that meander through the muddy litter. I see the dried mud where it hopped up on a log, then the deep imprint where it jumped heavily down.

In the evening there is time to catch up in journals, wash clothes, savour the cooking and eating of our dinner. In the tent we play a round of backgammon, this trip's game, before going to sleep.

The late-July weather turns hot. Each morning I mark the fact that the river has dropped noticeably in the night. Aspen and birch forests fill the valley, whisper next to us as we coast along. Shadows shift and move mysteriously in their depths. Black coal seams line the steep banks. Huge chunks of the valley have slumped into the river, trees at chaotic angles as if they had thrown out their limbs to break the fall. More trees crowd the rim, right at the edge, awaiting the inevitable. Clods of soil plop incessantly into the current, little rubbly avalanches cascade down, as the land settles, finding its balance after the floods.

As we pass under the Gold Creek bridge, cliff swallows burst out of their mud nests. A chick accidentally falls from one into the river. It flails desperately in the water, unable to fly, drowning as we go by.

Mountain Creek, Lignite Creek, the Wapiti River brown as topsoil, Simonette River. Grande Prairie, Sexsmith, Bad Heart, Teepee Creek. Farm country. It is shown white and cleared on the map, full of right-angle dirt roads following section lines. Yet the river valley is five hundred feet deep, coyotes chorus at night, and the smoke from our fire wafts unnoticed in the evening air.

The heat continues, day after day. Repeatedly we strip off our clothes and wallow in the cool, sediment-rich water. Shade becomes the most important factor in choosing campsites. When we don't find it we hide in the shadow of our tent until the day cools enough to cook dinner. Once, we stop beneath a power line because it's the only shade in miles. I can hear the faint charge passing overhead, feeding an inexhaustible appetite.

Smaller driftwood has been scoured away by flooding. We locate the line of dead wood dozens of feet up the banks, or well back into the forest. Mud coats the flats, sheathes tree trunks up to the first branches. I feel like I'm walking around on the drifts of a great muddy blizzard, peeking in at the second storey of things.

In one of our sandbar camps, after we've had a swim and I've recovered some of my equanimity after a day of unaccountable testiness, I approach Marypat.

"I'm sorry I was cranky today. The heat must have gotten to me. Some days everything seems like a struggle."

"Are you sure you're committed to this?" she asks, in an unexpected leap.

"Yeah, sure I am."

Her question concerns me, though. I thought we were over the early transition, the trip well begun. It startles me that she is still tentative, unsure enough to think that one day's bad mood might signal a lack of commitment to the whole endeavour.

For two years we have been trying to have a baby. The first

surprise, that Marypat was not becoming pregnant, was followed by a certain sheepish acceptance of our difficulty. The
jokes of acquaintances (Sure you've got it right, now?) have
become stale indeed. I've undergone the indignity of sperm
tests, and Marypat has had coloured dye shot through her
Fallopian tubes. Nothing is discernably wrong.

"After a certain age, it just gets tougher for women to have
babies," a doctor told us.

We've refused the expense and awful intrusion of more complicated medical intervention. The most we've been willing to
try is a mild fertility drug. Twice Marypat has been pregnant,
only to be struck each time with a miscarriage. She is taking a
daily dose of powdered Chinese herbs, a concoction that to me
sounds a lot like eye of newt and wing of bat, but which has made
her cycle longer and more regular.

At first we wanted to time the pregnancy conveniently, but
that was supplanted by our unconditional wish simply to have a
baby. Our intimacy became regulated by the thermometer
Marypat kept by the bedside, concentrated in the few days of
potential fertility each month. Sex changed from a source of joy
to a thing we failed at, something almost never much fun.

Marypat's mood, over the months and years, turned grim and
sad. Weeks at a time went by without my hearing her wonderful,
uninhibited laugh. When her sister got pregnant she couldn't
escape deep jealousy, followed by oppressive guilt. Nobody
asked us how it was going any more.

Having children had never been much of an issue for us; it
was one of those things down the road, when we were ready. Life
was full and rewarding. It never occurred to us, once we'd
decided, that we wouldn't be able to accomplish it. And it had
become, since then, the central issue, infecting our lives in
every quarter. A sadness Marypat couldn't surmount, a lack in
life we never before knew existed. By the time we began the trip,
I had resigned myself to our condition. Marypat, however,
continued to ride the monthly roller-coaster of hope and

disappointment, endured the physical manifestation of our inability, and didn't seem able to accept and overcome it.

This trip, at least in part, hatched out of that failure. We knew we were good at being in the wilderness, paddling a boat long distances, that we found joy and affirmation, even spiritual renewal, in big, wild country. But would it be enough, this time?

5

IT IS FINALLY cool. Thin clouds have moved in to screen the sun. Our camp is across from a huge muddy bank that periodically calves slabs of earth into the Smoky, like a dirt glacier. Coyotes are yipping and carolling up above, somewhere close, but out of sight.

"Look at that bird." I point over the river to where the tiny thing flutters erratically, almost falls in the water, staggering in flight, and then loops toward our camp.

It lands on a low bench of sand a few feet from us. A female American redstart. We move slowly and quietly, right up to her. The bird closes its eyes, exhausted and uncaring. We step back. For a long time she perches there, recovering from some trauma, while we go about making dinner.

"I wonder if she just barely missed being caught by a hawk or falcon," Marypat whispers. "It's too late in the summer to be tired out from migrating."

Our delicate visitor finally hops around a little, still occupied with her recovery, then flies under the shelter of our overturned canoe. While we eat we hear occasional chirps, soft flurries of wings, bumps under the hull. We stay quiet. It is nearly dark when she reappears, gets her bearings, perches briefly on one of our packs, then flies off, vanishing in the darkening forest.

It is rare to see animals in trouble in the wilds. Even rarer to witness death. It happens all the time, but the drama is somehow absorbed by the larger serenity. The quick killing stoop of a hawk, the dragging down of a fawn by a coyote are overwhelmed by the breadth of sky or overarching forest. Nature cleans up after itself, so that even the signs are quickly gone.

I remember the fawn we passed a day or two earlier, still spotted, hardly bigger than a coyote. We approached to within a few feet of where it drank from the river. It was slow to notice, then stared blankly at us before moving stiffly off. A chunk of flesh had been torn from its rump, a deep-bitten gouge. The mother was nowhere in sight.

During the night a terrific series of thunderstorms pound around us. The valley is lit platinum white, then immediately shudders under the crash of thunder. Our tent is buffeted, beaten on, and rain hits the beach so hard it flings sand two feet up the tent walls. I hear huge bombs of earth slap the river, loosened from the hillside. But by morning it's calm and warming up again.

Marypat is determined to stop in Watino, the first town near the river, and call Montana. She wants to find out if her sister has had her baby. We glide into the shadow of the six-span highway bridge and haul the canoe up on the mud, out of sight.

It is our first real walk away from the river, away from our canoe and all that sustains us. The highway is hot and hard, infrequent cars whoosh by. River shoes, shorts, already grubby T-shirts make us stick out like wild aliens. A small sign points us to the little town.

Watino exists because of the railway. The original town was known as New Smoky, situated just upstream of a hazardous bridge crossing. It was once a rough, unvarnished place, full of bootleggers and transients. The trains stopped here to take on water and fuel. On our map the town is a small circle on the railway track. From a distance it appears somnolent, shut up, out of the mainstream.

We have a few letters to mail, a phone call to make, small needs. A skinny man wearing no shirt is standing on a deck outside the door of a trailer-home, screaming angrily through the screen. He paces away, then comes back, yells some more.

Every house has a garden, some of them huge. In the middle of one, an old woman in a print dress is bending to some task. I go to ask directions.

"Excuse me," I call.

She straightens and peers myopically at a point about ninety degrees off.

"Over here." I wave. "We're travelling down the river and wondered if there is a post office in town."

"Oh, yes. Only, what time is it?"

"I don't know, but all we want to do is mail letters."

"Oh. Then it's no matter." Her accent sounds Eastern European, perhaps Ukrainian, Croatian. She looks pleasant, unflappable, standing there surrounded by her vegetables, the kind of person with whom it would be nice to share tea. "You just follow the road around the corner, past the trailer, and it's in a white house." Her gloved hand hangs limply from her wrist as she points the way.

Everyone we see is retirement age or older. Curtains lift softly from windows as we go past. An elderly couple sit in lawn chairs under a shade tree, shelling peas into buckets.

"Shelling peas, are you?" I say.

"Yes," they call back. And that's that.

Perhaps the post office she remembers was once white, but the dilapidated building we find is finished in untreated particle board, closed up and unpromising. We drop our letters reluctantly through a wooden slot, hear them clatter thinly on the other side as if they had simply fallen to the floor.

A public phone hangs outside another decaying building.

Marypat dials Montana. The idea that we might stop along the river, punch buttons on a box, and connect with home seems preposterous, but they answer. Marypat's sister has had a baby girl, but she isn't home. I hear the disappointment in my partner's voice, know that, more than the news, she wants to realign herself with Nancy. She says she'll try again from Peace River, a few days downstream.

As she talks, a telephone-repair truck pulls up.

"I had a report that this phone was out of order." The repairman hoists a tool belt out of the cab, looks around curiously.

"We're talking to Montana and it seems to work fine."

"Strange little town, eh?" He confirms our assessment. "Makes you wonder how somebody ends up here."

But I'm surprised he confides in us, out of place as we look.

Downstream, around a long bend, the railway bridge appears. Black iron trestles rise twenty-five feet above the river.

From a distance the bridge looks cluttered, fuzzy. We draw near and see that it's full of logs, entire tree trunks and huge battered branches. They sit on top of the concrete buttresses, angle out crazily from the ironwork, some hanging fifteen feet out into the air. I imagine an engineer sitting in the idling cab of a train, knowing well the history of washouts, weighing his chances, while the brown, tree-filled river sucks under the tracks.

Marypat is quiet through the afternoon, but I don't want to inquire, know only too well what her thoughts are likely to be. I struggle to regain my rapport with the water, find my pace again after the interruption.

"Isn't it strange," I say, "how you walk a quarter mile away from the river, into this weird little town, and *Wham!* there it is, the other part of your life."

6

THE SMOKY PICKS up speed for the final fifty miles before it meets the Peace River. The country has a semi-arid look, with sparsely vegetated, dry rock canyons rising sharply out of the valley. If I didn't know better I could be convinced I was on the Missouri River in Montana.

The heat reminds me of eastern Montana, too. Cloudless hazy sky, warm cliffs . . . I expect rattlesnakes when I walk on shore. A bald eagle watches us pass below its nest. Perched part-way up a sandstone wall, it is a platform of sticks and grass that probably weighs fifty pounds.

The canoe glides rapidly by the shore, as if hurrying to the next phase of the journey. A buck mule deer scrambles heavily away up a dirt hillside, making a trail as he goes. Waves greet us on the corners, little rapids through boulders make us pay heed.

The Smoky is the first stage of our 1,100-mile summer. It is over too quickly for me. I like the smaller scale, the sense of being embedded in deep canyons, the fast, heart-gripping whitewater. By comparison the Peace will be a long slog on a huge river. Vermilion Falls, Wood Buffalo Park, and other discoveries lie ahead, but I wish the Smoky had a week's worth of extra miles.

The brush becomes thick and tangled near the river junction. On a corner where the current sweeps us close under the bank I suddenly see a face through the branches. A sweaty face wearing a sheepish grin. A thumb sticks out, hitchhiker style. Almost as soon as I see the man, we've gone by.

"I'll bet he wants a ride!" I say. "It must be a hundred degrees."

What this person is doing, backpacking through that track-less stuff, and in this heat, I have no idea.

We stop for our final camp on the Smoky. The Peace, and all

it will bring us, lies a mile or two away. The town of Peace River is around the corner.

The hiker reappears on the other side of the river with a companion. I can almost see the sheen of sweat at half a mile. They speak a foreign language, perhaps German, but we can't make it out. Did they blithely assume they would come to Canada and hike a nonexistent trail along the Smoky?

Their progress is excruciatingly slow, with many detours. Finally they drop their packs and slosh, fully clothed, into the river. They kneel and drink the muddy water, pour it out of hats over their heads, splash each other and laugh, giddy with refreshment. Whatever gastrointestinal consequences there may be from drinking the river are the miseries of another day. Now it is too powerfully good to resist.

The grave of "Twelve Foot" Davis is somewhere nearby, at the Peace River townsite. He is a local legend, nicknamed not for any great height (he is reported to have been five foot two), but because he made his fortune mining gold on a claim only twelve feet wide. Originally from Connecticut, he settled in the Peace River valley during the late 1800s, establishing himself as a fur trader and businessman.

Alexander Mackenzie had also made his mark here. He and a crew of nine spent the winter of 1792/93 at Fort Forks, a few miles west of our camp. At that time the junction of the Smoky and Peace rivers was the western edge of known territory, and Mackenzie was on his way to find a practical route to the Pacific Ocean. He'd already been to the Arctic Ocean and back three years earlier, on the river that now bears his name.

The geography farther west was known only to the Natives, and most of them were familiar with little beyond their local points of reference. Several times during the winter, warm Chinook winds hit Mackenzie's fort. He interpreted the balmy air as a sign that the ocean was so near at hand that the warm ocean breezes hadn't had time to cool before they reached him. But the following summer he discovered that five hundred mountainous miles, and a long, arduous season of travel, lay in his way.

But I am brought to the present by the sound of a low-flying plane. A radio tower perches on the hill across the valley. Train whistles and loud engines intrude. A motorboat idles into view downstream, then drifts away, trolling for fish. When I walk along the gravel bar, I find the tracks of the modern-day vehicle of exploration, a four-wheeler.

II

SHEDDING CIVILIZATION

7

"I'M ALL THROUGH crying," Marypat announces.

We're riding the Peace River, heading toward town. The Smoky is big, but the Peace is huge. The two rivers merge in a jumble of islands and channels, so it's difficult to tell exactly when we leave one and join the other. A slight change in water – less cloudy green, a darker, clearer flow – and something more ponderous, like the difference between estuary and ocean, a leap in scale.

Single sections of current passing between islands are larger than the Smoky ever was. Our canoe seems diminished, at sea. The view is longer, the bends slower, throwing off my perception of our speed. And indefinable riverine qualities communicate through the shaft of my paddle, through my already callused hands, and translate in my muscles and nerves into impressions as clear as the those when I meet a person for the first time. I sense immediately that the Peace is easy to underestimate.

It's time for another phone call, the last for a long time, and Marypat's statement is part of her preparation. These town stops are awkward, and not only because they interrupt our rhythm. Our blind guess at a good place to pull out might saddle us with a half-mile walk through warehouse lots or put us beside a busy highway nowhere near a phone.

This time we're in luck. When we clamber over a stony embankment, where sandbags still lie around from the flooding, we find ourselves in a parking lot behind a small mall. A sign beneath a public telephone says, "Call Home!"

Marypat connects almost immediately with Nancy. I hear the relief, the emotion, in her greeting. Then she huddles into the phone, making herself more private, almost embracing it, and begins to sob. I know Nancy is equally emotional, a thousand miles away. The sound Marypat makes, even muffled and with her back turned, brings the sting of tears to my eyes. But it is a purging sound, too. It is likely to be a long call, so I wander inside the mall.

I'm a water hillbilly in the big city, wearing my river garb and two-week beard amongst the shoppers in tight jeans and fashionable clothing ensembles. My boat shoes slap along the tile walkways.

A local paper has a headline about forest fires started by a severe lightning storm, the same storm that hammered us at our beach campsite where the redstart took cover.

I converse with the owner of a deli bar. He looks Lebanese or Armenian and is thoroughly taken by the possibilities of his enterprise.

"I'll have all gourmet coffees soon."

He indicates a section of counter now filled with condiments, gestures expansively with his hands to show me the space he has allotted. "Four or five pots will be here, different flavours all the time. Something new for Peace River."

"You bet!" I say.

Peace River has been a regional centre since the turn of the century. Homesteaders who were restless and desperate to escape the depression years in the 1890s, or shot up with the same sort of enthusiasm for adventure that sent others hiking for the Klondike, pushed up here to farm in droves.

The way wasn't easy. Many laboured up the Athabasca Trail from Edmonton to the Athabasca River, a hundred-mile slog through bug-swarming swamps and bush. Then they took the dubious steamboat and portage route from Athabasca Landing to Lesser Slave Lake, as often as not foundering in shallows along the way. The final ninety miles to the broad valley of the Peace was made by wagon or cart, until the railway came through. Others took their chances in winter, making the long, bitterly cold overland trek by horse-drawn sleigh.

By 1916 the railway had been pushed to town and, in 1918, a 1,700-foot bridge was flung across the river, opening up the farming country to the west. And although the railway had its problems – mudslides and flooding regularly took out sections of track, sometimes closing the line for an entire season – whole settlements up and moved, buildings and all, to be next to the tracks.

The Peace River valley and the Grande Prairie region is a geographic anomaly. Follow the same latitude east into Saskatchewan and Manitoba and you hit boreal forest, jack pine, herds of caribou. If there are settlements at all they are Native reserves or mining operations.

Yet along the Peace the soil is rich and productive, the landscape as much plain and parkland as forest and muskeg. In the short growing season, the days are long and the climate conducive to crops. But insects can be a torment, frosts might come any night of the year, and winters are difficult and long. Agriculture is possible, however, and people came and stayed, even homesteading farther north along the valley.

"Feeling better?" I ask, when Marypat hangs up.

She nods, leans into me for a hug. I notice a change in her, a lightening of mood, something more alive and eager in her eyes.

Something lets go in me as well, and I grin at her. "Let's get out of here!"

The Peace River coffee mogul fills our water jug for us. Then we're off. This, to me, feels more like departure, more like a real beginning to the trip, although we have been out nearly two weeks already. With the phone call we seem to have made the transition, left something weighty and encumbering behind.

A train crosses the bridge as we glide under. Traffic overhead is distant, almost an abstraction. Nobody honks or waves, and perhaps they don't even notice us, tiny as we are on the watery expanse. The noise of factory whistles, airplanes, horns, and engines recedes, and the world of aspen and eagle, cliff and thunderhead reabsorbs us.

Then, eight miles or more downstream, our view is again interrupted, this time by a large pulp mill. A new bridge is being built across the river. Pilings force the flow to split, iron girders span the air. The mill is a fresh, newly minted white. A crane moves with methodical grace at the river's edge, taking huge bites of mud and rock and water, ripping them from one place, depositing them in another. Trucks and dozers manicure the surroundings, make roads and clearings out of flood plain. A helicopter flies overhead, hovering like a dragonfly, then swings away over the trees, perhaps to survey the stands of timber that will be cooked into pulp, made into computer paper, magazine pages. Nearby, a natural-gas vent sends its pale flame dancing into the warm day.

Pulp is the rage in northern Alberta these days, the latest way to fuel the economy and pillage the earth. Mills are either under construction or in the planning stages along the Athabasca River, the Smoky, the Peace, and other tributaries.

The Peace River pulp mill, like most other ventures under consideration, is owned by a Japanese company. They are after the aspen and birch left behind from the first phase of logging operations. The industry revealingly refers to these trees as "weeds," not worth the effort to cut down. But it has now found a use for them: a new bleaching process renders the pulp valu-able, saleable. And so they've come back for the weeds, like burglars returning to a house for a second haul.

The old arguments burn. Locals want the jobs, environmen-talists want the trees left alone, the water and air left unpol-luted. Statistics and economic figures are shot off like weapons, with plenty of ammunition for everyone. Facts are manipulated to fit each argument, like quotes from the Bible in a religious debate.

Industry representatives tout their clean technology, saying that these pulp mills are the cleanest ever, a claim that sounds a lot like a physicist heralding the safest nuclear bomb ever made.

I take the side of the river. I know what the wild, undammed, still drinkable rivers are like. I have paddled too many of them, camped along too many quiet banks, listened to loons and geese on too many twilight evenings not to take affront, not to take up the river's cause.

Economists and businesspeople speak of wasted resources, as though there is all this unharvested money standing around in the form of aspen and birch groves. But, unless they are more cynical than I think, they haven't paddled next to them, heard them rustling in a breeze, seen the deer peering out of their shadows. If they had, how could they think of that rich and mys-terious environment as waste?

And once the machinery is in place, once the groves have been reduced to denuded earth and the water sullied, once the industry's claims to environmental enlightenment are long for-gotten, once it's too late, we will come to understand what we've lost. Regulations will limit residents to eating one fish a week. Pregnant women will be cautioned not to eat any at all. Fish will have grown scarce in any event. This is, already, an old story.

The Peace and Athabasca watersheds feed the Slave, then the Mackenzie, flowing eventually to the Arctic Ocean. A system of interconnected current, wild rapids, placid bends, long unfurling ribbons of water, that drains one seventh of North America.

This is what we are talking about wasting, what we are in the process of wasting.

For a little while we rest our paddles across our knees and look at the scene. Water streams off the paddle blades, then drips, then stops. Marypat and I say nothing. We resume paddling, ignore the mill as best we can.

8

A DAY OUT of Peace River we encounter our old nemesis, the bear. Two of them. I see the first from a long distance, a coal-black smudge moving lazily through willows toward the river. It senses us while we're still hundreds of yards off, turns and lopes back to the forest, not panicked, but steady. A good bear.

The second we see across the river at lunch time. It clambers down a mud bank to drink, movements both heavy and lithe. Suddenly it lifts its head from the water. The bear looks our way, alert but calm, then scrambles up the bank, fast, quiet, suddenly gone.

I am determined not to be bothered by bears. It's been years since I had to kill one that tormented us on a portage along the Athabasca River. I've finally stopped dreaming about them, about their quality of quiet menace. I believe, in fact, that it's healthy to have bears around, good for my perspective, my humility. Fine philosophy, but emotionally I'm not always successful. When I see that black or brown shape, that fluid power, when a bear stands on its hind legs and scents for me, front paws dangling, I can't always suppress the upwelling of fear and memory.

Northern Alberta is crawling with bears. Without any effort to search for them, I've seen dozens of them along riverbanks, portage trails, at the edges of campsites. This is their home, I am the intruder. But I'd just as soon not see them, not have to confront them.

"I'll bet he was bummed he had to run off," Marypat says. "He looked like he wanted a swim in the worst way."

On the map the settlements grow sparse. Tamed and cultivated ground shows up as white blotches on a background of green – muskeg, forest, ranges of hills. I wonder about the Buffalo Head Hills, off to the east, an unsettled and rumpled landscape full of swamps and pothole lakes. Once an old haunt, perhaps, for bison, which even up here have been squeezed into tiny preserves. Looping river bends can take half a day to paddle around. I keep thinking we're moving slowly, but every evening when we tot up our mileage I find we've slid along twenty-five, thirty, thirty-five miles.

The flow of the Peace is turgid, almost appears molten. It takes a strong wind to ruffle its surface, and the weight of water, the volume and breadth and scale of the river, is so immense that it takes on a quality of some heavier medium, like pewter. Only when we turn against the flow and paddle upstream is the true velocity and strength of the river brought home. Then, the water leans into us, a power unimaginable, a patience and insistence almost geologic.

We have little trouble accomplishing our miles. Each morning we rise when we feel like it, enjoy several cups of coffee, cook breakfast over driftwood flames, soak up the coolness. Packing the boat is the part of our routine I like least, the part that becomes most repetitive and burdensome, like doing dishes or laundry at home, a job never finished. Everything has its own niche, every pack, the spare paddle, our lunch sack, the water container. All are lashed in place, made ready for whatever the day holds.

Mornings have become the time to paddle, to cover most of our distance. We talk only sporadically and let our thoughts roam as the tributaries and hills and points of land creep past. New stretches of river reveal themselves, one after another, in a slow unwinding of discovery. The stiffness in my shoulders works free, a knot in my back comes loose. Our paddling together has become, over the years, over the miles, a thing so intimate and synchronized that it requires no thought, a rhythm like breathing together.

No watch tells us when it's time to eat meals, whether we should hurry or slow down, when a work day is finished. By the time hunger forces us to shore for a lunch of bannock and cheese, we have usually made twenty miles or more.

The afternoons, unless we have a headwind to fight, are more relaxed. We drift, sometimes for miles, watch the shore for birds or deer, talk about this or that.

"What are you thinking?" I ask Marypat, a question one of us puts to the other almost daily.

"You won't believe this, but I'm thinking about stripping wallpaper off the living-room walls."

"Good God! Here we are, fifteen hundred miles from home, going down this quiet river, away from everything for more than a year, and you're thinking about stripping wallpaper?"

"I told you you wouldn't believe it."

Silence. Just the swirl of paddles, the sling of drops arcing across the water surface. Then Marypat says, "And about babies."

"What about them?" I ask, my voice impatient.

"That I want one."

When we have left enough miles in our wake, or the heat or fatigue is finally too much, we stop, undo the packing job, and erect our movable home. Daylight lasts until the middle of the night in August, so there is no hurry in camp. We swim and wallow, ease the heat from our bodies. There is time to scribble in journals or write a letter, look ahead on the maps, wander off to explore.

Already the campsites run together – the dawn with dew on spider webs, the beach where wind harried us with drifting sand, the tent site stuck in amongst tree trunks buried in mud.

It's odd how content I am in this life. On the surface it seems oppressively simple and repetitive, even boring. Day after day full of paddle strokes, the same chores over and over, hour after hour of nothing but my thoughts. No radio, no television shows or movies, no friends to visit.

Yet I shed the manic, compulsive tendencies that creep insidiously into my urban life, no matter how I try to avoid them. The tendency to gain weight, the fretful filling of time with meaningless activity.

On the river it is no matter to sit by the fire while the sky darkens and the sun slowly drops. There is nothing else I should be doing. And things come to me, gifts of thought, a peacefulness, memories long buried.

Almost always we are alone on the river. There are roads now, railway tracks, so the river is ignored, left as a strip of wilderness. We see a man and a woman, one afternoon, hauling buckets of water up the bank to their garden. They hardly pause as we pass by. Do they even see us?

One evening a powerboat comes thundering upriver, at full throttle toward our camp. It is calm, no waves break the smooth current, yet the boat is pounding up and down. A man stands in the back, pumping with his legs, letting out a shout with each knee-bend, holding his fist in the air. Marypat and I watch the show, hoping they'll go on past, but they spot us. The boat turns abruptly without slowing at all, a wide arc with a deep gash for a wake,

Two men and a large dog jump to shore. One man is lean and tall, wearing nothing but a bathing suit. The other is big-headed, lion-faced. He has a marijuana leaf tattooed on his upper arm and wears a T-shirt that says, "Instant Asshole." There is a woman at the wheel, but she doesn't get out.

"Wanna beer?" the skinny one asks.

Marypat and I each accept a warm Molson's.

They have to call their dog back before it lifts its leg on our tent.

The two men chain-smoke, drop their cigarettes in the sand, and pepper us with the usual questions. They also rail at the pulp mill.

"They're cutting everything this time," the woman in the boat says, her first words. "Even the aspen."

"We're always talking down the U.S. and how it pollutes everything," Instant Asshole says. "You'd think we might learn something."

We ask about the flooding and they point to the driftwood line fifteen feet up the bank. How much water is that? I try to calculate: fifteen feet deep and a mile wide.

"Did you see those big orange balls on the shore back there?" We nod. "That was the power line. Washed out by the flood. Our fields are just now drying out."

I imagine a huge tree somersaulting downriver, lifted into the air, slicing through electrical cable.

Suddenly they start leaving. As they back off I get in a few questions of my own.

"Where are you from?"

"Manning."

"What do you do?"

"Farmers." And they laugh, like it's an inside joke.

"Lived here all your lives?"

"Yup," the woman says. "Only he came from somewhere else." She points at Instant Asshole.

As the engine engages and they start heading farther upriver,

Instant Asshole calls out, "Rabbits are really good right now. Nothing wrong with a little rabbit stew!" He raises his fist in a power salute.

Later, while we're eating our spaghetti dinner, the boat comes back down. Instant Asshole yells a loud "Hey!" as if we wouldn't otherwise have known they were there.

9

THE DAYS BEGIN to roll, seamless as this unhurried bulk of water that bears us across a continent. Hundreds of miles already lie in our wake, weeks of storm and heat and calm, a trail of memory winding back – the exultation of rapids, the look in a dying fawn's eyes, the bruised glow of a sunset sky.

I am occasionally struck by an overwhelming sense of comfort. Foreign as we sometimes feel, there are also powerful moments when I am filled with a sense of belonging, like someone in a home they've occupied for decades.

My trip pants fit comfortably now. I have lost the extra weight not through half-hour stints of jogging or handball in a day full of half-hour allotments. It has dropped away because I live outdoors, because my body propels me all day long, because the life I lead is pleasantly strenuous, and my appetite isn't fuelled by manic habit.

In the long calm of a twilight we stroll down a new beach. No human footprints break the sand. An old trail of bear tracks follows the willow line, sandpiper feet stipple the mud. We stoop here and there for a pretty rock, speculate on the stories the tracks tell, listen to the settling sounds of the forest. As on many nights, we say little, but Marypat takes my hand, and when we walk back toward the pile of gear and overturned canoe that is this night's home, we feel connected.

We adjust our packing and camping regimen to cope with sand. Before dipping a cup into a pot of water, we automatically wipe the bottom first. Our steps around the tent or cookfire are careful and small, so as not to raise too much dust. Every pack and duffel bag is brushed off before it goes into the canoe. Last of all, we rinse our feet as we climb in. Even so, the boat is coated with sand and silt, the tent zipper sounds gritty, our food is peppered with inedible grains.

It is morning and already hot. This heat has become oppressive. Shorts, T-shirt, and a hat are all I ever wear. I forget where my jacket is packed, wonder why I bothered to bring a wool cap, long underwear. The windless days are particularly tough. The miles come slowly, and the heat, mid-river, is impossible to escape. A headwind is at least something to focus on and combat.

We start around the first ten-mile bend. Our paddles slice the water precisely together, the bow splashes its tiny wave, river sediment rubs against the canoe hull, audible as fine sandpaper applied with a light touch. I look for the day's first landmark, the mouth of the Wolverine River.

"What's that?" Marypat asks.

In the distance something blocky and shiny squats in the water by the riverbank. I get the binoculars and focus.

"I think it's a pirate ship."

"A what? Lemme see."

I lie back on the gear while she looks.

"Pretty weird. But it does look like a pirate flag. Should we go over?"

"I don't know. Who knows what kind of scene it is."

We paddle a bit closer, but still keep a safe distance. A cluster of people crowd the stern of a boat that looks like a shiny bread box on floats. The flag is definitely the skull and crossbones, limp but unmistakable.

"Hello!" someone calls.

"Hi. Are you going downriver?"

"Oh, we're out for a little swim, you might say. Wayne, here, is swimming from Peace River to Fort Vermilion, four hundred and fifty kilometres. He's raising money to build a swimming pool in Vermilion."

The black figure in the group turns out to be Wayne, clad in a wetsuit.

"Hot enough for you?" I shout.

"Just right for this," Wayne says.

We paddle on past this extraordinary scene. But two miles farther down the boat catches us. A stocky man comes to the rail.

"Coffee's hot," he calls. "Come on over."

He introduces himself as Mike and serves us coffee laced with Irish Cream. We soon learn that he and his wife escaped from Hungary in 1956 and have lived in Canada ever since.

He's not shy about expressing himself. "I built the houseboat because with all the regulations and bureaucracy, you can't even build a cabin along this river. Can you imagine that? This way I have my cabin *and* I'm free to move."

He shows us pictures of the boat at various stages of evolution, of family, hunting trips, fall foliage on the Peace.

"This is a beautiful valley. I never want to leave here." But he bristles at the mention of environmentalists. "They're a bunch of southerners telling us how to live, how to take care of this river. *Us*," he points at his barrel chest, eyebrows astonished, "who have taken care of it all along. And the pulp mills everybody's yelling about. They put out less pollution than a little town like Grande Prairie!"

Our canoe is tethered to the boat's railing, like a little pilot fish. The houseboat drifts silently. It is shady and cool inside. Mike gives us fresh fruit, more coffee, dollops of Irish Cream. A comfortable disarray of books, maps, binoculars, guns, clothing litters the boat. Although the bread-box craft looked cobbled together and ungainly from a distance, it has been thoughtfully constructed and is perfectly functional.

Mike has donated his boat and time to Wayne's cause. Wayne is an Olympic-class swimmer who owns a hotel in Fort Vermilion. He became distressed when a local kid drowned in the river, a thing that happens with some frequency. He thought a town swimming pool would allow kids to learn to swim, and he took on this marathon as a way to raise money. His support team comprises his family and Mike.

"Greenhorns from Edmonton," Mike calls them. They are barely in sight behind us, upriver. Wayne tows a large red balloon, and the rest – father, sister, and fiancée – putt along close by in a little motorboat. "They would have tried this swim just like that," Mike says. "You could see it would never work."

I feel like I'm playing hooky, drifting along, making slow miles, escaping the sun. Neither of us says anything about venturing back into the heat. The thermometer on board creeps upward to one hundred degrees (37°C).

"Lived in Toronto for eight years," Mike says. "The scary thing is that you can get used to living like that. All that time and I never saw the inside of my neighbour's house. What's worse is that I didn't even realize how strange that was till I moved away."

It soon becomes clear that Mike can take any conversation and lead it quickly to his favourite topic, the evils of socialism.

"I'm proud to be Canadian now, but I'm ashamed of the way the country is acting. It's like Hungary before the Communists, the same thing all over."

He and his wife have settled in High Level and run a string of small-town newspapers. "I've been burned out twice, and I'm in court all the time. I'm the most burned out and sued publisher in the country. But I promised never to run away again after I left Hungary. And I've never lost in court because I tell the truth and can back it up."

"Socialized medicine is killing people." Mike has momentum now. "They won't allow it to evolve. Canadian journalists are socialist scum. Over the years I've hired twenty-two writers out of journalism schools. Only two were salvageable!"

We steer the conversation back to the river. He sees what we are doing and chuckles. "I've been accused of being half a mile to the right of Attila the Hun, politically." Mike flicks the depth-finder on, and we see the shifting numbers – fifteen feet, thirty-five, nineteen, twenty-six. "I've seen it go to sixty feet in places," Mike says. "It's eerie when you're going over one of those deep spots."

Eventually Wayne catches up, swims alongside. The family is huddled under the shade of a funky awning in the little boat. Marypat and I make it an international effort by taking turns joining Wayne. Twenty minutes in the Peace without a wetsuit and our teeth are chattering, lips purple.

The group obviously dotes on Mike, knowing that without him the swim would be impossible. He is always threatening to keelhaul one or another greenhorn, to demote them in rank, and they banter back happily.

Before long they invite us to join them for a picnic that evening at the La Crete ferry crossing. The Métis community of Paddle Prairie is putting on a feed for them. The day slips past at the Peace River's pace. It's disorienting to see shoreline going by without the accompanying ache of muscles, or the small discomforts of long hours in the canoe seat, or the warm spots on my hands where the paddle turns and twists. Disorienting, but like a vacation.

The campground at the ferry crossing looks like a newly bulldozed construction site, with deep, hardened ruts scarred in the earth. The outhouses wear a high-water line halfway up their doors. We pitch our tent on the worst site of the trip and join the party.

The people from Paddle Prairie have come across in pickup trucks and are serving up moose stew and bannock. Wayne makes a short speech, thanking them for their support.

"No problem," the Métis chairman says. "My brother dropped the moose last week anyway." He smiles readily. His ballcap reads, "Life Is Too Short to Dance with Ugly Women."

A woman named Nora is responsible for the stew. Her long hair is ebony black. She and Marypat strike up a conversation, and within minutes they become intimate.

"I lost my boy last year," Nora says, in a voice so gentle you have to lean in to hear. "He was eighteen. Died of cancer in two months."

Paddle Prairie, along with Fort Vermilion, is one of the oldest settlements in northern Alberta. The Métis people who live there now are of mixed Indian and European blood, a birthright that has saddled them with a long fight for recognition and social status. These men and women are descendants of the unions between Cree and French, Chipewyan and Scots, Beaver and English, which began with the first European contact. They were not covered by the treaties negotiated with the various Indian bands, nor were they granted the rights of Europeans. To some extent that no-man's-land legacy still lingers.

Before long the mosquitoes get thick and the party breaks up. Marypat and I scurry to our tent to escape the insects. A short-eared owl perches on a post near the ferry, its silhouette barely visible as the twilight descends.

10

IN THE MORNING we ride the ferry across to say goodbye to the swim team. The deckhand is a middle-aged man wearing white overalls, with a nice smile full of bad teeth.

"My family moved here to farm in 1941," he says, waving off to the east. "There were only horse trails back then."

Wayne, with his fiancée, is off trying to get medicine for a bothersome ear infection. The group is at loose ends and a bit testy with each other. They have taken to calling us the Boat People. We stay long enough for pirate-ship coffee, then ride the ferry back to our loaded canoe.

The deckhand tells us that the other day a brand new car had been left in neutral and rolled right off the ferry. "It's still in the river. Right over there." He points to a spot in the unruffled current and chuckles.

It is nice to be off again, to leave people behind. We paddle over the sunken car and wave back at the houseboat, then lose them around the first bend.

The floods have dropped huge sections of bank into the water. Whole groves of aspen, still alive, poke up out of the current, waving slightly as if in a thick wind. We paddle through them, picking a watery path through forest.

A brown bear comes down to the river ahead of us. I can almost hear its sigh of relief when it walks into the water, turns, and lies down. Only its head rests on the bank, and though I can't tell, I imagine that the bear's eyes close in bliss. Then he catches our scent, rises wearily, and lumbers away.

The wind begins to pick up. For the first time I see the surface of the Peace lose its molten quality, break up in wind-driven waves. The already long bends become excruciatingly slow and the canoe grows unmanageable. At least the moving air is cooling. We bear down, don't talk or watch the slow parade of shoreline, just dig in, heads bowed, arms aching with strain.

Black clouds finally convince us to quit. By the time the canoe hits shore the waves are white-capped and sand on the beach swirls in small funnel clouds. It takes both of us to wrestle the tent up, in conditions like a windy day on the Sahara.

But the air is blessedly cool. Squalls of rain patter down, and for the first time in weeks we can get into the tent without sweltering. Once we are cozily inside, the sounds of the storm are comforting. I climb into long pants and a heavy shirt. Marypat extends her winning streak in backgammon by several more games, until I get huffy about it and we turn to reading instead. My reading for the summer is Paul Theroux's *Riding the Iron Rooster*.

And it is still blowing when morning comes around. For ten difficult miles we battle on. There is a bit of shelter right next to shore, and we inch through the shallows. Any conversation has to be shouted. Gusts of wind punch heavily into stands of trees, whipping the branches. Clouds of sand pelt us and get in our eyes.

"This is ridiculous," Marypat shouts. "What about stopping over there?" She points to a flat, green patch on the far shore.

But crossing is very nearly our undoing. The current slews the boat in one direction while wind shoves it in another. The canoe wallows in steep wave troughs. I draw the bow straight, Marypat pries with her paddle in the stern. All our effort is spent keeping upright and head on. We are like a twig caught in the fray.

"Look back, Al."

A spotted sandpiper has landed on our deck. We quit the battle for a moment while the bird walks around skittishly and tries to get a grip in the fabric. Then it is snatched away again, leaving skeletal tracks that dry almost immediately.

By the time we make shore our arms are rubbery with fatigue. "We need a good day in camp anyway," Marypat announces.

Soon she is busy with a beading project, then tackles some laundry. We heat water and wash our hair. A nearby spring provides a supply of clean water, seeping down the hillside in the midst of lush grasses.

"You're really having fun, aren't you."

"You know I like these camp days." Marypat looks fresh and sunburned. Her hair blows around her head. I remember how pretty she is, how infrequently I've seen this kind of happiness in her eyes lately.

"Let's go for a walk," she says.

At the top of the steep hillside the woods close around us. The wind is a thing that happens in the tree tops, and without it I start to sweat again. Game trails lead us along the top of a wooded ridge, through cranberry and blueberry bushes. The tracks of wolf, deer, bear, and coyote make me think that eyes are watching from the near shadows. It's a good feeling, not at all like being spooked in a dark house.

At a break in the forest, we get a view far upriver, a wide brown rope coiling off in the green distance. It's strange not to hear the sounds the water makes, to be distant, suddenly, from the medium we are so intimate with, so dependent on.

The remaining fifty miles to Fort Vermilion come gradually, each one tough, like a long uphill grade. Wind harries us, not strong enough to make us stop, but enough to make it a struggle, and I keep thinking of Wayne breast-stroking through the brown waves, pulling his balloon down the long miles.

The Peace has become a mile wide, more than that in places. I am surprised again and again by how long it takes to get across it, how steady and powerful the flow is, even though the river drops only one foot a mile. The water level continues to recede in the hot summer days. We have to watch for sandbars, running aground when we're not careful, and become increasingly adept at reading the water's texture for deep channels.

Several bends above town our canoe passes under the final

highway bridge of our journey. For the next year we will not see another. It is the last road that connects south, another layer shed.

"That's it," I say, as a car drones above our heads.

We park the canoe on a mud flat on the outskirts of town and climb up to the main, river-front street, appearing suddenly, as if from out of a utility hole, carrying our small sack of laundry like hobos. Right away we see a large billboard with a map of the Peace River on it. At the top it says, "Where Is Wayne?" and an arrow marks the swimmer's last known position. Beside the map a fundraising thermometer measures up to $500,000, but is coloured red barely above the bulb, at $25,000.

Fort Vermilion has that just-scraped-out-of-the-bush look so typical of the North. Dirt side streets, dirt yards, as though the town had been erected in the last year and nobody has gotten around to planting grass yet. Except that the area has been occupied since the fur-trade days in the early 1800s. In 1897 Fort Vermilion was already populated by 168 people and a variety of livestock.

The laundromat is sandwiched between a convenience store and Fonzie's Arcade. Listless teenagers hang around in the dusty heat. We pick up a few things at the store, buy stamps at the post office.

At Wayne's hotel I order a Mighty Peace Burger. We tell the waitress that we spent a day with Wayne, that he could arrive in town any time.

"Maybe it's just that I'm from down south," she says. "But it sure doesn't seem like anybody cares. You'd think they'd have the streets decorated and be planning a big welcome, but nobody even mentions it. The poor man might show up after swimming all that way, and have twenty people there. It could happen!"

In barely two hours we have managed to spend more than fifty dollars. Even this brief stop brings home the extent to which we have gone over to wilderness living. Now it is the town that seems strange. The air in the post office is oppressive and stagnant, cigarette smoke in the restaurant a noxious cloud.

And our return to the river feels like an escape. We stroke away hard, away from the noise, until we are, once again, enveloped by the sound of the eddying current, the whispering leaves, the nearby croak of a raven.

By the time we stop again, the town is a faint memory. Camp goes together smoothly, and then with relief we wade out for our daily swim, as much to wash off town as for relief from the sun. Afterward, still wet, we make love. Our bodies feel lean and strong together, muscular and weathered. The sun dries us off and breezes wash across us, cooling, healing, and we hold each other tight.

I I

WE ARE COOKING up dinner when a wood skiff drones toward us from upriver. A big man rides in the back, his weight forcing the bow out of the water. He angles in, dodging sandbars, running aground once or twice, but persisting until he lodges against shore.

He clambers noisily out of the flat-bottomed boat as we walk down to meet him. His snap-up western shirt is soiled with mud, the crotch of his pants hangs halfway to his knees, a week of beard roughens his heavy face. He wears cowboy boots with broken-down heels.

"Going up or down?" he asks, without introduction.

"Down."

"You know you have a big five-mile portage at Vermilion Falls in a few days, eh?"

He doesn't stand still when he talks, keeps shoving his hands in his pockets, then taking them out to gesture randomly.

"Well, we hoped we might sneak through some of the chutes and just portage the falls," I say.

He starts to pace in front of us, his hands making erratic sweeps.

"Christ, I don't know about that!" he explodes. "All I can say is, you better have a damned good look before you try anything like that. I heard of people who ran those things and showed up later in pieces! You throw a stick in that water, and it gets sucked in and spat out again twenty yards away."

He begins to draw a map in the sand.

"Here's Adam's Landing," he says, digging a divot with a rock. "Then the Lawrence River comes in." A long slash. "The chutes cross here." A broad band made with his boot. "Oh, shit, you'll hear those things miles upstream!"

"Want coffee?" I ask.

He takes his grubby life vest off and sits down on it. "Always wear this on the river, eh?"

"Do you live near here?" Marypat asks.

"My place is about nine miles down. The last homestead around here. Been here and on another place down by John D'Or about thirty years."

"What do you grow?"

"Oh, most anything. Wheat, rape . . ." He looks at Marypat. "Sorry. Canola is what they call it now. Shot a nice brown bear in my fields the other day. Thought he'd make a good rug, so I shot him."

While we talk, he grooms the sand with his hands, builds little mounds, draws circles, then wipes it clean with a boot, starts over again.

"Now I'm glad I stopped to visit," he says, finishing his coffee. But he stays on.

"Any family?" I ask.

"No," he replies, in a tone that means there's more to it. "I'm baching now."

"Kids?"

"All grown. Moved south by the cities." He studies the sand.

The sun is making peach and purple colours in the sky. A nearly full moon pulls itself above the trees across the river. We offer him dinner. He declines, but still lingers, loneliness hovering around him. I notice him assessing our gear, appreciating the efficiency of our camping style.

"This is a beautiful, peaceful river." All during his visit his eyes are out there, watching for fish, for animals across the way, again and again pulled to the water. "It's all changed since they put that Bennett Dam in up in B.C." Something strident comes into his voice. "That's not what the dam people would tell you, but it has. They let out the same flow all the time, now. Used to be this river was changing constantly, almost like it was alive, eh? I'd drive up a channel one day and come back the next and run aground. Even the islands moved. No more. The dam killed all that."

Someone shoots a gun in the distance, back toward Fort Vermilion. "Indians on the warpath," he says, looking at the moon.

"We don't even know your name," Marypat says.

"Probably just as well, eh?" Then, after a pause, he says softly, "Vern." There is no shaking of hands.

"Do you think this country will ever fill up with people?" I ask.

"Nope. Never will."

He stands up, groaning, knees popping, dusts off a cloud of sand and dirt. We follow as he shambles back to the skiff, shrugs into his life vest.

"I do the same thing you do on this river," he says. "Getting to know it. Spending time out on it. Just in little bits, eh?"

After he starts his motor and navigates to deeper water, Vern lifts his hand in a long stationary wave.

By lunch time the next day, shade is the only thing we crave.

"There." Marypat waves her paddle at a steep mud bank.

I have nothing better to offer, so we head there, land in muck and crawl crabwise along the gunwales to reach the relative cool. We have to tiptoe on driftwood to avoid deep mud, then perch on a bleached log, backs against the dirt wall.

A hermit thrush is loud in the brush around us while we eat our dried fruit and bannock, drink water by the quart. Dirt from the bank dribbles down our backs, but the shade is bliss. My exposed skin gradually stops throbbing.

Later, heat again makes us give in for the day. We camp on a shrubby island, backing ourselves against a screen of willows to escape the sun. There are bear tracks in front of us. The bears use the islands and sandbars like stepping stones as they swim the river. Again and again we find their tracks emerging from the water at an island's upstream tip, then trailing along to the far end, where they disappear again into the river.

I don't read, can hardly think in this heat. Just sit numbly, with the big, rustling silence and the slick river all around.

"I think we made a mistake," Marypat blurts out. "I never want to do one of these huge, muddy rivers again."

Her tone alarms me, the defeat in it. It sounds like more than just the effects of a long day under the sun.

"It won't be long. We should be up to Lake Athabasca in a week or ten days." I try to think of something more encouraging, uplifting, but Marypat is distracted, not listening anyway.

My thoughts wander back to the falls we will negotiate tomorrow. I try to imagine a mile-wide river, a river that is sixty feet deep in places, dropping over a ledge. What kind of power is that? I feel the adrenaline pump picking up inside, the old familiar mix of dread and eagerness, the urge to be there now, and the hope that it will never come.

When we again take up our paddles in the morning, we chatter back and forth about our families, then about the life of the *voyageurs*, and the way the river has since been abandoned, like a long, meandering ghost town.

But after a few miles, when we stop to pee, a light upriver wind brings us the far-off grumbling of big water. It is still five miles away. The placid, silty expanse is as sedate as ever, but the irrefutable evidence of the coming conflict wafts up to us and shuts off our diverting talk.

The sound is solid, heavy, unvaried, a drumming in the air. It is a long time before we can see anything, but we paddle tight against shore, quiet now. Then I see the huge islands of rounded rock at the head of the chutes. The river cants downhill, and the drumming closes around us.

A raven coasts out of a tree, flies ahead, and lands downstream. When we come near it does it again. I take it as an omen, as if the black bird is encouraging us, telling us to come on. Or is it playing the trickster?

The huge rapids are indistinct, impossible to read. Rocks the size of trailer-homes break the current, and spray from the waves catches the sunlight. Whole trees, battered and bare, lie on the rocks, left there by high water. Some are balanced delicately, with a kind of random artistry. We pull in and tie up below the ruins of a large old building. Both of us have anxious bladders and need to pee again before going to scout. It is our style to look over an entire run in silence, each searching for the best way, and then to negotiate strategy.

"This isn't so bad," I shout, after we walk the length of the upper chutes.

"Hard to say. The river's so big that it might be easy to underestimate. But it does seem like we've done lots worse."

"We can do this!" By now I'm hopping around on the rocks, pointing out the linked moves that will bring us down the narrow passages, through sets of waves. The five-mile portage will at least be substantially shortened.

After all the slow, ponderous miles of the last weeks, I welcome the anticipation of action. It is the first time since the Smoky that we snap up the deck, put on life vests, and kneel in the boat. The whitewater is something joyous after the unrelenting heat, the daily search for clean water and campsites free of mud. The flood-rounded rocks loom over us, our canoe sneaks between boulders, ferries out around obstacles, lines up to slice through waves. It is a dance, this play of current, boat, and paddle, and we are laughing together in smooth water again, the ride over too quickly.

But the falls are still coming up. The canoe hurries toward them, and we tense for surprises. Marypat stands up repeatedly to look ahead. By the time we see the ragged, sharp break in the river, we are nearly on top of them. The pounding water is endless thunder. The current pulls us closer as we backpaddle, inch toward the brink, gaining as much distance as we can before landing a few feet above the drop.

We rest the canoe on a flat shelf of fossil-filled limestone. The jagged ledge of rock crosses more than a mile of river. The far side could well be a postcard. And all this immeasurable fluid weight, this monstrous draining of a continent, piles over the rock face, froths and eddies, then pushes on relentlessly.

Barring any surprises, this will be the only portage in our 1,100-mile summer. The canoe stays parked and loaded while we explore the falls and look for a good put-in. The noise is like an exhilarating wind, water dances in the sunlight, and the rock seems to shudder beneath our feet. Marypat is busy with the camera and tripod. After a while I just stand there, soaking it up.

When steamboats plied the river they had to stop and offload where we first pulled out to scout. Their cargo would be freighted around on a cart track, then transferred to another boat.

Once, a sternwheeler ran the falls – the *D.A. Thomas*, 167 feet long and 40 feet wide. The Hudson's Bay Company had bought the boat in Peace River and wanted to bring her to Lake Athabasca. Captain Cowley and pilot Louis Bourassa thrashed through the heavy water to the falls, lined up for the broad slot they had chosen, and then stuck fast, like a cork in a bottle. Water piled up behind the huge boat, lifting and tipping her until she crashed down. Tons of water flooded over the bow, half of the stern wheel ripped away, but the boat rose, bobbing in the froth below. After repairs to the wheel, the *D.A. Thomas* went blithely on. I look for a place a boat that size might have run, and try to imagine the gumption of any man willing to try it.

We may have shortened our portage to fifty yards, but the put-in will still be tricky. Cliffs drop sheer into the water, and downstream they rise higher, with no way around, no way down. Right at the base of the falls, we find a spot that will require handing the packs down a seven-foot wall, but the water there is turbulent and rough. We eat lunch while we think about it.

"Maybe we should camp out there, take the rest of the day off to enjoy this place." I point to an island formed by a remnant limestone ledge, surrounded by sand beach, sitting in the middle of the river just below the falls.

"It looks like a tugboat out there," MP says. "Think we can get to it?" The water is frothy and full of waves.

"It'd be fun if we could."

"First we have to get back in the river!"

When we lower the canoe down the cliff by its bow and stern ropes, it rocks and bucks wildly, bumps in against the wall, then tries to escape into the current.

"You sure about this?" Marypat has the stern line and is looking down sceptically.

"I don't see another choice, but we'll need to tie the ropes off so we don't have to hold the canoe while we're loading."

I belly over the side of the cliff, scrabble for a foothold, then stand carefully in the centre of the canoe. Beneath the hull the river is alive, agitated, full of itself. The light boat jumps around erratically, tugging against its tethers.

"We need more weight in here," I call up. "Bring me a pack." I cling to the crumbly rock, smell its musty, ancient odour, try to visualize myself keeping my balance with the bulk of a pack descending on me.

"Here it comes."

I grab on, spread my feet, but am not prepared when the full weight hits. My feet adjust, but the canoe tips abruptly, throwing me against the rock. I half drop the pack, grab limestone, steady myself, then breath again. Marypat is above me, shaking her head and chuckling.

"Whoa!" I gasp. "If I'd fallen away from the cliffs instead of into them, I'd be in the falls now."

12

THE MAPS OF this land are an unbroken expanse of green. The only white spots are natural clearings or swamps. Cut-lines from old seismic surveys and occasional cart tracks are shown here and there, and the Caribou Mountains rise to the north, uninhabited, seldom penetrated, a wild presence, soothing to the imagination.

The notations that have to do with mankind indicate either

relics of the river-oriented past, or Native settlements. John D'Or Prairie Reserve, Fox Lake Reserve, Tall Cree Reserve, are squared-off blocks, tiny land grants in country once unbounded.

The morning we leave Vermilion Falls an upriver wind snatches away their thunder. I have to glance back west to remind myself that they are there, like a broad mural filling the view.

"This is a wonderful place," Marypat says, sounding wistful. "Yesterday was the first time I didn't think about home."

We stop to explore the Little Red River settlement, just downstream, where there are cabins with caved-in sod roofs, dilapidated ruins left over from the busy days of trapping and portaging. But a new outdoor chapel, longhouse style, is filled with wood benches. The Virgin Mary occupies a glassed-in shrine. She is surrounded by plastic flowers, thick candles, a string of rosary beads. Several wall tents are pitched nearby, but no one is around. Two kittens approach through the tall grasses, keeping a wary distance.

The winds fight against us, stop our conversation. We pace ourselves, heads down, trying not to notice how slowly we progress. At Fox Lake Reserve a few houses are visible from the river, a plume of smoke, four or five boats along shore, but no movement.

Part-way along a shallow channel that we take to avoid the wind, I see people near the water's edge. Three small boys play in the shallows. They cluster together when they see us, arms at their sides, pants rolled up, no shirts. Skinny kids, who watch us as soberly as if we had just dropped from the sky. A young woman stops along a path leading up the bank, half turns toward us. When I wave, she lifts her hand, then seems to catch herself and pulls it back down.

Although these people almost certainly have television, a microwave, connections to the outside, we seem irrevocably distant from each other. I wonder, as we paddle on, what sort of man I would be, what passions would drive my life, if it had been my lot to be born on this quiet reserve along the Peace River.

The day has been lightly overcast and relatively cool, but the afternoon heat comes on fiercely. The air feels heavy with change. Winds die off, then gust fitfully. Massive thunderheads build up, towering against the pale blue sky, brooding.

We are back on the main channel, mid-stream, when I turn and see a black squall behind us.

"Wow! That looks like rain. Is it coming for us?"

Marypat turns and automatically reaches for her camera.

"I don't think there's time for that." My voice is tense. I can see a lather of whitecaps under the darkness. Big trees on shore are bent over at impossible angles. "We better get our rain gear out and snap up the deck!"

I see that what I thought was rain is actually a cloud of wind-driven sand. The whitecaps are charging toward us. Wind sounds like an approaching train.

"Hurry up! Hurry up!" I mutter, fumbling with snaps, tightening the skirt around my waist.

It pounces as we're still struggling. There is no prelude, no build-up, just this grit-filled blast smacking into us. The smooth river is transformed into a welter of three- and four-foot waves. When the squall hits, it turns us broadside. The downstream gunwale tips under. Momentarily I think we're over. Without the cover we would be.

"For Christ's sake, brace!" I scream.

We give up trying to turn the boat, both hang out, bracing with our paddles like outriggers, helpless as driftwood.

"We gotta get to shore," Marypat calls.

But just as the words are out we hear a splintery crash and see a mature tree fall in the forest. Then another.

"Holy shit! Did you see that?"

Slowly, we alternate between bracing and paddling and come closer to shore. The wind is a steady gale, with no break. It catches against the hull, keeps trying to shove us over. Waves heave us up, twisting, wallowing. More than once the gunwale goes under, water breaks over the deck. Trees keep snapping, their broad, leafy heads toppling over, taking out saplings as they fall.

Eventually we reach a muddy spot on the bank that seems out of reach of any trees, and we hold ourselves there, watching first the churning river and then the tortured forest.

"I've never seen anything like this," I say. "It can't last long."

In relative safety, now, we can afford to be awestruck.

The wind finally dies a bit, but the water is still rough, the clouds threatening. We creep along shore to the very tip of a skinny island, a sharp prow of land safely away from falling trees, and stop to make camp. The largest bear tracks we've seen all summer, fresh-looking, an inch deep, mark the mud out the door of our tent, but there is no other place to go.

Then something catches my eye. I get the binoculars and focus on a point a mile or more downriver. It is two people, running away from the water, carrying a canoe. The first canoe we've seen.

"I wonder if they're in trouble," Marypat says. "There's no way we can get there if they are."

It is still windy the next morning when we pull to shore near the white canoe. A small tent perches above us at the edge of a sand escarpment. A large duffel bag, presumably containing food, dangles over the edge from a tree root. It's a steep scramble up the slope.

"Anybody home?"

We stand outside the closed-up tent.

"Hello?" answers a muffled male voice, accented. Rustling, a zipper, then a small, lean man dressed only in underpants pops through the door.

"Saw your canoe and thought we'd visit," I say.

"Yes. Fine." The accent is German. "My name is Wolfgang.

This is Rosemary." He points at the tent, indicating a companion we can't see.

"We saw you yesterday, in the wind. Thought you might be in trouble. Are you all right?"

"Yes, yes," he nods vigorously. His skin is goose-bumped and he is shivering. "We had to move the canoe. We were hiding from the storm."

Rosemary hands him a pair of pants and emerges shyly from the tent to be introduced. Her English is not fluent and she mostly lets Wolfgang talk.

They have come from Germany to paddle from Fort Vermilion to Fort Smith, in the Northwest Territories. Wolfgang has already done a Canadian trip on the Yukon River. "After the Yukon," he says, "I knew I had to come back. So I saved money until I could return."

After we talk awhile we wave goodbye and slide back down to our canoe. But the winds are powerful. Waves hump up in the river, and while we ready the boat, sand whips us until we have to turn our backs. The heavily loaded boat rocks and shivers.

We look at each other, shrug, and start back up to where our new friends stand watching.

"I was just saying to Rosemary, 'See, they can paddle in such a wind as this!'" says Wolfgang. "But maybe not."

"We'll make a fire down by the creek," Marypat says. "Let's have coffee together."

All day the wind funnels upriver and the forest shudders and moans. The four of us huddle together in a thicket of alder. The tiny creek that flows nearby is full of silt, so our coffee has a thick, muddy taste.

Wolfgang and Rosemary keep referring to West Germany and then correcting themselves. The Berlin Wall has fallen only the previous year, and union is something very new.

"Can Germany afford to rebuild the East?" I ask.

"It is our obligation," Wolfgang says. "The Americans rebuilt our economy after the war. Now it is our turn to help the East Germans."

Between pots of coffee and tea, snacks and lunch, the conversation ranges from the new German team for the 1992 Summer Olympics to family histories, and then back to the present. This river, this wilderness.

"I am a forester in Germany," Wolfgang tells us. "But forests in Europe are nothing like this. Nothing so wild."

When I go out once from our sheltered grove to check the weather, a bear is swimming away from shore, fifty feet out. We watch the black head, facing upstream, waves breaking around it, slowly angling for the far shore a mile away. It has left tracks that lead right to Wolfgang and Rosemary's camp, then turn to the water. By the time the bear reaches the other side we are watching with binoculars. The black shape heaves out of the water, shakes heavily, disappears like a smudge of charcoal into the tangle of woods.

The inevitable bear stories start up. Wolfgang tells of a morning on the Yukon, frost in the air, when a brown bear ambled into camp, licked hot chocolate from the bottoms of their unwashed cups, sniffed their packs, then wandered away. We relate our adventure on the Athabasca, explaining that we take a shotgun along as a last-resort defence. Rosemary is intent on our story, quiet afterward.

"That was a very rare situation," MP reassures her. "We've seen dozens and dozens of bears. Mostly they are like the one just now. They don't want anything to do with people."

It becomes obvious that we will travel nowhere today. Before we retire, Wolfgang says, "Perhaps tomorrow we would paddle together?"

13

THE BOUNDARY AT Wood Buffalo National Park is nothing more than a line on the map. If there were signs, the high water has taken them out. The ruined settlement of Fifth Meridian hunkers in the weeds. On the topo sheet a dotted track extends back to Vermilion Falls, an overland route used when low water and sandbars made navigation impossible.

And yet something indefinable changes as the four of us enter the new jurisdiction. It is a place watched over by wardens and rangers, where permits are required of travellers. The land is managed and studied here, and somehow it seems more tame than where we have been.

The banks are low and muddy, the current slow. No wildlife in sight. At the Native settlement of Garden Creek we make our way through a litter of plastic bags, Pepsi bottles, and discarded lengths of rope to the main dirt street. Older log cabins are crowded by newer, prefabricated houses and trailers. In the general store Rosemary and Wolfgang look for more food supplies, but the shelves are spotty and all they find is a box of spaghetti and a bag of cookies. Kids loiter in the aisles, silent and shy. It is a long time before someone comes to the cash register. As we leave town a skinny dog howls at us from the top of its little house.

Rosemary and Wolfgang stay with us for nearly a week. They are good company and we are going the same way. In the international spirit we refer to each other as the American Team and the German Team.

"You never stop paddling," Wolfgang protests. "But I think it is good for us. We wouldn't finish on time if we only drifted."

Their food supplies are meagre. Tiny bags of granola, tortilla-like bannock, noodles without sauce, some soup mixes. We share our dinners with them every night, ignoring their protests.

Each evening they are up late making their stack of bannock for the next day while the mosquitoes grow thick and the grey light falls. The Midnight Bakery, we call it. But they are in good spirits, love the wild country, are uncomplaining about the clublike paddles and below-par equipment they've rented.

At a campsite that we reached by wading across an expanse of ankle-deep mud, I watch from our tent as they bake their bread. It is twilight. The waning moon, still heavy, shines a path of light across the rippling river. The two of them are silhouetted against the flickering fire. An owl ghosts through the air above their heads, silent, almost batlike, looking for its prey.

The weather becomes changeable. Steady rain falls one day and the German Team in their inadequate ponchos and open boat are miserable. But the coolness is a relief, the cloud patterns and play of light a refreshment. The next day the oppressive heat returns, along with a headwind. We catch whiffs of forest fire in the air, and the sunlight is hazy and red.

Near Peace Point the river quickens through Boyer Rapids. Lining the shore are limestone cliffs studded with gypsum deposits so white I pick up a rock and lick it to be sure it isn't salt.

A few wall tents are set up amongst the poplar and aspen that provide shade at Peace Point. In the late 1700s the Cree and Beaver bands negotiated a treaty here, and it is designated as a holding of Native land within the park.

The site is indeed peaceful, but Marypat is cranky. "I want a rest day!" she demands. It has been a long haul since the early, easygoing miles on the Smoky. The heat and monotonous paddling have taken their toll.

"We'll get wind days on Lake Athabasca," I say.

"I need one now!"·

Once in camp her mood lightens. She cools off in the river, changes clothes, makes herself a cup of tea. Her bare feet knead the sand as she writes in her journal.

"This is the best time," she says later as she presides over a dessert baking in the Dutch oven. "But I still want a rest day."

At dawn I find bear tracks behind our camp, tracks that I'm sure weren't there the night before. But nothing has been disturbed. The trail is a straight, purposeful line, ignoring whatever temptations we provide.

We start out trying to sail, erecting a tarp between the two canoes to catch an erratic wind. No good. Soon we are paddling again, watching the sky. A pair of sandhill cranes fly over, their broad wings set to the wind in an effortless economy we cannot hope to match. The sound of their watery talk comes through miles of air. They coast north, not once flapping their wings.

The only wild population of breeding whooping cranes summers, along with thousands of their sandhill relatives, in the remote northern section of the park. The birds, on the brink of extinction, were spotted by chance when a helicopter pilot flew over the area in 1954. At that point the entire breeding population of the species was twenty-one birds.

Beleaguered over the years by habitat destruction, pesticide poisoning, and unrestricted hunting, the flock has made a slow but steady comeback to its present population of roughly 140. They nest in this northern remove, then take their chances against storms and misguided hunters on their yearly migration to Texas. A single calamity of weather or disease could still wipe out the wild population at a stroke.

Around a corner the fires we've been smelling for days are suddenly in our face. Flames run up the trunk of a spruce, smoke and spit, then bloom out in a consuming explosion. Smoke billows out of the deeper forest, and as we coast by we hear the sounds of crashing limbs. The same winds that harry us sustain and encourage the fires. Occasionally a helicopter whirrs past, but it is only monitoring the blaze, not fighting it.

Unless the fires threaten settlements, it is too expensive for the park to battle them. I read that in dry years as much as a quarter of the park's lands will burn. The vastness of the wilderness allows the luxury of letting nature take its course.

When Yellowstone Park burned out of control in 1988, our local Montana papers were full of emotional letters to the editor. People bemoaned the burning of "our park" and chastised authorities for not "taking control." As if it is our right, our mandate, to control nature. As if such events are subject to our ownership.

At lunch we dine at the river's edge beneath a section of forest blackened by recent fire. Wolfgang finds a way up the steep bank by climbing a downed tree, and we soon stand in the eerie silence of devastation. Wolfgang is barefoot and keeps hopping on the hot ground.

Puffs of ash, like moondust, cloud around our feet. Spruce and jack pine are black and broken, skeletal. On the ground lie ghost shadows, lines of ash left under fallen trees after they were consumed. Little trails like capillaries wind here and there where the fires followed root systems. Nothing moves among the ranks of trees. No birds, no squirrels, only the tendrils of smoke which snake upward and then are taken by the wind.

When we camp, it is on an island that we hope is at a safe distance from either shore. The sun is a weary red eye. At times the crackling, crashing sounds come to us, and I think of the animals in its path fleeing, or dying. I try not to breathe deeply, taste wood smoke in our dinner.

Overnight the wind shifts and cleanses the air, as though the fires were nothing more than yesterday's dream. We battle against it, but the clear sky and smell of live forest is worth the struggle.

Although I have grown accustomed to the bulk of the Peace, I am struck again by its enormous size as we near the delta that marks its end. Studying the map I see old channels and oxbow lakes, the signs of an aging river's slow writhing dance across its valley; a dance in which a move takes thousands, even millions, of years. And yet the river has such sudden, effortless strength.

When we fight with our small strokes to miss a snag, the sinews of water are inexorable and unrelaxed, gigantically strong.

Sweetgrass Landing is a place where the herds of bison cross the river. On the far side, an aisle of beaten-down brush indicates where their path continues. Around us their tracks are sunk deeply in the mud, leading off into the interior grasslands near Lake Claire.

There is a picnic table up on the riverbank, a park sign, and an unmarked trail heading inland. No road comes here, you must travel by boat. But nevertheless there are discarded tea bags and scraps of toilet paper on the ground, along with a healthy mound of bear shit.

The wood buffalo, slightly smaller than their plains cousins, once roamed the North in large herds. Their range included the southern shore of Lake Athabasca and the parklands throughout northern Alberta. Their near extinction is an old story, the same old story.

The species was in dire peril by the time a hunting ban was enforced in 1893. Then in 1922 the park was created in their name. Between 1925 and 1928, six thousand transplanted plains bison were brought north from the former Buffalo National Park near Wainwright, Alberta. These beasts had to be shipped on the Northern Alberta Railway to Fort McMurray, on the Athabasca River. Then barges took the bovine cargo down the Athabasca, through the delta to Lake Athabasca, and into the park.

Since then the bison herd has interbred, established a range, and lived in balance with the wolves that feed on them. Their numbers drop in flood years, when many drown, or in harsh winters, and rebound in other years. At present they number some 3,500 to 4,000 animals, the largest free-roaming bison herd in the world.

Yet their future is hardly assured. The Canadian government has recommended the slaughter of the entire park population.

Its crime, tuberculosis and brucellosis. The diseases were introduced by the transplanted plains buffalo, and have become
chronic and widespread.

Livestock ranchers and the agricultural lobby are strident in
demanding the eradication of these diseases. A government
panel charged with finding a solution finally settled on the most
drastic, albeit effective, course of action.

As far as we can tell, contact between domesticated livestock
and wild bison is a fairly remote possibility. We haven't seen a
domestic animal all summer. The nearest ranch is a long hike
from here through formidable wilderness.

Evidence of the diseases being transmitted from wild to
domesticated herds is scanty. The greatest irony of all is that the
bison almost certainly contracted these scourges in the first
place from infected cattle brought over from Europe.

Studies continue. Government panels discuss alternatives.
Meanwhile, the bison graze in the sweet clover and marshy
grasslands, swim the wide river, watch for wolves, unaware of
their precarious future at the hands of humankind, whose convenience takes priority over all else.

We walk a little way inland, through fields of wildflowers,
native grasses, sun-dappled aspen groves. The river is abruptly
gone, and I feel the absence of its weight and supple sounds as a
vague uneasiness, as something gone wrong. Water, over the
weeks, has taken possession of me. Away from it, I am lonely.

Just down from Carlson's Landing a powerboat is staked to the
mud bank in an eddy. A high sand bluff rises above it with a fire
tower perched on top. The four of us follow a trail up the bluff,
climb a long crude ladder made of spruce logs, and make our way
into the clearing. Wind stirs the branches of jack pine. A picnic
table rests at the edge of the bluff. Log buildings squat nearby, a
Canadian flag stands out in the wind, and the metal fire tower
rises above the trees.

A heavy, pleasant-looking Chipewyan man stands at the

screen door of a cabin. "Come in," he beckons. Inside it is cool and dark, confined, the moving air kept at bay. Our host arranges a few chairs for us. In the next room two women play cribbage, and children peek around the door.

"I saw you from the helicopter," the man says. "We were looking at the fires."

"Have you been here all summer?" we ask.

"Three and a half months, every year. We go back to Fort Chip next week. The summer is over now."

"Can we climb the tower?"

"Sure. Go on up."

On the metal ladder I am quickly past the point where I want to look down, well above the trees. I concentrate on the trapdoor at the top and try to ignore the swaying sensation. Rosemary is afraid of heights and refuses to come up, but the rest of us crowd into the warm square box with windows all round.

The country that has been, all summer, something to be imagined, hinted at by marks on maps, now spreads below us. The Peace is broad and dominant, sinuous and so huge that even at this distance and this height, it is undiminished. The Caribou Mountains, with a faint haze of smoke over them, shoulder against the horizon. The country is a green ocean, broken here and there by clearings and bogs, traced by the winding loops of tributary streams, pocked with lakes. I think to myself that we have paddled eight hundred miles and, for most of that distance, have been surrounded by such vastness.

When we descend, the Chipewyan man is at the picnic table.

"You didn't want to be in a canoe down there in June," he gestures over the river. "Full of sticks, all the way across."

By "sticks" he means huge logs, entire trees, brought down by the flooding, collected from rivers like the Smoky, the Wabasca, and the myriad other tributaries, until, near the delta, they made a jostling, bank-to-bank raft of wood, bumping and herding past for days on end.

"Do you go up the tower every hour or something?" I ask.

"I go up when I'm not lazy," he laughs. "When it's really hot I stay up most of the time."

"Are the fires being fought?"

"No," he looks off. "Probably burn until snow puts them out."

In our sandbar camp that night, we are crowded by the trees and stumps and weathered logs brought down by the floods. The water is low now, even our canoes run aground if we're not careful. It is our last night with the German Team. Tomorrow we start through the delta in order to reach Fort Chipewyan on Lake Athabasca. Wolfgang and Rosemary will paddle on to the Slave River.

Late at night I crawl out of the tent to pee. It is cool and quite dark. Northern lights move in the sky like pale white scarves. Mid-August already, with a hint of fall in the night air and the sun starting south. It is the first time I think about the coming winter, and about the big cold lake we must cross before it hits.

In the morning we go our separate ways. In mid-river we gunwale-up. Marypat hands Rosemary a bag of food we've put together. "We'll send lots of cookies and chocolate for the winter," Rosemary promises. Then the sleek boats drift apart, the two wakes slowly diverging. I picture us in the aerial view, how tiny we must seem, and imagine the other meetings and partings that have taken place between boats on this river.

Just before we disappear from sight into our tiny side channel, I hear a distant booming. Wolfgang is beating a frying pan on the side of his canoe, a farewell drum. We answer, banging our paddles on the hull. There is the hollow sound of our goodbye a little while longer, then silence.

14

THE CHENAL DES Quatre Fourches, our route through the delta, is the only river I've ever heard of that flows first one way and then the other in the same summer. Early in the year, when the Peace is high, the water is forced into Lake Athabasca. But by August the Peace has dropped, reversing the Quatre Fourches. The river then drains the lake and becomes one of the final tributaries to the Peace. It is our bad fortune to be late in the year.

A powerboat catches us just before we hit the current. Another Chipewyan man throttles back, then shuts off his engine to drift with us. He lights a cigarette while we talk.

"Water's low," he observes. "But the channel is good. That's how I'm going. Too bad you can't fit in my boat." He looks along the distant bank. "There's something down there."

We squint, see nothing, then finally make out a tiny black speck.

"Bear or something," he shrugs.

We talk a little longer, then take up our paddles. He is looking over our boat, our load.

"Let's see if we can tie you behind, give you a tow."

"Oh, no," Marypat says. "We like to paddle."

When we nose into the current, it fights us to a draw. I had hoped for a sluggish flow, something you'd have to study a while before telling which way it went. But it's fresh and strong, no question about its direction. We turn our paddling up a notch, then another, lean into the work.

"Oh, no. We like to paddle," I mimic my partner, after a few minutes of this. She doesn't respond.

I had no idea how cushy we'd had it all summer, coasting along with the helping current, getting a free ride. We angle as close against shore as we can to find slower water, where it is just deep enough to paddle. Still our pace is creeping.

It takes an age to get around the first bend. Along the mud shore I watch muskrat and bird tracks pass, an inch at a time. With each heavy stroke we first regain our position, then shove a little forward. Yellowlegs and spotted sandpipers keep ahead of us at a comfortable walk. Forty miles of this, I think.

Another bend falls slowly behind. I take to focussing on short goals – a large tree, rock in the stream, the next curve – piling up the small victories without thinking how tiny they really are.

The small river is refreshing after the immensity of the Peace. An intimate, winding back alley. I watch the muscles in Marypat's back and shoulders. She bows her head now and then, just working, not watching, losing herself in the effort.

It is all a matter of getting my head right, accepting this new pace. I start to notice the rewards of our slow passage. I smell the musty odour of beaver and muskrat, pass their fresh tracks, the worn slides where they belly into the water. A belted kingfisher, blue and white and rusty, perches on an overhanging branch with a loud rattly call. It flies out over the water and returns half a dozen times before we pass beneath it. Intricate spider webs slip by inches from my face.

All these things were there to be noticed along the Peace and the Smoky, but we passed too quickly, or were so far away that we never noticed. Once I realize that we're actually making progress, I concentrate on relaxing, forgetting the miles yet to go, accepting where I am.

The combined waters of the Athabasca and Peace rivers form the largest freshwater delta on earth. Silt and mud scoured from thousands of square miles, a massive block of North America, create a delta that covers a million and a half acres of wilderness. This region, the size of Prince Edward Island, contains lakes, ponds, rivers and erratic channels, bogs and marsh, grasslands, impenetrable stands of alder and willow.

There are birds by the millions: geese and sandhill cranes, pintails and yellowlegs, fox sparrows and yellow-rumped warblers, great horned owls and Cooper's hawks. Through the trackless vegetation wander fox and wolf, bear and moose, mink and otter.

But places for human beings to rest or camp are rare. Mud, swamp, and thicket are the norm. Dry spots are miles and miles apart. Late in the day, in evening light, we find a rock outcrop, a knob of Canadian Shield bedrock in a sea of wetland. I've no idea how long we've been paddling, but my shoulders and back are knotted into one big ache. The tent goes up right on rock, yards from the river. After the weeks and weeks of sandy camps, rock is a joy under our feet.

We reward ourselves with a cocktail before dinner. It's nice to be alone again. We lean tiredly against each other, watch the small river gurgle past. Thoughts of tomorrow's struggle can wait. I relish the miles behind us, listen to the owls welcome the coming darkness, feel the warmth of Marypat's body through my clothes.

"Here's to the Mighty Peace," Marypat lifts her cup. "And to being alone again."

"To the Mighty, and Interminable, Peace."

Mist clings to the water when we start up again in the morning. Without rushing we are still on the water at dawn, our old streamlined efficiency coming back. I'm in the bow, muscles warming up, trying to keep track of bends on the map. A red fox trots along shore ahead, then notices us and disappears. Long dark legs, huge brush of tail, utterly quiet.

The day warms, and the pace seems less brutal now that we're used to it. Hawks and falcons and eagles are everywhere, roosting in trees, circling overhead, diving through the air. A falcon stoops on a spotted sandpiper right in front of us, a sharp, deadly dive. The frantic shorebird zigs and feints, finally eluding death by diving underwater.

Hour by hour the heat intensifies, wearing on us as the bends pile up. In places the current is fast enough that we are slowed almost to a stop. Then a helping eddy will pull us forward. I begin to think about Lake Athabasca. Pure, drinkable water, an end to silty camps. There will be blueberries on the islands, wide views full of blue.

But we are mired in the delta. The muddy river and thick bush could be somewhere in Indiana.

"Good thing we stopped where we did last night," I say. "There hasn't been a dry spot since."

When fatigue and hunger tell us it's lunch time, there is nowhere to rest. We find an overhanging tree, tie off to a branch, and perch unsteadily above the river, a couple of ungainly buzzards.

"I was going to save this for the lake," Marypat says, once we've taken up the gruelling toil again. "But it seems like we need a discussion topic now. I've been thinking about adoption."

"Yeah?" I try not to sound wary.

"If I can't get pregnant, I still want kids."

"We've been at it for more than two years," I agree. "Seems a fair bet that we won't succeed."

"I'd want to adopt a Black baby," she adds.

"Hold on," I protest. "Don't you think that's going from the frying pan to the fire? I mean, we've had these emotional times, you've basically been depressed for a year or more, we're still unsteady, and you want to jump into something like that?"

"Why not?" She's getting belligerent now. I feel us polarizing, even as I fight it.

"Because, dammit, it's going to be hard enough as it is. Maybe we *should* adopt a minority kid, maybe that's what's best, but you present me with this incredible statement, your mind all made up."

"I've thought about it a lot."

"Not with me you haven't!"

The debate is immediately acrimonious and heated. We fall silent, both recognizing that it is fatigue as much as real anger. But I'm reminded how close to the surface it all is, how little we have to scratch to open wounds, and how fine the line is that separates love from this near-loathing. It shocks me how quickly we're shouting at each other.

I bow my head, dig in harder. Marypat is too far out in the current, I think, so I draw us in. She pushes out again. We stop arguing, but lose our paddling rhythm, communicate our discord in a subtle battle of wills.

By the time The Forks come into view we've been paddling in silence a long time. Each of us feels sheepish, wants to apologize, but won't be the first. Instead we fasten on the lake, only a few miles off.

"Lake Athabasca!" I sing out. "We're coming!"

There are cabins on the high spots near The Forks, summer camps. As we pass one a string of dogs erupts into a bedlam of barking. Through an opening, I see a man standing on the front step, looking around curiously.

"We're not a bear," I call, and wave. He watches us go by in silence. It is the last dry spot for miles.

The current slackens, and our speed picks up. I can taste the lake in the air. I am tired but exultant.

But the day isn't over, not nearly. The final length of water opens before us, and beyond it the amorphous blue of open lake. But down its throat funnels a brutal east wind, right in our faces.

The current slowed us to a crawl, but this wind stops us cold. We push our aching muscles harder. Still nothing. I fasten my sights on a driftwood log lying up ahead, but it moves no closer. We push into marsh grass, pole against the mud bottom, inch forward.

"God dammit!" I yell. "This isn't fair. I thought I was paddling hard before."

"There's nowhere to stop, either."

Watery swamps surround and entrap us. Our argument is forgotten, now, as we battle together.

I don't know how long I can keep this up. My hands are numb with the strain, shoulders on fire. But we have no choice.

Fort Chipewyan lies in the distance, clearly in view but utterly unattainable. I can see the heaving lake. Blade by blade the marsh grasses pass by. The all-out pace becomes a dull monotony of effort.

After an endless stretch we pull into a quiet spot amongst a litter of bobbing driftwood, hold our position by grabbing handfuls of weed.

"Where the hell can we go?" Marypat sounds exhausted.

"The only place on the map that looks like a sure thing is Potato Island." I point ahead to a distant high spot. Miles of unvaried wetland stand in our way. While Marypat ponders I guzzle a quart of muddy water.

"I don't know if I can go that far."

"I know, but there's nothing else."

We start again, arms protesting, wind, solid and implacable, muscling against our faces.

"Look at that, over there." I wave my paddle toward a lump of rock with the lake pounding against it. "It's a hell of a lot closer."

"Can we get through the waves?"

"Worth a try, I'd say."

All we want to do is slip sideways, hold our own, and let the wind push us across. But the waves are steep, breakers crash in the shallows. The boat is a bucking horse under us.

"Hold our angle," I shout.

"I'm trying. Help me if I lose it."

Slowly the rocky hill comes near as we get used to the crazy ride. The boat handles the chaotic waves while wind drives spray in our faces, drenches us with cold water.

There is no calm spot to land, but we are past caring. The bow crashes against rock. Each wave heaves us up, then slams us down. I scramble over the deck, grab the bowline, and leap for solid rock. Marypat follows, skittering over the load and getting doused by a wave.

"Jesus holy Christ, welcome to Lake Athabasca!" We stand together, shaking from exertion, and contemplate the wind-lashed lake.

III

CRISIS IN CONFIDENCE

15

THE LAKE I'VE been fantasizing about is nowhere in sight. Brown, churned-up water rumbles through the shallows and slams driftwood together. The sky is hazy and dull. The same east wind, not as strong as yesterday, but cold and steady, leans into me.

Marypat is in the tent, writing letters in anticipation of the post office in Fort Chip. The sticky griminess of my body drove me out early to stand crotch-deep in the silty waves and wash, shivering with cold. Now I'm hunched by the fire, swilling coffee, warming up.

My head keeps turning east, into the wind. Two hundred and fifty miles of lakeshore – cliff and sand, calm and storm, deadly cold water, intense beauty – the final leg of a summer with a groove already more than eight hundred miles long worn through it. It still seems a long way to go, without a helping current, out in the open, with fall coming on and our food dwindling. I shake off the bleak mood. Just another challenge to meet. If it could only have started well, with a few days of calm . . .

"I know you want a rest day," I begin, when Marypat has a warm cup of coffee in her hands. "But if we can fight our way to town, we could take our break there, get our mail, wander around."

She looks at me sceptically, then at the lake. "It's not exactly calm."

"No, but once we cross to the mainland we could just creep along shore. It looks a little out of the wind there."

"Let's see after breakfast. But if we go, I'm not going to let you talk me into pushing on any farther."

The lure of mail is strong enough to sway Marypat. Without it she'd never budge on a day like this. We take our time packing up, then launch the canoe precariously amongst the rocks. Away from the little island the waves are less broken up, but still large, and I can feel the pull of current draining the lake toward the Slave River and on farther north, thousands of miles to the Arctic Ocean.

By the time we pull in beside a large metal barge at Fort Chipewyan, our sore muscles have been reawakened and our bodies tingle with the sensations of rough water. On firm ground I sway a little, adjusting. I'm not the least inclined to go on. We tie the boat and walk off without a backward glance.

Our mail is more than we hoped for, a big bundle held together with a thick rubber band. We're still grinning when we go to the Northern Store to buy treats – evaporated milk for our morning coffee, some oranges, a bag of chips, cookies.

All the while the words sent by our families, the friends we've left behind, seem warm and alive in our hands. We ration out the wealth. Just a few letters while we eat a snack, then off to the Wood Buffalo Park building.

Natalie Bourke ushers us inside the new Visitor Centre. She is warm and talkative, perfectly willing to chat at length. Although she's lived in Fort Chip for some time, her job with the park is only a year old. Her husband is a local man, and she talks of the trap line they run together on the north shore of the lake, when she has time.

We relate our journey, talk about the lake crossing.

"It's been rough this summer," she says. "We haven't had a calm spell at all, just lots of wind."

When we ask about the park Natalie skirts the plight of the bison, concentrates instead on the state of the delta.

"The whole delta is drying up," she tells us. "We have satellite studies going back seventeen years that show it. And not just drying up a little. It's bad. The worst-case guess is that the whole delta could be gone in twenty years.

"It's the unexpected effect of the Bennett Dam, up on the Peace. Nobody thought of this problem back in 1968 when the dam went in. But it stopped the normal flood cycle that used to recharge the water in the delta. Even on a flood year like this one, the 'perched basins' aren't replenished. Those are the lowland areas behind the riverbanks, the real wetland habitat."

"It didn't seem very dry to us!"

"Maybe not, but the local trappers have been telling us for years that they can't get to places they used to. There aren't nearly as many animals. It is drying up."

We allow ourselves a couple more letters, then wander up to the RCMP office to leave our itinerary. The man in charge seems quite off-handed about it. I wonder how overdue we'd have to be before anyone got concerned. While we're there a call comes in and somebody reports a drunk lying on the side of a road.

Fort Chipewyan seems thriving, busy, cleaned-up. An imposing new lodge and restaurant crowns the rocky hill where the old Hudson's Bay stockade used to stand. It's a government-subsidized business venture, an attempt to generate jobs for local Natives.

During the eighteenth and nineteenth centuries, Fort Chipewyan was the hub of the North. *Voyageurs* and explorers came and went through this confluence of routes. Alexander Mackenzie, George Back, Samuel Hearne, Peter Pond – some seeking fur, others heading north in search of the lost Franklin expedition. Missionaries followed later, bringing their religious fervour to the untamed wilderness.

Fort Chipewyan was the great crossroads, the convergence of trails leading east to the St. Lawrence and the Great Lakes, north to the Arctic, west to the Pacific, south along the Athabasca. While the United States was still in its infancy, hardly explored, this northern outpost was throbbing with the energies of bold men and great plans.

The Indians were the unsuspecting pawns. Their existence was first transformed by the arrival of steel needles, metal cooking pots, knives, axes, and guns; then nearly snuffed out entirely by the awful, mysterious plague of smallpox. They were caught up, without understanding, in the economy of the fur trade. Capitalism, to these people, was as foreign a concept as Christ dying for their sins. Sometimes traders would claim men's wives in lieu of a debt.

At Fort Chip, the North West Company and Hudson's Bay Company battled for twenty years or more to control the treasures of the North. Potato Island, English Island, and the mainland bristled with the forts of vying factions. Hostages were taken, whole brigades of men systematically starved to death, all for control of the fur trade.

By the mid-1800s, the Church had established itself as the dominant influence over the northern peoples. On September 5, 1847, Father Taché held the first mass in the region. Before he left he had baptized 194 Natives, mostly children. In 1851 Father Faroud built Nativity Mission in Fort Chipewyan and began what was to be a busy and largely self-sufficient settlement. Men and women of the cloth put up with all the hardships and rigours of travel faced by the *voyageurs* and explorers. And they came to stay.

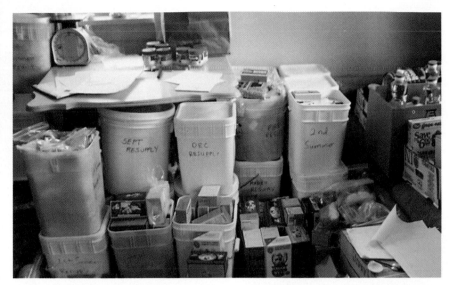

Supplies for more than a year of wilderness living consume a staggering amount of space, even when most of it is dehydrated food. Winter clothing and equipment, food, books, and other necessities are packed into labelled boxes. Once over the Canadian border, we will mail it all to Stony Rapids, Saskatchewan, where it will wait for us until fall. (Photo: Marypat Zitzer)

Camp routine quickly becomes familiar and efficient. Everything to sustain us over a thousand-mile summer fits comfortably into our canoe. The nomadic lifestyle develops its own rhythm, set to the tune of flowing water, long days, and changeable weather. (Photo: Marypat Zitzer)

The rain-fly cooking tarp is a common
camp feature as the summer wanes and
volatile fall weather moves in. Wool
caps and gloves are frequent camp attire
by the end of August.
(Photo: Alan Kesselheim)

Fall colours dot the boreal landscape by mid-September. To the north the forests grow increasingly stubby and sparse as trees give way to tundra. Clearly, the best way to travel through this landscape is by canoe.
(Photo: Marypat Zitzer)

Top left: An alert deer watches us descend the Smoky River. Sightings of deer, coyote, beaver, elk, and bear are far more common during the trip than encounters with our own species.

Bottom left: A black bear heads for the safety of the forest after a mile-long swim across the Peace River.

Top: A dreary tent-bound camp in thick brush on Lake Athabaska. Winds and storms on open water make travel problematic at the best of times. Our two-hundred-mile lake crossing at the end of the summer tests our resolve almost to the limit.

(Photos: Marypat Zitzer)

The judgement calls required in rapids are made weighty by the rivers' remoteness. Losing food, equipment, or even the canoe in a capsize would be like becoming shipwrecked in mid-ocean. (Photo: Ed White)

The rhythm of water and land weaves itself into a tapestry of images — campsites, storms, sunsets, the quiet wilderness — with days and even weeks at a stretch without human contact. (Photo: Marypat Zitzer)

In October the paddling season is
plainly over. In a matter of weeks slush
and ice force us to put the canoe up for
the season. Athabaska Camps hunkers
in the background, almost obscured by
fog, with our winter home nestled
against the forest at far right.
(Photo: Marypat Zitzer)

The local museum is crammed with old photographs, canoes, trapping hardware. Fuzzy black-and-white pictures taken at the turn of the century show the large white mission surrounded by tepees. Priests are making shoes and running fish plants, as well as ministering the faith. Records show that in 1860 the mission gardens produced four hundred kegs of potatoes.

No one else patronizes the museum while we're there, and the woman on duty follows us around, more a nuisance than a help. She has been in the area for some time, but has no sense of local geography, how the lake drains, where the Peace River is.

At the lavish, and empty, lodge, we are served ice water and hamburgers by a Chipewyan teenager in a suit. The burger is a side dish to the mail we devour. The lake outside is a wind-tossed picture framed in the large windows. We are cut off from it, for the moment, and I try not to watch the spray dancing around the islands. But there is nowhere to camp in town. We have to paddle at least to the outskirts. The canoe waits patiently for our return.

Back on the water, we barely travel a mile, and that at a snail's pace, to a shoulder of lichen-covered bedrock just out of town. As we pass in front of the lodge, I wonder if anyone is watching, whether they would come if a rogue wave capsized us.

Still, it's a rest day, a mail day. I tell myself that any progress is a bonus, even a mile, and after the tent goes up we read all the mail a second time, ignoring the surf around us.

I can't sleep. News from home jangles around like loose change on the brain, and I think, too, of the delta drying out. Another thing not foreseen, another number left out of the equations flashed by confident engineers. They thought they would tame the river, provide power, a lake for recreation, there'd be no more terrible floods. Twenty years later, the largest delta in the world is drying up like a sponge left on the counter. Where are those engineers, those politicians, those construction moguls now?

Marypat is restless, too. When I look outside, the soft purple sky is alive with green lights dancing through the branches of jack pine. We both crane our necks out the tent door for the late show.

All night, even after I fall asleep, I am aware of the wind. It tugs on the tent, finds its way inside, won't leave me alone. In the morning it is still with us.

Yesterday was a rest day; today is a travel day. We gird ourselves up, batten down the deck in the calm water behind a rocky arm, then start out.

For a few miles the route is relatively protected. A cluster of islands shields us intermittently. I read the map, choose a defensive, winding course down the watery back streets. The paddling is manageable, but the wind still sings, makes us work all out to get anywhere. And the islands will run out.

"That looks like a good spot. Let's stop." Marypat has an island home in her sights.

"We've only come five or six miles!" I object. "It's not even lunch time."

"This is the last island. It's all cliff down there. It's too hard and we won't be protected."

"You heard what Natalie said about wind this summer," I protest. "If we just wait for good days, we'll never make it."

"It's too soon to be in this frame of mind," Marypat says, adamant. "I don't want to battle all the time. Anyway, it's too rough."

I look ahead, see the white spray against the cliffs, and know she's right.

16

IT'S JUST DAWN, two days later, and I'm all business. No sleeping in and snuggling. No way am I going to spend another day on this island. Marypat groans sleepily when I shake her, but starts to dress.

The first afternoon had been tolerable. At least we had made some progress that morning. I read a magazine someone sent, even the classified section, and wrote letters. But then a second day came and went with the waves still churning and the wind howling. We tramped around the domed, rocky surface of the island, the lichen as dry as potato chips underfoot. I took a picture of Marypat squatting at the edge of a rocky escarpment, looking out at the waves. Behind her, nothing but water in the frame. We played backgammon, took naps we didn't need, ate food we hadn't earned, the sun making its dimly visible circuit through clouds.

The high point of the day was a visit by a merlin. I looked up from a book to see the falcon perched on a rock twenty feet away. Then it flew to the ragged tip of a spruce just behind and above me. We watched each other for a long time, neither of us moving, and when it flew off I wished for the freedom of those fast wings.

It's still windy now, but not as bad. I ignore the waves, don't look at the distant cliffs. I'm up to my knees in the frigid water, stabilizing the boat enough to take off. It is the fifth day of wind, night and day.

At first the paddling doesn't seem difficult. The islands slowly drop behind us, and we cross toward the short cliffs that extend all the way east to Shelter Point. Then the winds pick up, the waves grow huge and turbulent, and it turns grim.

Waves rebound off the rock face, slamming back across the swell. Water slaps at us from every direction, so that I'm always changing the angle to keep us head-on. Irrationally, I want to paddle right up against the rock, as if its solidness is a thing I can count on. But it is rougher there than in the open lake, the water chaotic. Besides, what help would it be anyway? If we capsize, if we could swim to the rock, would we cling to handholds and wait it out?

No, there's no going back now. It's Shelter Point or nothing. I steer far enough out to avoid the rebounding waves and we struggle ahead. When I ask Marypat how she's doing, she shakes her head and says nothing. Not good. Her stomach has never handled sailboats or small planes well, and she's obviously queasy. But seasickness in a canoe? It's never happened.

Even as I think this she lays her paddle down, grabs the gunwales. "I'm gonna puke," she mumbles, and starts to lean over. I lean the opposite way and brace with my paddle, feeling puny and foolish as hell, while she retches over the side.

By the time we pull in to a cove behind the very tip of Shelter Point, Marypat has thrown up twice more, losing the cinnamon rolls she ate at dawn. For miles the big swells have raised and dropped us with that sinking-elevator effect, while the chop worked its twisting, slamming, corkscrew action. Miles of unforgiving bedrock dropping sheer to the water, the lake piling relentlessly against it. Miles during which the only sounds are the hiss and curl of breaking wave and the bullying air in our ears. We are focussed, numbed, intent as warriors.

Shelter Point must have been named by just such people as us, on just such a day. It is what comes at once to mind, rounding the final rocky finger and entering the cove. Shelter! Safety! It is quiet and calm. The wind whistles overhead but doesn't reach the water, and the canoe glides silently to the smooth, welcoming rock.

Marypat wobbles to shore, pale and trembling, and immediately lies down in the foetal position, still wearing her life vest. I find a rock to sit on, rub her shoulders, but she moans, wants only to be left alone.

For me, too, it takes some time before I'm steady on land. My body is still righting itself after the ride. From the vantage point of a nearby ridge of rock, I watch the stormy lake, study the grey, leaden sky. We must have started very early. Behind me the branches of jack pine wave stiffly, the forest is quiet, carpeted with moss and bear berry. A raven rows through the treetops, croaking faintly.

While Marypat naps I study the already-worn map, make calculations based on days of food, protected or exposed shoreline, wind direction, the capability of our boat. Nothing is changed by my fretting, only a little more time slips past.

My partner stirs, rolls over. "That was horrible," she says.

"I'm sorry. I didn't think it would be anything like that bad."

"The only good thing is that maybe the seasickness is really morning sickness."

"That's one way to look at it," I say.

We eat a little granola and afterwards just sit together hunched up, watching the day come on. It is a lonely place.

Then it begins to calm. Both of us sense it, perk up, even before the waves diminish. For the first time since the delta channel, the wind slackens.

When we're convinced it's for real, we shove off again. This is more like it!

As the wind and lake die down, our muscles loosen and I realize that my face is unfurrowed, my jaw unclenched, for the first time all day. The sun comes out, our jackets come off, and the lake relaxes until the canoe glides on a surface as calm as the protected water behind Shelter Point.

We jabber at each other with relief, point out the pretty crescents of sand beach, rehash the news of home, watch for the shape of a peregrine falcon in the sky.

Miles drop away: around the long peninsula of Sand Point, where terns and gulls fill the air with their screeching; past Bustard Island; down the long straight shore. Map study is now a matter of accomplishment rather than frustration.

When we camp our arms are sore with satisfying fatigue, the morning of fear and danger a memory from another place, our spirits buoyant. We have finally left behind the silty, cloudy sediment from the Athabasca River that fills the western end of the lake. Our canoe has earned a thorough cleaning. The muddy water-line left by weeks of river travel gets rubbed off. All the grit and sand and mud prints slowly disappear. When we turn it over the hull is a glistening red symbol of a fresh start.

For the first time the lake works its magic on me. Our camp is on a wave-smoothed ledge of rock that shelves into the water. Sand dunes rise behind us to an open forest of birch and pine, a northern parkland full of animal tracks and sunlight. We wade out to swim and wash, sputtering with cold, laughing, quickly warmed by the sun.

Like contented home-owners we enjoy a sunset sky and the sound of lapping water while we eat dinner. Marypat is fully recovered, rejuvenated. She searches the shoreline for bird feathers, finds one from an eagle, and adds it to her collection.

Neither of us mentions the chances for continued calm weather. I think to myself that we are certainly due some. While I'm caught up in the lake's spell, the dread I felt earlier in the day, my dreary calculations, seem the preoccupations of a neurotic.

When I wake in the morning the lake is rustling, coming alive. Nothing serious, but we gobble breakfast and pack with haste and efficiency, listening to the growing surf. By the time we launch I'm muttering to myself. The polished, exposed bench of rock is a tricky place to leave. Waves break over the gunwales while we hop in, cinch the deck, and start to paddle out.

Within a mile we are back on the roller-coaster. Marypat is in the stern, where she is less likely to get queasy, but the waves build and build. The wind is mostly at our backs. We sluice along, hissing down wave fronts, hurled ahead again and again.

It is as exhilarating as it is terrifying. In six miles our route bends sharply east and the wind will be at our side. Impossible. Even at our back, even on the joyride, it is a test of nerves. We shouldn't be out here, I think, when a bad wave throws us to one side, twisting us like a waterlogged tree.

A raven circles above a nearby cliff, its wings constantly playing on the powerful winds, watching us, assessing. Again I take it as a good omen, a helping spirit. Stupid, maybe, but I'm soothed by the sight. At the base of the cliffs waves boom in hollow grottoes of rock.

"We have to stop somewhere in the next half-mile," I shout back. "One of the shallow bays up ahead."

"These waves are huge!"

I hear the tension of fear, mixed with risk-loving elation, in my partner's voice.

The landing is through a minefield of boulders and crashing waves. The canoe is dumped down on one rock, nearly tipping us out, before surfing up onto the sand.

Trapped again.

"Dammit, this lake won't give us anything!" I explode. "Times like this I think we ought to just make our way back to Fort Chip and hitch a ride on a barge."

"Al, stop it!"

"Since we got to the lake we've had half a day of good paddling. All the rest have been risky, maybe even foolish. We could just as easily still be in sight of Fort Chip."

She ignores me, but I'm on a roll.

"We might not even make Uranium City! Fall will come and we'll run out of food ten miles from here."

"Al!" Her tone stops me.

"I know. I just can't stand it." And I heave the canoe farther up, start unsnapping the deck.

We leave the boat packed, ready for calmer water. Marypat is immediately excited by the beauty of the spot. A small waterfall purls over a rock ledge and fills basins that are perfect bathing holes. I find a wealth of bald eagle feathers scattered below a jack pine perch.

Little mottoes for lake travel keep coming to me. *Every mile earned today is a mile we don't have to paddle tomorrow. We take what the lake gives us.* You'd think I'd be better at this after all the open water I've paddled, after crossing Lake Athabasca once before, paddling Lake Superior, and all the hundreds of others in between. But I find it hard to be stoic.

And there is something more, this time. An insidious foreboding that crept in that first windy night on the lake, a feeling that we shouldn't be here testing it.

"I like the feeling of not having control," Marypat pipes up, after lunch. "But then, if it were only me setting the pace, we'd still be back at Vermilion Falls. So we make a good team."

"I don't mind the quiet time," I admit. "I just hate starting the crossing so far behind schedule."

It's twilight before we give in and turn the boat over. Inside the tent I say, "I really want to paddle tomorrow."

"That would be nice," Marypat agrees.

It is cold and clear, the stars like jewellery against the deep blackness. I sleep fitfully and when my bladder gets full I ignore it, using it as an alarm clock. Only, there is still a lot of night left, and it's so uncomfortable that I lie awake. The winds die, then gust through the forest. Should we get up and paddle in the dark?

When I rouse Marypat, the eastern horizon is only faintly less black.

"Geez, Al, it's the middle of the night. I'm sleeping!"

"It's time. And it's calm."

As the sun rises through the spruce trees we pass Lapworth Point. The waters are still, quiet, lovely. Loons wail in the distance, swim through the rounded rock islands, sleek and sharp-eyed. Watched by an otter, we pass Fidler Point, named for a Hudson's Bay man. It's been only five years since I last crossed this lake, but I had forgotten its beauty. The wave-worn rock, the untouched sand, the warm sun splashing down, the smell of northern forest. I had forgotten. And as we arrow swiftly over the miles, I am amazed at how completely seduced I am. It's the same lake that just yesterday was my enemy.

I shake my head. "I love this place. On a day like this I could say I'll be back every year."

By the time afternoon winds roughen the lake we've just crossed the Saskatchewan border, put thirty miles behind us, and are ready to stop anyway. Singed Dog Island is our home, and an old burn scars the nearby mainland. What fiery adventure gave the island its name?

There is lots of day left. We happily pick the small raspberries that grow among the rocks and eat dinner thinking of the hunk of shoreline in our wake. It seems to me that we have turned the corner.

A peregrine falcon perches in a tree behind us. While we sit, enjoying the waning day, it glides on a silent, deadly line right in front of us, into a bush full of songbirds. There is a flurry of tiny wings, birds scurrying for cover, and the peregrine flaps back to its perch, a feathery meal in its hard talons. Seeing such things, I cannot express how fortunate I feel.

Before we go to bed, I notice a heavy line of clouds in the west.

17

IN THE VAGUE, grey light that passes for day, we don't even need to look out the tent door to know we're going nowhere. Rain began during the night and now it is a hard, steady noise, the surf a booming kettledrum behind it. Singed Dog Island is only another prison, after all.

We sleep through breakfast, then lie there, listening. The old east wind again, a headwind, moving wisps of grey cloud fast overhead. I am determined not to fall prey to my dark thoughts, not after such a wonderful day. When Marypat goes out to pee, a trio of sandhill cranes crosses the frame of the tent door. Their wings are wide, prehistoric sails in the mist, and they talk their unmistakable talk into the muffled distance.

Not just windbound, but tentbound. We read *Riding the Iron Rooster* out loud, go through the mail we've almost memorized, play games. The storm is so undeniable that we don't even discuss it. Desperate for entertainment, we play crazy eights.

I can't believe it. Another day of storm. This is too much.

I am on my elbow, lying in my sleeping bag. "Look, Marypat, I think we have to consider stopping in Uranium City and working out some other way to get across the rest of the lake. This weather is really starting to spook me. It's like we're not supposed to be here." It all comes out in a rush.

"I don't want to hear about it," she says and turns to the wall.

"It's not just difficult. It's foolish. We can't even average ten lousy miles a day. Except for a day and a half, every mile we've made has been dangerous."

She sits up abruptly. "I can't listen to this." She begins thrusting her bag into its stuff sack.

"What are you doing?"

"If we have to make miles, let's go!"

There is no stopping her. I am bullied into following along, knowing how risky this is, but so taken by surprise, so shamed by her outburst, that I start packing, too.

No breakfast. Our tent, jammed into its sack, is a sodden, sandy mess. The weather is cold, grey, and the lake is rough. Marypat is in the stern. We paddle in silence, hands quickly numb.

She strikes off on an angle across a wide bay rather than sticking close to shore. I am fatalistic, say nothing for a while, but in the middle of the crossing I'm truly scared.

"We shouldn't be here!" I yell. Nothing from the stern. The angle stays the same. Waves are twisting us, hitting broadside.

"Christ, Marypat, if we're going to be out in this, at least stick to shore! This is crazy."

"That angle is too hard. I can't fight the wind that way."

"So we should drown instead?"

All the while I'm paddling as hard as I can, watching the far shore. Is it really that bad, or am I just making the most of it for the sake of argument?

When we finally come close to land again Marypat slams the boat into the rocks. "Okay, I can't do it. Let's camp."

"Now you want to camp? No way!" The shoreline is inhospitable, all boulder and willow. And I'm convinced now that we actually can paddle in this. "Why don't I stern for awhile, see if I can keep us close."

We go on. The wind is steady, the waves big, but we can manage. The shoreline is low and rocky. Even if we go over, we can save ourselves. We work hard, largely in silence, trying to keep warm.

Somewhere along Maurice Point we stop for a cold breakfast. A broken-up wood skiff is half-buried in the gravel. We jog in place, holding our metal bowls, gulping down lemonade. Like anything, given enough time, it begins to feel normal, even mundane, being out here.

A moose lifts its broad head out of some shallows, water streaming from its mouth. It studies us across the misty distance with myopic concern, then crashes off, high-stepping through the boulders. "How can it possibly not have a sprained ankle?" I wonder. It is the first thing all day not said in an argumentative tone.

Near Lobstick Island I see smoke. Then a wall tent, two people, an aluminum boat on the shore. They are the first

people we've seen on the lake. A couple out from Camsell Portage for the weekend? Is it a weekend? They watch us, apparently amazed to see someone on the water, then wave. By now
I'm feeling smug having made twenty miles on a day like this,
like we've snuck one in.

But the wind rises another notch, and soon it is clear we must
stop. Near shore the chop is heavy, and we're wet through,
shivering. There is nowhere to camp. All the shore is large rock
and thickets of willow. But we have to stop! I aim for a slight
gap in the bush and we stumble ashore, hauling the canoe into
the weeds.

The primitive need for a fire is the only thing on my mind.
But it's been raining for two days and we've chosen wet lowlands
to camp in. Stringing the blue cook tarp, our hands are numbed
to blunt knobs, each knot a slow frustration. I trudge off, without confidence, in search of kindling, anything that will hold a
flame. Marypat wrestles with the sopping tent. Adversity has
made us a team again.

Birchbark is the key. A pile of bark wisps with large curls
heaped on top. My fingers, trying to strike a match, are pale
wrinkled slugs, stiff as wood. Resin in the bark hisses and snaps,
tries to burn, then dies. I make a second attempt, rearrange the
pile, keep from dripping on it. This time it smokes and crackles,
flames lick up. More bark, then tiny damp twigs that dry in the
minuscule fire. It is a sluggish, halting success, never a roaring
blaze, but we are heartened beyond description, hover close
with our hands cupping the heat.

A small hawk is suddenly with us. Cooper's? Sharp-shinned?
It's too fleeting to identify. It coasts, silently hunting through
the thicket, almost comes under the tarp, then flares its wings
two feet from Marypat's face. The summer has been marked by
these avian visits, these encounters. They have the feel of bless-
ings, or some communication we are too dense to understand.

We now have hot drinks and food in our bellies, warmth back

in our hands, but it is nasty out. Soon we retire to the damp tent, snuggle into our bags. "I never would have picked this for a camp," I say, when we're nestled together, "but it's actually pretty protected and comfortable."

"Hmmm." Marypat is nearly asleep already. We are friends again, safe as rabbits in a burrow, with the wide, dangerous world outside our door.

In the morning that world is white. Wet slush weighs down the tent, clings to leaves, and carpets the forest. And waves still crash against the rocks. Even snow I could handle, if we could only paddle.

"This is unbelievable."

It is all I can think to say, and I lie back down.

Another day in the tent, this time dressed in layers of long underwear, wearing wool hats. Wet socks hang limply from a line above our heads. At twilight the neighbourhood hawk tries to perch on our tent, can't find a hold, beats its wings against the nylon as it takes off.

When day comes again we are both bustling with pent-up energy. The wind is gusty but fitful. Patches of blue sky encourage us. It is never calm, but the storm is over, the sun becomes warm, and the lake is beautiful, undeniably beautiful.

"I think we need to discuss our options."

I've chosen lunch time to bring it up. We are near Camsell Portage, a tiny settlement named for the illustrious Camsell family. J. S. Camsell, the patriarch, assured his place in local history in 1877, when he established the record for an overland snowshoe march. That winter he tramped from Fort Liard to Crow Wing, on the Mississippi River, a jaunt of some 3,500 miles. Another day's paddle will bring us to Uranium City, roughly halfway across the lake. All morning wind and rough chop have shoved us around, but at least we have made progress.

"Uranium City is our only chance to stop and get help."

"We're making it, Al." Marypat doesn't want to give in. "And it's so beautiful here."

I outline my fears, admit my emotional malaise, but argue that it is no shame to acknowledge that the elements are too strong, too dangerous. "Think of all the mountaineering expeditions that haven't made their goal. And the polar trips."

Marypat tries to be understanding, allows that conditions have been incredibly bad, but also says, "They have to get better. I keep thinking we'll get our break."

"But it's almost fall. In nine days we've still only had a day and a half of good paddling."

When we paddle off the air between us seems cleared, we understand each other better. I wonder if I'm overreacting. Perhaps it's as much the strain of not knowing, the daily anxiety, as it is the actual danger. Marypat is, in this phase of the journey, the strong one. Where earlier I encouraged and pacified her, now she has the emotional steadiness, the resolve. I can't explain my fears, not fully, even to myself. Neither can I deny them.

In under two miles we are windbound again and have to hurry with the tarp to beat a rain shower.

18

WE HAVE DECIDED to quit.

We were up this morning with the stars still sharp in the sky. So intent have we been on sneaking in miles that we skipped breakfast and coffee. There was frost in the air, the tent covered with ice crystals, so that packing up was chilly work. Still night when we began to paddle.

Easter Head is the day's objective, a hard fist of rock thrusting out into some of the deepest water of the lake. Beyond it lies Crackingstone Peninsula, an even more forbidding headland of sheer cliff and black, fathomless lake.

In the pre-dawn darkness huge swells picked us up, then dropped us, passing beneath us in an ominous march. We said nothing, kept to ourselves, paddling in darkness so complete that everything about the water was felt rather than seen. But we are intimate with this lake, know exactly what it is telling us.

We travelled along rocky shoreline as daylight faded the stars. The deck became wet with spray and wash, the swell developed the roughness so familiar. When it began to grow light, the first visible things were whitecaps, almost luminescent blinks of light in the velvet expanse.

Only one bay offers shelter before the long headland, and Marypat turned us into it without a word. We had no business being on the water, crashing through the cold waves. Just as we turned east, into the protection of the island-filled bay, the huge orange sun lifted over the hills, blinding us with its brilliance. The island we chose is another gem, with a gravel beach, enduring rock underfoot, wind-twisted pines gripping the stony surface with tentacle-like roots.

"I don't know," I said. "That was spooky."

"Let's rest."

Marypat looked haggard and seasick. By now we know it isn't pregnancy. She pulled out her sleeping bag and curled up, finishing her night's rest.

All day, while the sun poured down, the lake stayed wild. For the first time, when the inevitable discussion came up, Marypat seemed as dejected as I. Our decision came with surprising suddenness and was strangely anticlimactic. All the points had been made before, and as we talked, we faced an aspen grove already tinged with yellow. We would stop in Uranium City, give in to the unrelenting lake, the coming fall, our dwindling food supplies. Give in.

For the rest of the day, we have been subdued, thoughtful. Why should this be any different from deciding not to drive your car when it's icy out, I think. But it is different, dispiriting, personal. The wind stiffens even more.

It is afternoon and we are picking at lunch, half-reclining in the gravel near our boat, staying low and out of the wind. A raven appears, like that, landing on the shore not fifteen feet away. It is huge and black, heavy-beaked. But the eyes are what hold us. The bird's gaze is piercing, unwavering, intimate. I see the thin membrane blink across its dark eye, the wind shift a stiff feather. There is some communication going on, something personal being said. It is a judgement that I feel, an assessment. Finally the bird hops away and takes flight.

"Did you feel that?" Marypat asks. "Like it was questioning us, making us think."

"All summer it's been like that with birds."

"You've noticed it, too?" This is the first time we've discussed it. "It's as if whenever things are tricky or dangerous, when a decision is being made, they appear."

Morning again. Another morning when nothing needs to be said. The hammering water says it all. I begin to think that even the last eighteen miles to Uranium City aren't a sure thing. How long can we sit here? At least there is no longer anything to discuss.

Halfway through a desultory, mid-morning game of Scrabble, I sense some change. The whitecaps are fewer. It is subtle – the lake still rough, the wind fresh – but it is changing.

"Let's go," I say.

"The last thing I want to do is pack up, only to stop on an island fifteen minutes from here," Marypat complains.

"I think we'll be able to paddle."

It *is* better, although the deep-water swells are gigantic. At least they're steady and broad, lifting us up like the backs of whales. The canoe fits lengthwise in the wave troughs, with room to spare. Like an ocean. Surf beats against Easter Head, froths among the jagged rocks, loud and close. We are kneeling, shifting our weight, leaning together as the water tosses us. To be out in the midst of it is exhilarating, delicious. I find myself dawdling, savouring our final day alone on the lake, saying goodbye.

Then we duck into a protected narrow passage between islands, out of the wind. It is warm and summery. We snap pictures, stop at an eagle's nest to hunt for feathers, find an eaglet carcass on the ground, either fallen out or pushed. Without the pressure of another hundred miles ahead of us, the day has become a jaunt.

Marypat pushes for us to get close to Uranium City. I don't understand her drive. Why hurry now? By the time we stop it is twilight and we are at the tip of the water channel that leads to Bushell. The road from there will take us to Uranium City.

Before dinner we hike up the sharp ridge of rock for a look. Down the channel, close up, loom squat fuel-storage tanks and several large buildings, a jarring sight. We stand side by side, looking. When we turn away we have said nothing.

"Now I don't want to stop," I admit.

"I know."

"Did you plan this? Wanting to get here today?" I wonder if Marypat could have been that cunning.

"No. But I did think it would be good to be right at the start of Crackingstone Peninsula, just in case."

"Look, we both know how much lake there is left. I'm not at all sure I want to start up the battle again," I argue.

"I know, I know." Marypat picks up driftwood for the fire. "What about this? If it's calm tomorrow, we go. If it's stormy, we stop. One shot."

19

FOR ONCE MARYPAT is up first, peering out the door at the view, then shaking me awake. The lake is undulating satin. Not a word is said about stopping. I realize that when Marypat made her proposition, I knew with certainty that it would be calm. It is another pre-breakfast dash, this time down the twelve-mile cliffs to the safety of St. Mary's Channel. For eight miles the black water is benign. Slow lifting swells, the lake's slumbering breath. Dark cliffs throw their chilling shadow over us and our strokes are hard and steady, eating up distance. But the last four miles become another battle in the long war. I am plunged again and again into waves. The sound of wind and water, our dogged companions all along, engulfs us.

"How are you doing?" Marypat calls up.

"Making it," I answer. "Making it."

I am not tempted to turn back, to reverse our decision. Even though that option is only a few miles behind us, we are past it, the door has been closed. I'm soaked by the time we have breakfast in the channel, but my thoughts aim forward. We'll have a tailwind on the far side of the peninsula, if the wind doesn't shift.

Along the protected channel our canoe passes the ruins of Gunnar Mines. Broken-down tar-paper shacks litter the islands, huge dormitory buildings, machine shops, the big water-filled mine pit stained a shocking yellow. When it became economically unfeasible to mine uranium, the company closed up and went away, leaving everything behind.

Uranium City is almost a ghost town as well. The area once had more than four thousand residents, modern schools, suburban homes, a paved airstrip, a hospital. People would fly south at the company's expense for a day of shopping, movies, visits to the doctor.

Now the town's population hovers around one hundred, people who refuse to leave, who grow gardens and scratch a living somehow, because they love the North and won't give it up. The land of Crackingstone, Goldfields, Eldorado, is covered with the evidence of men grubbing for gold, silver, uranium. Weathered claim-stakes poke out of the moss, pits and tunnels and ore piles testify to the lust for minerals. Slowly the patient lichen grows over the scars, frost and exposure erode the rock, buildings collapse and decay.

Luck stays with us. The wind urges us on, all along the east edge of the peninsula. The canoe sails down the fronts of waves, is pushed over the miles.

The eastern half of Lake Athabasca is narrower, less exposed, fractured into a jumble of channels and islands and narrow bays. Travel is a game of calculations, our opponent the wind. Our tiny craft is a red dot gliding ever so slowly through the northern maze. Whoever is in the bow is the day's strategist, choosing our path, weighing distances and wind direction and exposure. Although the battle is still joined, we now have an ally in the broken shore.

Geese stream south overhead. It is almost September. Their talk is with us all day, from miles up. Distant ragged V's, constant friendly chatter.

Since we were last here, a power line has been punched east from Uranium City, lighting up Fond-du-Lac, Stony Rapids, Black Lake, marching through the bush. We see the stark poles and looping wire only rarely, and it has absolutely no effect on our travel, yet the mere sight of it, the knowledge that it exists, somehow compromises the whole lake.

Another twenty-five-mile day, then another. The lake drops behind us in great chunks, huge spans on the map. For thirteen days we fought and stuttered across the first half of the lake, and now, after just three more, we camp ten miles from Fond-du-Lac, within a hard day's paddle of our winter home. If it hadn't happened, I wouldn't have believed it possible.

"I knew we'd get our break!" Marypat is tending a blueberry pie in the Dutch oven. When it's done we draw a line across the middle and each eat half. Then we make dinner.

Northeast winds funnel down against us during the slog to Fond-du-Lac. The distant white church taunts us, but we are determined, as implacable as the wind. There is a new building, too, with a huge, blue roof.

"Is that Philip?" Marypat asks. On shore next to the dock stands a familiar figure, one of the local fishing guides we got to know during our last winter in the area.

"Hello!" he waves, as we come near. He grabs the bow and hauls us up. "We watched you coming."

The first time here we paddled right past Fond-du-Lac, feeling foreign and uncomfortable. Now it is like a reunion. We are surrounded by old friends, people we know, who remember us.

The new building in town is a just-completed school, variously reported to have cost from eight to twelve million dollars. It is like something plopped down from southern California – carpeted classrooms, computers, potted plants in the foyer. The rest of town looks weathered and run-down by comparison.

The post office is a disappointment, the woman behind the counter brusque. "I didn't know you, so I sent it all back." Dejected, we trudge over to visit our old friends from our previous northern winter, Eli and Angela Adams.

Following the local custom, we walk right in without knocking. The house is exactly as I remembered, spare and clean. Pictures of Jesus on the walls, a television, one or two pieces of furniture, a wood stove with a kettle warming. They are in the kitchen. "Hey, hey," Eli calls out in greeting, but he is old-looking, slumped, his face lined and lifeless.

"My heart is bad." He puts his hand to his chest. "They call me Old Man. I take the medicine, but it's no good. I get tired carrying five gallons of gas across the yard. I have to rest even when I'm just taking my rifle to the boat."

Angela and Marypat talk about beading. A few of the Adams' many children drop in. Their youngest girl, barely a teenager, comes in with her baby.

When we leave town Philip shoves us off. "Stay to the north shore," he tells us. "Wind is from the northeast. Lots of islands to hide in."

We had fully expected to camp one more night, but our goal is close and our arms work their smooth, practised cadence, ignoring fatigue. Miles slip past, island by island, despite the wind. The fishing camp, our winter home, is suddenly only a few miles off.

"Want to go in?" Marypat asks, and I agree.

Through Olson Islands, in big waves across to the south shore, then into the familiar protection of Otherside Bay.

"We're coming home!" I shout. "Here's our bay."

Closing in on the camp, I see Cliff Blackmur's floatplane, a Beaver, taxiing in circles, warming up. Then he turns toward us, opens up the throttle, and roars across the wave tops, straight at us. The floats lift off the water, wings waggle, I see Cliff's face peering down through the Plexiglas at us.

"Hey, MP, tomorrow we can wake up and not even think about wind!"

IV

FREEZE-UP

20

BIDING TIME. IT is, for a while, an exquisite relief not to wake up listening for wind, not to mould my hands to the shaft of a paddle, not to pack and unpack the canoe. But the summer of constant motion, strenuous travel, exposure to the elements, has instilled in me a deep restlessness. Letdown is inevitable.

For months we have been captive only to our own routine, our own basic needs. Suddenly that is overwhelmed by life in a busy fishing camp. Our home for the winter, the cabin that five years earlier we helped build and then lived in, is still filled with fishing clients. We pitch in on the endless dishwashing, laundering, cabin-cleaning, wood-cutting, that is the staff's part in making "fishing dreams come true." As much as anything, the challenge is to stay out from underfoot.

Our friends Cliff and Stella make us welcome and at ease, but for us it is a period of stagnation. Soon we will be alone again, will assume the chores and rigours of the winter season. For now, we try to relish the human contact, give each other breathing room, and often feel at loose ends.

Several mornings I sit in the back room of the lodge and chat with Norbert, one of the guides. He is a large, angular Chipewyan, with huge brown hands and a stooped posture, as though he were always ducking through a doorway. His English is broken, and my Chipewyan nonexistent, so our language is pantomime as much as talk. He uses the word "sometime" the same way I'd say "well" or "you know."

"Sometime," he says, "every year go up Territories. Long time. Trap everything." He describes a route north, his hands mobile and his eyes distant, as if seeing the rockbound lakes and fast rivers, the bends in the trail – landmarks as clear as street signs. He makes as if to carry a canoe, describes summer portages from a time when canoes were still used by local people.

"Snowmobiles no good for slush," he tells me. "Always break. Have to use dogs."

It has been many years since the caribou came all the way south to Lake Athabasca, even longer since they crossed at the Fond-du-Lac narrows. But Norbert remembers. "Sometime, make drymeat." He slashes his hand delicately across his other palm, like a knife, and I imagine hide falling away, strips of dark red meat hanging above a smoky fire.

He tells me his father died when he was young, that sometimes he was very hungry and would walk a long way, hunting, to find even a little food.

"Chicken coming soon," he says, referring to spruce grouse. "Hunt early in morning. By nine o'clock you stop."

One evening a group of us talk in a room off the kitchen. One of Eli's daughters, Jean, tells of a man buried on the shores of Scott Lake, to the north. Eli and some other elders had Cliff fly them there for a ceremony. From what I gather it was something like a last rite for Eli, who is convinced his heart will soon fail.

Cliff asks Jean who is buried up there.

"He was a man who was sometimes a wolf, then a man again." She is completely matter-of-fact, as if such transformations are accepted knowledge. In Native tradition, of course, they are. Catholicism, it seems, hasn't entirely wiped out ancient beliefs.

"People go there to pray," Jean continued. "Then they leave clothes and other things at the grave."

She goes on to tell of an Englishman who lived with his Native wife at the edge of the tundra for many years. His English wife wouldn't go with him, so he took a Native woman instead. Apparently, the man held a life-long vendetta against wolves, and poisoned or trapped them by the score until he died.

"He left all his money to his first wife," Jean adds. "The second wife lived in Stony, died just two years ago."

Within days of our arrival Cliff has to fly to Stony Rapids, and offers to take me and bring back a load of our winter supplies, boxes we mailed north before starting our journey. Thirty-five miles in twenty minutes. Below us the lake is dark and rough, flecked with white, and I am glad to be finished for the season. The slash of power line mars the landscape. Otherwise it is pure and wild country, horizon to horizon, with the tint of fall highlighting the bogs with gold and rust, the ridges with yellow.

I drink coffee in the White Water Inn while Cliff runs errands. For a time I talk to a young white woman whose husband manages the Northern Store. She has a distracted, nervous air, bumps a baby on her knee while she talks, smokes one cigarette after another.

In a year and a half she and her husband have been stationed at Fort McPherson, John D'Or Prairie, Fort Resolution, and now Stony Rapids.

"We want to get District Manager," she confides. "Then we can live in Winnipeg and just visit the stores."

She shudders at the thought of a transfer to Baffin Island. She's seen pictures of sheer cliffs backing the town. "If that cliff slides, you'd be gone!" she says emphatically. As if rock that has endured for millions of years would choose their short stint to crumble.

The boxes – full of winter food staples, warm clothes, boots, candles, books – make up a Beaver-load. "Light ones in the back, heavy up front," Cliff instructs. Then I cast us off and climb in. We motor into the current of the Fond-du-Lac River, a landing strip Cliff has used hundreds of times.

Headwinds slow our return, make the plane fly nearly sideways. Still windy, I think, looking west across the lake, amazed that Marypat and I have made our way across all of what I can see, and a great deal more, one paddle stroke at a time.

When we land there is a sphincter-tightening moment in a crosswind. Cliff looks at me and grins. "I knew it would be squirrelly in there."

A few days later Cliff takes both of us back to Stony. There is nothing we can do to prepare for winter while the camp stays busy, and we feel we are just another distraction in the meantime, more people to deal with. We want to stay with our friends Ed White and Margy Michel and return when the fishing season winds down.

Besides owning the White Water Inn, Ed and Margy operate a fishing camp of their own on the shore of Black Lake, where the Fond-du-Lac River drains out. We join them there, take up the same camp chores, acquaint ourselves with another patch of northern geography.

We are anxious to soak up their company because they'll be gone after Christmas and won't be able to visit us in our cabin. I can't say that I envy them their life style. "I love running the camp," Ed says, "but it's not the romantic life people think. All I am in the summer is a human forklift!" Then, over the winter, they travel south on the sport-show circuit in search of fishing clients. Denver, Minneapolis, days spent in barnlike convention centres, trapped in their little booth answering the same questions over and over.

On an Indian summer afternoon Ed drives us down a dirt track to see the wild section of the Fond-du-Lac River at

Elizabeth Falls. Sheer rock walls rise out of the gorge. The water is so clear we can see river bottom from hundreds of feet above. A recent fire has left the forest black and skeletal. Fireweed and a few grasses have just started to recolonize the area. Our pants are soon striped black from charred twigs.

We scramble down a break in the cliffs and stand next to the furious river noise. The water mesmerizes me; its heavy, dangerous roar is seductive, and I let myself be seduced. What would life be without these places? Marypat is perched on a rock, as far into the river as she can go, held in the same exultant embrace. Ed, too, is rejuvenated by our little jaunt, a rare vacation for him in a summer full of chores and responsibilities.

When we climb out of the canyon I notice that Ed still has trouble going up steep slopes, a slight gimp from his ultra-light accident five years earlier. In March of 1986 he set off to fly an ultra-light plane from Wollaston Lake to Stony Rapids, over hundreds of miles of empty bush. He made a trial takeoff and landing, circled a few times, then headed off, bundled up against cold.

He barely made ten miles.

"I just fell out of the sky," he told me once.

The cause of his fall, whether he stalled, or got caught in a wind sheer, or fell prey to a mechanical problem, is still a mystery. He dropped from four hundred feet, levelling out briefly at about sixty feet before crashing on the frozen surface of a lake.

"That little break in the fall saved my life," he told me.

For twenty-two hours he lay pinned beneath the plane, waiting for rescue. His pelvis was broken in three places and the pain wouldn't allow him to lie back, so the entire time he held himself up by a strut. He ate snow to slake his thirst, but had no food.

Searchers had a massive quadrant of bush to scour. If Ed hadn't had the luck to land on a lake, he would never have been spotted. When they did find him, fresh bear tracks were all around the area.

His bones mended rapidly, but there is still some nerve dam-age, which may never completely heal. Understandably, his interest in flying ultra-lights waned dramatically, but within a few years he had his pilot's licence and was flying small planes.

Every afternoon, Marypat and I gather cranberries along the crashing river. Between picking over the patches of deep-red berries, their tart sting fresh in our mouths, we stand above the rapids and discuss how to run them, or how to survive them.

Doug, the camp pilot, takes us to an island on Black Lake, dropping us off to pick berries while he trolls for lake trout in the shallows. It is misty and cool, the sky almost within reach, and we are conscious of the coming winter. I think of all the ways we will eat these cranberries in the dark months – muffins, pan-cakes, bread, dressing.

"I like doing this together." Marypat is stooping next to me, doesn't stop picking to talk.

We work along, filling our bags.

"This social time is nice," I say, "but I'll be ready to be alone again."

In Stony Rapids, the centre of male gossip, like a small-town barber shop, is the town dock. If you hang around there long enough, you'll know who is on a drinking binge, who isn't pay-ing their bills, which charter service is undercutting the rest, who pushes the load limit in their plane. The talk is punctuated with fuel-consumption figures, talk of the latest navigation sys-tem, the landing characteristics of various planes.

On September 25 the barges arrive at the dock on the last run of the year. The *W. H. Horton*, a staunch-looking tug, pulling a flotilla of six barges packed with fuel drums, pickup trucks, pro-pane bottles, semi-trailers crammed with goods.

"We go back to Uranium City, then home to Fort McMur-ray," a deckhand tells me. "We've run as late as October 20 before, but the water was freezing as we moved, that year."

I am replete with all this socializing, ready to get back to Oth-erside Bay. But Cliff's schedule doesn't bring him to town. The fall colours peak, then die away, the first snows come and go.

Ed and I fly over to the Fond-du-Lac River one evening to call for moose. Small planes are the northern car. It is nothing to pop here and there, droning over the northern bush as routinely as taking a trip to the store. We nose in to a sand beach and tie up the plane.

Ed starts up one of the boats he has parked there and motors against the current. It is a river I have paddled, years earlier, and memories flood back as we pass the points and bays lit in sunset colours.

The moose bugle is made from a thick slab of birchbark formed into a funnel. Out of it come mournful cow-moose howls, grunts, and belches, noises that bulls supposedly find enticing. As he blows, Ed closes his eyes in concentration, stands with his legs wide apart. Then we wait. Waves lap the sand, a squirrel scolds in the distance, evening falls silently.

On the way back to the plane Ed trolls for fish but catches nothing. It is a wonderful failure, this quiet trip. No generator noise, no other people, just river and forest and the sunset-flaming sky.

Suddenly we are back in Otherside Bay, September almost over. As usual with northern travel, we have had to wait and wait, then be ready to go in ten minutes.

Stella has already gone south. The fishermen have all left, allowing us to move into our old cabin. Only Bob, the camp mechanic, and his wife, Darlene, the cook, are still here. Cliff and his son, Craig, have one final group to host. Moose-hunters whom they will take north of the lake.

Every morning the water pumped out of the lake to supply camp has frozen in the black pipes. The boats are hauled up on shore, turned over. Motors are packed away, everything shut up.

Bob and Darlene fly off to their farm in southern Saskatchewan. The moose-hunters come, eat lunch, and leave again. We are alone. Winter is closing in.

"Let's go for a paddle," Marypat suggests, once the hunters have gone.

The canoe hasn't been wet since we paddled into camp, weary of the wind and our battle with the lake. Without a load the craft is light and buoyant, fast. Water speeds under the hull, glassy smooth, our strokes quick and in time. The light in the late evening sky is purple.

The motion of us paddling together is sweet. So sweet, and so easily forgotten.

21

FREEZING NIGHTS AND warm days mean perfect blackfly weather. It is as though the insects know their end is near and step up the intensity. Camp is at the outlet of the Otherside River, and blackflies require moving water to lay their eggs, so the location is vulnerable.

But firewood for winter is a need that can't be ignored, and we want to harvest good, downed timber before snow covers it all. The flies are furious little clouds around our sweaty heads. They land and crawl, searching for openings in our clothing, finding them. Rising in hordes out of the deep moss, they creep into our ears, noses, mouths, eyes. Mosquitoes are a delicate, minor-league pest compared to these demons.

Our tools are axes and a bow saw. Chainsaws are loud and

obnoxious, besides being dangerous, and the extra work is welcome after our soft month in camp. The two of us cut and trim
until we have a good stack of long logs, then carry them out to a
pile by the cabin. Thick, heavy logs are "two-ers" that require a
person at each end. The rest are "one-ers," and we follow each
other down the trail with these canoe-length hunks of tree,
winter portaging.

We become intimate with the fuel that will warm us through
the nine months of winter, through forty-below nights and
weeks of sombre days. The way, for instance, birch cuts as if
there is soap in the wood – quiet, soft, lubricated. The strong
resiny tang of spruce, the centres of jack pine honeycombed
with carpenter-ant burrowings, the propensity of poplar to
become waterlogged.

A single standing jack pine can consume an entire morning.
We take turns notching with our axes, then cut with the saw.
Old trees have trunks wider than the saw's bow. At some point,
invariably, the perfume of sap gushes out, as if we have cut
through an artery. By the time we have climbed over the trunk,
lopped off branches, cut the tree into lengths, we know the tree's
individual traits, and even months later will be able to remember the look of a certain grain or a quality of bark.

Sometimes there are berries and seeds tucked under slabs of
bark and in woody crevices, tiny food caches left by the small
birds that winter here. Birds like the chickadee hide their morsels in dozens of such safety deposits scattered throughout the
forest. Much later, in the bitter, hungry light of midwinter, they
return and are sustained.

When I find these I feel guilty, picturing a starving bird cast-
ing about for the food it knows should be there, but which has
mysteriously disappeared. I see that, indirectly, we are competi-
tors. And I think of miracles – how we search for them, but miss
the ones under our noses.

People will make a pilgrimage to some Latin American

town where someone has found the face of the Virgin Mary in the burn marks on a tortilla. Yet the fact that a little bird, five inches long from beak to tail, flourishes through a winter of minus forty- and fifty-degree nights, and maintains a mental map full of all the seeds and berries it has tucked away, passes as unremarkable.

About halfway through our laps with logs we take a coffee break on the front porch. Our shoulders are sore from the knotty weight of wood, scraps of bark and sawdust are under our clothes. The morning's sweat dries, cooling our skin.

"It's so easy to lose touch," Marypat remarks. "Even here, when the camp is running, or in Stony, I forget to notice whether the moon is full, what the wind is doing. I just go inside when it rains."

"Then, when you regain it," I add, "you think what a fool you've been."

Like animals reclaiming a territory, we go for long tramps in the afternoons, along trails we walked many times during our first winter here. It is deeply satisfying to recognize the bends, the shadowy lanes of forest, even individual rocks and tree roots.

Bald eagles still roost in the large poplars upriver, and on the island hill where we stand for a view over the shallow rapids. We collect their feathers, find whitefish carcasses pierced by their talons, ripped by their strong yellow beaks.

Spruce grouse burst from the ground or out of trees in a startling flurry. The brittle river grasses are rusty and golden. Muskrat tow their quiet wakes through the backwaters, busy and intent. On a knoll far upstream we find wolf scat and a rotten log torn apart by a bear rooting for grubs and insects. I am conscious of my own mental map, redrawing itself through the country of our trampings, touching and passing the spaces claimed by our wild neighbours.

The camp dog, Bandit, accompanies us while Cliff is away. She was our companion over the first northern winter, but will go south this year. She has lost none of her enthusiasm for chasing squirrels, although her success rate is as dismal as ever.

At home our winter supplies crowd us uncomfortably. Each evening we sort through bags of food, boxes of clothes and books, tuck things away as best we can, until our living space is somewhat restored. The mountainous pile of food, and the knowledge that we will eat our way through it all, makes me realize how long winter is. Marypat arranges her desk and I see her actually rubbing her hands together, anticipating the many projects she has planned.

When Cliff and Craig return we are thrown into a final burst of camp chores. The last boat comes out of the water. Doors are secured against the winds, valuables locked away. The radio-phone and its antenna, strapped to a tall pole of poplar, come down to our cabin.

"Let's buzz over to Fond-du-Lac," Cliff suggests when we're done. We have mail to pick up, a few supplies to buy, and we want to visit Brian and Jackie Van Stone, a couple we hope will come see us during the winter.

Before the Beaver even reaches the dock a small crowd has gathered. Cliff is assailed as soon as he steps down from the plane. Several guides want advances against their next-year's pay. The Band wants to charter him to fly trappers north. He wades through requests good-naturedly, manages to fend off most.

Brian arrives to rescue us in his official vehicle. He is the RCMP officer in town, and he drives us up the dirt street to the police compound. His house is clean and modern, ranch-style, with all the conveniences. Jackie greets us as we come in. She is a nurse, stationed at the local clinic. They have been married less than a year.

"Somebody is thinking of you!" She points to a large pile of mail she has picked up for us.

Over cups of coffee we talk. Brian complains of the recent

hectic work. "Full moon and the Band cheques at the same time," he says. "I don't care what anyone says, the full moon always makes things worse.

"Mostly it's like police-work anywhere," he goes on, referring to his posting. "Family quarrels, somebody beating his wife. Keeping booze out is the biggest headache."

Although Fond-du-Lac is a dry reserve, bootlegging is a flourishing trade.

When we get ready to leave, Brian and Jackie promise to continue to collect our mail and to visit. "Oh, we'll come," Brian asserts. "I like getting into the bush."

Cliff is happy to get away. "It's always crazy when I come here."

On their last night in camp Cliff and Craig have cocktail hour and supper in our cabin. Bandit's tail thumps the floor. She makes the rounds to be petted, then lies down with a sigh.

I catch myself wondering how long it will be until our next human contact.

Cliff and I spend the rest of the evening tinkering with the thermostat on the propane cookstove. The oven temperature is way off. There are, of course, no spare parts, no repair manuals. We guess our way into the mechanism, end up manufacturing a screwdriver out of a large bent nail, then sit in front of the oven door for the next two and a half hours, watching a thermometer inside and making tiny calibrations. By the time we're done the cabin is sweltering.

Marypat has been scribbling letters to send south and she and I spend the rest of the night opening packages and reading the words of our far-off friends.

By mid-morning the next day the plane is packed, camp is shut up, and there is nothing left to do. We hug and clasp hands, say what is always said at such moments, free the plane from its moorings for the final time. While Cliff warms up, circling on the water, then roars away across the lake, we stand together at the end of the dock. They circle back, low overhead. The wings waggle dramatically in a final salute, and they start south, over hundreds of miles of bush, to civilization.

"I just got butterflies," Marypat says looking at me nervously.

"I felt a little jolt of reality myself."

Keeping busy is the best therapy. For the afternoon our employment is cabin-remodelling and digging a new outhouse hole through the rock and sand, seven feet deep. Near the end, Marypat stands in the hole with a coffee can, scooping up dirt and sand, then throwing it out.

"We're really alone." She looks up out of the deep pit. "It keeps hitting me."

When we take a late-afternoon walk, the scent of winter is in the air. The leaves have fallen. Only the tamarack clings to its golden fur. The lake is black, cold, dangerous. The woods, today, seem eerie, unnerving. As we walk through the dead leaves I keep catching elusive movements at the edge of my vision, can't shake the feeling of being watched. The forest seems full of cover for quiet, lurking things that might mean us harm.

On other days, most days, the woods are inviting, the light clear and sharp, the trees and game trails welcoming. But not now. The forest is a place I hurry through, thinking of the cabin.

Then later, after dark, I go outside again. The night is black, the sky obscured by cloud. The light from my lantern shines out a few feet, then is overwhelmed. At that moment the little cabin, and the heat of my own body, seem tiny and insignificant. Something could be out here, I think. Something at arm's reach that I am not acute enough to sense.

It comes to me, then, that what is out here is the absence of humanity, nothing more or less.

I am reading Conrad's *Heart of Darkness*, and pick it up again when I retreat into the cabin. Almost immediately I read: "The silence of the land went home to one's very heart – its mystery, its greatness, the amazing reality of its concealed life."

22

THE BALD EAGLES are massing along the river. An immature bird fishes over the bay, twice plummeting, talons outstretched, into the water, then labouring into the air without a fish. It screams shrilly, as if in frustration, as it flaps away. As many as a dozen of them sit in the big, naked poplars overlooking a stretch of fast shallows. Dark, silent blots hunched against grey sky, with wet snow falling. Otherside River must be a staging ground, where the birds feed up in preparation, gather themselves. Day after day they collect and wait for the primitive mounting restlessness to reach its height.

Besides stocking up on firewood, our other chore is to groom a network of ski trails. Snow falls, clinging to the ground, and nights are already cold. It seems an indulgence, a recreation, to be out snipping twigs and cutting deadfall so that we might more easily glide through the woods. Our cabin still isn't tight, our woodpile remains small. But skis will be our only transportation, our physical release, the antidote for cabin fever. Maintaining the trails is as important as staying warm.

Paths go up both sides of the river, out parallel to the shore of the bay, and along several cut-lines through the forest. Cut-lines are the legacy of oil and mineral exploration. When Alberta struck oil in the 1940s, it set off a frenzied search throughout Western Canada. Exploration camps and seismic crews combed the outcrops, cut the provinces into grids along which they set off explosions and charted seismic waves through the bedrock.

The exploration goes on. Uranium lies underground in large quantities, along with other precious minerals. For now it is too remote and expensive to exploit; more accessible deposits are available. But it is only a matter of time before mineral extraction becomes more economical, or we become sufficiently desperate for them to come back. Exploration teams regularly frequent the North, go furtively about their business, feed rumours and speculation.

Meanwhile, their old cut-lines, straight as rulers, provide us with additional ski trails. Through bog and thicket, with no attention to the sensible way to travel, the gashes they make are a precise and foreign gridwork branded across the landscape. Temporarily, we claim them for ourselves.

Ice is forming in the bay. At first it is thick, waxy slush, elastic and tough, but breakable. The canoe is still out, and we wrest a trail through new ice to the river channel, where the current keeps the water open. We wear hats and gloves, and go to great lengths not to get wet. River otters are active in the moving water. Their heads break the surface like periscopes coming up for a look. They bob up and down, eyes glistening soberly, inhale our scent in sharp snorts, then dive again. At a distance they haul out on the thin ice, recline near the dark water, supple and quick and full of confidence. When the shadow of a raven passes nearby, they slither quickly into the safe, frigid water.

Muskrats poke through the slush, but seem to have no interest in us, no time to waste. A loon, already in winter plumage, rests in the open lake, drab as the sky, all alone. Mergansers spend an entire snowy day crouched quietly on the ice near the river mouth. Constant flocks of ducks fly silently above the black water.

The sense of girding up for winter, of escaping the coming harshness, of patience and deliberate focus, is as palpable as the snow that melts on our warm skin.

Our time is equal parts exercise, chores, and indoor projects. Reading and writing consume a solid chunk of every day.

"Imagine what it would be like to spend a winter here with nothing to read," Marypat says.

"I guess you'd take up whittling or play an instrument." But I can't imagine filling the dark season without books, paper and pencil.

By the time we exercise with the wood, haul water, cook meals, take a walk, there is hardly room to cram in the projects we've set for ourselves. How can there not be enough time, up here?

The pace seems profoundly sane, and the salient parts of a day are things we are too busy, or too preoccupied, to notice in civilized life. The rich amber grain of a jack pine trunk falling open under an axe; tree sparrows migrating through; northern twilight shading from rose to purple to black; a good conversation.

Snow on the ground shows up the movements of other members of our neighbourhood. Without it we make only the most obvious discoveries – tracks in mud, big piles of scat, the rare sighting of an animal. In the snow, squirrels reveal their busy traffic patterns, concentrated now around winter dens made of spruce cones. The runs of snowshoe hare are dense in the thickets, beaten-down trails between points of protection. In the thickets, too, we find the clawless prints of lynx, that most dedicated predator of the northern rabbit.

Along the river the dainty meandering trail of red fox and the broad track of wolf wind against the banks. Here and there, still, the humanlike foot of bear. It will be a relief when they are gone for the winter.

We leave behind our large blunt trail, to be sniffed at, assessed, taken into account. These tracks are certainly no revelation to our neighbours. They have been smelling our wood smoke, hearing our racket, encountering our scent, perhaps even watching our movements, for weeks.

Marypat lasts several weeks with her desk in the back half of the cabin. The woods nearby screen out light from the side windows, and she is cloaked in gloom back there, bent nearsightedly over her beading and drawing. "I can't stand it!" she finally explodes.

We rearrange things, cram her desk up against one of the front windows. I write in front of the other window, eight feet away, at the same table where we eat and play cribbage and backgammon. All that is left at the back of the cabin is our bed, stacks of supplies, the radio-phone.

Light is a kind of drug, a thing we crave and observe with obsessive attention, that affects our moods, our ability to work. Sunlight, even a few hours of it, turns a dull day radiant and upbeat.

From my seat, where I spend a good portion of every day, I can see nearly the entire arc of the sun's passage. The mouth of the river is in view, and the end of Otherside Bay. It is like a stage, across which the play of northern winter is enacted, events both remarkable and ordinary.

A red fox regularly trots along the far edge of the stage. It tests the rim of ice, near the current, even breaks through with one foot, makes forays into the woods, but always returns to the margin of open space.

Marypat takes her camera one afternoon and sets herself up to intercept the fox as it reaches the river. She is gone a long time.

"I couldn't believe it," she says, when she returns. "I only had three pictures left on the roll! And the fox was right across from me. It hunted mice in the grass, paced back and forth. I could have played rock 'n' roll and it wouldn't have cared. Damn!

"But, you know, it doesn't matter. It was so pretty to watch, and it knew I was there, but somehow it was okay. Even more than that, it was like the fox stuck around longer because I was there."

Snow falls every few days, but the temperatures aren't bitter. If it continues, freeze-up of the open lake could take a long time and slush will be a problem. It is always cloudy, and we feel robbed. Sunlight is in short enough supply as it is, and overcast days, one after another, never brighten beyond dusk.

When the sun does break free, we are immediately drawn out, as though by a magnetic pull. On the final day of October it is sunny. We skate on our boots along the brittle shore-ice to the point, where the open lake fights off winter. Broken tents in the ice show where muskrats come up to breathe. The rocks wear frozen hats where waves break over them. A flock of redpolls chatters in some nearby alders, almost frantic in their attacks on the catkins they feed on. Sunlight catches the warm red spots on their heads.

I notice, on our way back through the woods, that Marypat is particularly chipper, full of enthusiasm. I am following her along the snowy trail. She carries a branch in her hand and taps lightly on tree trunks as she goes by, her step bouncy, like she might be keeping time to a song in her head.

When I calculate, I realize that her period is overdue. This jauntiness has come before, these last years, always for the same reason. Her hopes are up. It is unfathomable to me, how she can be so radiant with expectation, after all the disappointments. But I say nothing, enjoy her happiness, the flush in her cheeks when she turns to me, pointing to the distant orange sun flaming at us through the spruce.

November 1 is my thirty-eighth birthday. My partner rises early, kindles the fire, brings me coffee in bed as the air thaws. She cooks me cranberry pancakes, studded with tart reminders of moss-carpeted ground and yellow aspen leaves shaking in a fall breeze.

But this morning Marypat's mood is as downcast as it was buoyant the day before. Her hopes have been crushed for another month, one more in a string that winds back out of memory. After breakfast we sit together. She cries against my chest.

"I just get so sad," she says.

"I know you do." This meaningless acknowledgement is all I can think to say.

"I don't know how to get over it."

Sooner or later, I think to myself, you have to. We have to. Already it has been too long to wallow in depression. I don't have the physical connection to failure that she does, can't fathom the emotions, can only try to comfort. Today the grey-ness of winter is inside as well as out.

23

SNOW KEEPS FALLING. At the mouth of the bay the lake surges against newly formed ice, breaking the thin sheet into jostling cakes. Where ice and water meet, a slurry of broken crystals sounds like the tinkling of a thousand chandeliers. Swells advance into the ice, visible for a long way, even under the unbroken surface.

Ed calls on the radio-phone one night. "Slush everywhere," he reports. "Too much early snow. None of the trappers can do anything. Prices are low to start with, eh? Lots of people aren't even going out.

"You've got mail piling up," he goes on. "I'm collecting it here, thought I'd fly over one day and drop it air mail."

Two days later the sound of a plane circling overhead makes us stampede out the door. It's been a month since our last human contact. This plane has come on our account. We know the people one hundred feet above us, can just make out their faces. It is as close as we'll get, but it has the warmth of an embrace.

After several reconnoitring passes, the plane comes in low over a stand of poplars, heading for the frozen inner bay. Should we be wearing hard hats? I have a flash of us laid out by a bombardment of mail. The passenger door opens and Ed's companion shoves a bag out. It drops like a stone, at terrific speed, and tumbles along through cushioning snow. Perfect aim. They make another pass, a box hurtles toward us. When it hits, the seams split open and a can of beer flies out, foaming. Miscellaneous other items scatter across the snow – a book, canned oysters. Another pass, and another box. This one spews red, bleeding in gouts along its white, snowy trail.

The plane zooms low one last time, waggles at us, then turns east. Before we pick up our packages we watch until it is a speck in the greyness.

The damage is considerable. A bottle of sticky liqueur has shattered in a box of books and magazines. We peel pages apart, pick out glass shards, hang magazines above the stove to dry. The bleeding package had a six-pack of cranberry juice in it. Two of the six survive, and everything is dyed red. Five or six cans of beer, sent along by Ed and Margy, all appear punctured or dented in some way. Rather than risk them going flat, we set about drinking without delay. One hard-boiled egg out of a dozen is salvageable.

Later, Ed calls, gleeful over his accuracy. When I report the casualties he only giggles. "The eggs were a test," he says. "We didn't think many would make it."

Despite the losses, we are wealthy, once again, with camaraderie, overwhelmed by the thoughtfulness of friends. This is the only thing we miss, these human connections. How taken for granted is the luxury of visiting at someone's house, talking over coffee, having friends to dinner.

"Where's the sun?" Marypat says irritably one morning. Human contact is not quite the only thing we miss. In the first two weeks of November, we catch glimpses of sun on only three days. At its height, it is now barely a hand's breadth above the spruce line, and we rarely see it through the clouds.

Daylight is evaporating in discernible chunks. We eat dinner by candlelight, not for the romantic appeal, but to conserve lantern fuel. Also, because we don't want to admit that it is already too dark to see.

The lack of daylight saps our ambition, cripples our spirits, makes us irritable and snappy.

"You need a project!" Marypat turns on me. "All you can do is pace around."

"I'm thinking," I flash back. "It helps me write if I can move and think."

"It makes it impossible for *me* to think!"

There is a venom that has crept into our arguments during the past year, a well of anger that is tapped unexpectedly at these times of stress. I don't know where it comes from, how we can speak in such a tone and still love each other. Absurd things, like the scoring in a backgammon game or whose turn it is to make dinner, will fester, unresolved and petty, but poisonous, through an evening.

"We need to talk," I say, later. "If we don't get at the little things that bother us, it'll always be bad."

Marypat waits for me to say more, her face tight and discouraging.

"Okay," I push on. "I'll tell you something that's been getting to me. Every time you make bread, you leave the doughy stuff on the board after you knead. By the time we clean it, it's all hard and crusty and petrified. Why can't you clean up after yourself right away?" My complaint, as I hear it spoken, sounds ridiculous, but I let it hang there.

"All right." Marypat is ready, hardly hesitates. "Your booties drive me crazy. When you pace around the cabin, they drag on the floor and I can't concentrate. If you picked your feet up, you wouldn't make so much noise."

It's like water breaching a dam, first a trickle, then a stream, then a great bursting torrent. The niggling complaints that have been pent up, quietly bothering us, eroding our tolerance, all pour out, one on top of another – eating idiosyncrasies, my tendency to check the fire too often, Marypat's clutter.

Eventually there is less heat and hatefulness behind our charges, greater detachment. We laugh sheepishly at the pettiness of our rage, and at the relief that comes from uncaging it.

"We have to do this when things come up," I say. "I can't believe all the stupid stuff that we've kept inside, how important each thing seemed at the time. I had no idea those things were bugging you."

It's easy to blame discord on the lack of sun, on our confinement in a wooden box sixteen by twenty feet. These are undeniable factors, but also convenient scapegoats.

More profoundly, we are adrift with our emotions, our lives, not sure with each other or about our future together. The trip will end, we will return to pick up the threads left hanging back at home, and, perhaps, nothing will be resolved. That is the fear that hovers between us, manifesting itself in these frightening outbursts, in brutal tones of voice. We came on this journey, in part, because we didn't know what else to do. Now here, the same anger and disappointment, the same unresolved future, lurks in the corners. And here there is no escape.

We fall into a pattern of discussion, setting a period aside each day for talk. If the air needs clearing, we work at that, but just as often we take tangents. For a day or two it is life-style choices that occupy us: work and money and the priorities that inevitably seem to come unglued. We make resolutions to keep ourselves honest.

Something in a book or issues in the news will come up. The topics don't matter. The talking, the interaction, does. How could we drift apart, become estranged, when we do so much in tandem? Paddling a boat, sawing logs, working in a crowded space. Yet, without words, without giving time, our awareness of each other, that tenderness, goes slack. The other person becomes only the other half of the machine that is the two of us surviving, travelling, making do.

Our time together alternates between periods of harmony and discovery, of love and descents into conflict, with its impotent, unfocussed frustration. Week after week we trudge through the forest, do our chores, sleep belly to back through the long nights. We are without human company, balancing between light and darkness, making our way through an inner wilderness more impenetrable, more forbidding, than any external terrain.

More often than not we make love on shower days. Funny how clean bodies encourage an interest in sex. Warm water in a black bag is hung from the roofbeam behind the cabin, tied off to a propane bottle. One at a time we scurry out, wearing only rubber boots, then stand on a plywood sheet to lather up. In bone-numbing, frigid cold the water steams off our bodies in great clouds. Chickadees watch from a nearby spruce. If the wind is blowing, the run back inside after shutting the water off is a numbing dash. Once a week we endure this ritual.

Although Marypat continues to take her Chinese herbs, we no longer chart her daily temperature in hopes of hitting her ovulation. It is too painful to be clinical, too calculated and hopeful to follow a strategy. We talk, now, about adoption.

"What about an Indian baby?" Marypat asks.

In mid-November we admit, finally, that the paddling season is over and store away the canoe. At about the same time the last eagle flies south. The river is being shrunk by the inexorable advance of ice. Bear tracks are gone, and we ski what I think of as our territory, seeing no human sign but our own, as we glide across miles of country.

One evening we go upriver in the light of a fat, cold moon. Frost crystals glitter, suspended, in the luminous air. Trees near the open water are frost-rimed, their branches clouds of feathery ice. The open water sounds treacherous, and I imagine being taken down through a hole, swept under the impenetrable crust, into the liquid darkness.

Away from the water there is no sound at all, the silence so compelling that I strain to hear the movements of stars.

24

LYNX ALMOST NEVER appear, but when they do they are unmistakable. We are playing cribbage in the late-afternoon twilight when I glance out the window and see one on the bay. The cat has a particularly feline way of moving, flowing over ground. The only other one we've ever seen was a fuzzy glimpse along the Porcupine River in the Yukon.

We leave our cards scattered on the table and tiptoe onto the porch. The lynx is the same grey as the sky. It moves steadily, without the nervous hyperactivity of a fox or the heaviness of a wolf. Its body cants slightly forward from hips to shoulders, a dragster built for bursts of speed.

This species has highly defined dietary tastes. Its only food is the snowshoe hare, and its fate is tied inextricably to the fortunes of that other northern species. When hares are plentiful, so, too, are the lynx. When the hare population plummets, every ten years or so, the cats inevitably die off as well. Often they will starve to death rather than change prey. Less aggressive and adaptable than its close relative the bobcat, lynx have been pushed farther and farther north, their territory limited by the hares they eat and by their retiring nature.

A hunting stalk nearly always culminates in a final intense sprint. The hare loses faith in its camouflage and explodes in a dash for cover. The lynx pursues, running low to the ground in a soft streak, its broad feet like snowshoes, dodging as the hare dodges, gaining bit by bit. Snow flies along the path of the hunted and the hunter. At the last, still going full speed, the lynx reaches out with its oversized front paw, claws unsheathed, and bats the hare off its course. The twenty-pound cat is on top of its quarry, ignoring the death scream, with the unwavering ferocity that allows it to live to the next meal.

These sights are only occasional gifts, but frequent enough that I schedule long glances out the window into the day. Marypat sees our first wolf out the window by her desk. It is abruptly there, sitting on its haunches by the water hole, looking at our cabin.

"Al, Al, there's a wolf!" She is stammering with excitement, flapping her hand at the window.

For a long time we stare at the wild animal across the short distance. The wolf is patient, unafraid. Its coat is full, creamy white, and its attention is on our home. Eventually it stands, walks off upriver, its long legs taking it quickly from view. Although we watch intently much of the day, that's all we see.

The next morning wolf tracks are in the deep snow outside the cabin. They were everywhere, within yards of where we slept. Their trail leads along the river; eight of them, we decide.

My mind is full of wolf as we follow the cold spoor. I imagine them stopped where the tracks group up, sniffing each other, nuzzling, taking stock. Yellow pee-spots mark their route, staying along the bank, following the meandering water, the trail beaten hard from their weight.

There is a place in a thicket of willows where several of them lay down. Their bodies left melted circles in the snow and I picture them there, curled up, ears twitching, heads lifting now and then, their breath smoky in the cold. Perhaps they howled together, made that hungry lament that is so great, so primitive, filling the night.

Slush plagues us along the ski trails. Deep, insulating snow hides lakes of mush underneath, and we ski right into them. Our skis immediately gain twenty pounds. The efficient glide becomes a laborious trudge. We stop to scrape and chip off the frozen layers, our hands slowing with cold. Twenty feet farther another trap may await.

The river writhes and slithers, avoiding the final shackles of winter. The ice is like travertine deposits at a hot spring. Layers of it build and harden in thin sheets. Fantastic, dynamic sculptures. Canals bordered by high walls of ice build up, freezing along the bottom, so the river is actually elevated above the surrounding land. Whenever water overflows the wall, huge skating rinks are formed overnight. Or huge ponds of slush that wait for our unsuspecting skis.

Even past mid-November the lake stays open. We break a trail along a cut-line to the shore, but except for a rim of ice, open water extends to the far side. We turn back, disappointed. Then, for two days solid it is bitterly cold. Thirty below (−35°C) at night and hardly warming each day. The next time we ski to the hill overlooking Lake Athabasca, it is solid white, shore to shore.

Despite the near-darkness and deep cold, despite not knowing whether the route is good or treacherous, we are lured by the expanse of ice into trying to ski home on the lake. For miles we skate with our skis on the glazed surface. Daylight wanes, the line of forest turns black and shadowy. The sky to the west is pale orange, cool pastel, then purple.

We surprise the red fox whose tiny tracks we've been following through frost crystals. It scampers into the deep snow, disappears into the forest, its huge tail bouncing as it leaps. By the time we round our bay it is night – black, star-filled night, with new ice singing as it firms and settles. Slush hampers us for the last hour, our hands are spotted white with frostbite from scraping it off, but the discomfort is minor compared to our exhilaration.

"The skies are so big here," Marypat says. "You can see stars right to the horizon, right into the trees."

We dive into the safe burrow of our cabin, warming our hands painfully over the stove. For the rest of the evening we are drawn back out into the cold again and again to watch green and pink lights snake through the sky. Through them I see Orion's belt and the cluster of the Pleiadies. Over our cabin, above the windows glowing with candlelight, hangs the Big Dipper. And faintly, very faintly, the sound of open-river water is audible from half a mile's distance.

On our anniversary Marypat gets her period. In matters of love we are dogged by these ironies.

"I don't feel like celebrating," she says.

She was up reading a good part of the night, unable to sleep with the cramping. She tells me she had intense chest pains at one point. "Like someone stabbing a needle in my chest," she says. "I could hardly breathe. But I was so calm. I just lay there a long time wondering about it, massaging my arm. Then it disappeared."

"Maybe it was gas pains or the cramps," I suggest. "You're about the least likely candidate for a heart attack I know."

She shrugs listlessly and I want to shake her, make her care, make her overcome this addiction to depression. It is one of our tough days. Even a pair of willow ptarmigan snipping willow buds out front doesn't elevate the mood for long.

The next shower day Marypat wants nothing to do with sex.

"It's just too depressing," she complains.

"For crying out loud, Marypat. Can't you think of it as making love, not making babies?"

"It's always there, no matter what."

We dress in silence, and in the afternoon I take a solitary ski, my mind chugging along the same dead-end streets and my eyes seeing nothing of the landscape.

As December begins we anticipate visitors. The snowmobile road between Fond-du-Lac and Stony Rapids will be in use as soon as the lake solidifies. We are counting on Brian and Jackie to make good on their promise. Two months have passed since our last human contact. Two months of grey light and alarming mood swings.

Much as we hunger for visitors, we are strangely reticent and introverted. When the radio-phone sounds, we look at each other. "Your turn," we say and point at each other, stricken with shyness.

My parents are planning to come for Christmas, only a few weeks off. The first time we paddled across Canada, they were full of reservations, couldn't understand our need to do it. This time they are determined to join us, to share the adventure. On the solstice they will fly in to Stony Rapids. From there they'll charter a ski-plane and come to our bay, stay in our cabin for ten days. It seems impossible, even as the time approaches.

We are skiing out on the bay when our isolation ends. A snowshoe hare has been hunkered out on the open snow for half the morning. It seems suicidally exposed out there. Any passing owl or fox or lynx could have it at will. And it isn't the first one we've seen do this. Is it soaking up the feeble rays of sun, combating the claustrophobia of willow thickets?

"Let's see if we can get a picture," Marypat suggests.

At twenty feet the hare hasn't moved. I slide forward, to ten feet away. The large back paws twitch nervously, the nose is busy, but it stays, utterly dependent on its camouflage. I can reach it with my ski pole. Marypat is busily clicking away, and the hare hasn't budged.

Then we hear the far-off sound of a motor.

"Hear that!?" we say, simultaneously.

The hare is forgotten. We turn toward the open lake, listening intently. Unmistakable, the snarl of snowmobile. But is it for us? Then they are in sight, black spots bearing in on us from two miles out. People are coming! We are suddenly tempted to hide, like the hare, which bounded away when our attention wandered.

V

ICED-IN

25

WE MEET HALF a mile out on the bay. Our visitors are unrecognizable under their heavy clothing until they are right in front of us. Brian and Jackie, on the RCMP snowmobile, and Philip, from Fond-du-Lac. We barely know these people, yet are hugging them and slapping their backs, babbling with excitement while their machines rumble and smoke.

"You're the first!" I exclaim. "The first people in nine weeks!"

The import of this doesn't seem to sink in. They grin and nod, rub their mittened hands together. They are just out for a little adventure, an escape from town. How could they know what it means to us to have other human beings in our reach?

"Slush off the point," Philip says as he looks out to where we first saw them. "Almost got stuck."

At the cabin we can't sit still, bustle around warming up a pot of chili, make coffee. Marypat mixes a batch of our favourite muffins. Our guests shed layer after layer of clothing, tour the cabin, shake out the inevitable cigarettes.

"How do you fill your time?" Jackie asks, clearly impressed by the smallness of our quarters, the quietness of our location.

137

We tell her, but she isn't convinced. "I'd go crazy," she says.

Brian is a career RCMP officer. He is sturdily built, concise in his conversation, restless in his movements. His tone of voice and summary statements seem the outgrowth of his vocation, a job that requires unwavering authority.

"Scholar!" he says, when I bring him coffee. It is short for "You're a gentleman and a scholar," and he uses it instead of thank you.

"What's your opinion of Americans?" I ask him.

"Never had much time for 'em. They think we still ride horses and use dog teams up here. Whenever I meet one they want to know why I'm not wearing my Mountie outfit."

They each brandish cigarette after cigarette, stop only to eat. The cabin is blue with smoke.

Philip sits by the window after lunch, looks outside much of the time. "Lots of snow this year," he observes. He is one of the most gregarious Chipewyan I have met. His English is good and he loves to gossip and joke.

He has known this bay all his life, from a time when only seasonal Native camps existed here. When he was young very few people actually lived year-round in Fond-du-Lac. The Chipewyan still moved nomadically with the caribou and worked their trap lines, only coming to town to trade and visit. He has been a fishing guide here for years, spends his summers in the company of clients who might as well have been born on another planet from the one he grew up on.

Too quickly, twilight is on us, and our guests prepare themselves for their return.

"Don't worry, we'll be back," Jackie reassures us.

By the time Brian unloads our mail there is hardly anything left on his toboggan. They disappear into the falling snow, the sky like gauze, and we can hear their engines for a long time.

The visit is a watershed, not only because we have connected with people again. The knowledge of the potential is, almost, more important. We can ski to Fond-du-Lac, people can come to us, ski-planes can land in the bay. Even if weeks go by without visitors, we know it is now possible, at any time.

Going through the mail takes half the evening. Each of the letters and packages is savoured. We read every letter aloud, one after the other, talking each one over before opening the next. Someone has snuck a bottle of whisky by Customs, so we indulge in a cocktail. Another box is full of nothing but bags of potato chips, which we devour on the spot.

Our invigoration lasts through the next day. During the afternoon ski, low sunlight warms the trunks of birch and poplar in a rich glow, light pools in open glades. It is an inviting light, cheerful as our mood. Four spruce grouse explode out of their insulated snow burrows, land in the low branches of a jack pine, fluffed into corpulence. On the way home we are stopped by a strong, musky odour. A dark fisher, a large member of the weasel family, bounds across in front of us, tail flowing luxuriously.

"Must have been marking its territory," I say. "Pretty big smell!"

The cold grows intense and the river finally gives in. Only a few fast corners remain open. The rest is entombed under hummocky armour. Only a faint gurgling through cracks gives away the continued flow. Steam rises off the tiny patches of open water into the brittle air. It instantly freezes on the trees, coating the branches, making feathery sculptures.

Even skiing hard we barely stay warm. "Your nose is white," I tell Marypat. She holds her mitten to it while she looks me over.

"Spots on your cheeks," she points out.

In the cabin our stove maintains a temperature as much as 120 degrees (68°C) warmer than outside. One night I stay up late, reading. It is minus forty-six degrees (−43°C) on the other side of the wall I lean against. Although the stove is well-stoked,

I feel the tendrils of cold creeping under the door, through cracks in the logs. Layers of frost collect on the inside corners at the back of the cabin.

The cold, then, reminds me of a tide coming in. Water feeling its way through rocks, lifting seaweed out of its limp repose, inching up the sand, inexorable, until, suddenly, it laps at the beach towels. Only, the cold is invisible as well as inexorable. The refrigerated ocean filters down, settling, claps hard over the cabin without any warning. When I step outside to pee, the startling air numbs my lungs, stings my nostrils, and I think of the hunkered-in life all around me, flourishing outside without any fire.

Prolonged below-zero (below −18°C) temperatures make us bold in our explorations. Far upriver, where the channel has been frozen for the longest time, we hazard a crossing. The critical area is twenty feet across, maybe even less, but it is a moment of tension. If we go through the ice, we could well die. I unclip my ski bindings so I can kick out of them if I have to, push off, gliding in long, tender strides, and am across. Marypat follows, holding her breath.

We giggle, there, in the quiet air, over our little triumph. All afternoon we ski the far side of the stream. Old landmarks, seen from a new vantage, are fresh and different. Another network of animal tracks comes to light. We point out fox trails, lynx scat, the snow burrows of ptarmigan.

No life reveals itself, not even the croak of a raven rends the stillness. All we see is a hairy woodpecker, feverishly shredding dead bark in a stand of alder. Yet it is remarkable what a change in routine, some new country, a few little discoveries can do for our mood.

The camp is smothered under snow. When we return, through the back way, there are drifts to the eaves of some cabins, propane bottles are buried, and the woodshed roof is bowed down under the weight. We stop on top of a high drift.

The white lake spreads across the miles to the foot of distant hills of rock.

Marypat tips her head back and lets out a wolf howl. It sounds pretty good to me. I even get a little chill up the back of my neck. Nothing answers. She howls again into the silence, and we stay there, breathing clouds, before gliding home.

There is no way to forecast the bleak, downcast episodes. One day, for no discernible reason, my writing goes badly, a lethargy overwhelms me. There is nothing I want to do, nothing that excites me. This box of a home in an ocean of cold is the very last place on earth I want to be. A remote panic, a claustrophobia, tugs at my consciousness, saps my fortitude. Why am I here?

These are the times I conveniently forget when I'm planning an adventure. I remember the sunny days, the exhilarating paddling, the quiet contentment, while the bad weather, the dull monotony, the suppressed fever of confinement, all fade out of mind.

What brings me back is equally mysterious. An inspiration in my writing, ten minutes of chipping ice out of our water hole, a good night's sleep, reading the right poem.

We are capable, the two of us, of outbursts of giddiness, wrestling bouts on the floor. One morning in bed Marypat clambers on top of me, lies naked on my back. Our bodies make little farting sounds against each other. We can't seem to stop it. Every move elicits another rude noise. We chuckle, more farts. Soon we are roaring with laughter, goofy as eight-year-olds playing in their bedroom.

Our relationship seems to be on a sounder footing. We talk freely when a thing bothers us. The little grievances don't grow out of proportion. I think of all we have been through together, even since the start of this trip, and a kind of pride in our endurance wells up. We are truly partners. It has nothing to do with marriage vows; everything to do with being there, face to face, through the dark, grubby, insane times, as well as the periods of light and grace.

And my dreams are finally coming freely. In the wilderness I am usually assailed by a nightly outpouring, but on this trip the vivid, memorable dreams have been rare. My theory is that in society the hectic pace and usual neuroses tie knots in my subconscious, knots that loosen up once I have been long enough on a trip. It seems to me a mark of how tight those knots have become, these last years, that it has taken six months of quiet living to open them. Now when I drop into sleep, I anticipate dreams, welcome them, even the disturbing ones.

My parents are coming, and soon. Out on the bay we probe for potential landing strips, dig pits in the snow to discover any slush pockets. In this cold it seems impossible that slush can persist, but it does, and a ski-plane mired in icy water is a nightmare I want to avoid.

We find what we think will be a good strip and mark it with a series of small spruce saplings we cut down and drag out of the woods. Each day I check again for slush.

On solstice morning, sunrise isn't visible until eleven o'clock. It is bitterly cold. As the sun reaches its low peak, the mercury inches up to minus thirty degrees (−35°C). We are resolved to take showers, regardless. I am the second one out this time. Marypat scurries back in, buck-naked, teeth chattering, covered with gooseflesh. By the time I venture out the board is iced-up solid and sticks painfully to my bare feet. The hot water is wonderful, but too brief. It hardly blunts the deep cold.

Since we can't concentrate on anything, we take a long, vigorous ski up the river. Miles out we see the first silver fox of the winter – tar-black, its coat long and beautiful. The little guy prances with curiosity, sniffs in our direction, then bounds off, flashing a white tip on the end of its tail.

I know that the northern economy to some extent depends on the trapping of fur, that the history of the fur trade is illustrious and exciting, and also that the trapping life style is an independent and hardy one. But when I see these vibrant, hot-blooded animals going about their lives – the grey lynx, this fox, a fisher – I am utterly repulsed by the thought of their lifeless pelts warming the backs of high society.

When we ski home at sunset, on this the shortest day of winter, we are granted an extraordinary show of light.

"Amazing," Marypat says, "that there really are these colours in nature."

26

BY MIDDAY, WHEN the faint sound of an approaching plane finally reaches us, we have been outside to listen dozens of times. I have slogged to the strip on snowshoes and made a final check. Two pots of coffee have been consumed.

We race for the bay, loaded with sleds and packs, extra snow-shoes, a camera. The plane appears, arrows toward the frozen lake, drops low over the willow point that protects the inner bay. Skis thump down heavily in a cloud of snow, obliterating our view. The pilot roars up and back, tamping down his runway, then turns the plane in readiness for takeoff.

The day is somewhat overcast, slightly warmer, only fifteen or twenty below (−26° to −29°C). The engines die, a door pops open, and my parents unbend from the inside. They have endured a bitterly cold three-day odyssey from Wyoming to reach our cabin on Otherside Bay.

But they are here. The pilot tosses duffels and packs through the door, and it is too cold to stand around gawking at each other. As soon as the plane is unloaded the pilot is back in the cockpit, turning the engine over. We hunch our backs against the bitter slipstream as the plane starts to move, slewing its way through the snow. It is soon lost in a thick swirl, and I listen for the dying pitch that a pocket of slush would cause, but takeoff is successful.

For once we don't stand around, watching, savouring the human contact. We are busy with our own gathering. The pile of stuff, once we labour with it to the cabin, is huge. They have brought us fresh cheese, bottles of Christmas cheer, film supplies, gifts, as well as their substantial stack of personal gear.

"We can organize later," Mom says. "Let's go for a walk while it's still light."

Marypat and I compete as tour guides. The four of us tromp through camp on snowshoes while we point everything out, talk on top of each other. We add a short loop up the Otherside River, then back through the forest. In the cracks between our jabbering my parents exclaim at the beauty of the North.

"When we flew up here yesterday," Mom says, "it seemed so huge and featureless. All these little rivers and lakes and no real landmarks. I wondered how anyone finds their way."

All we can do is talk. We hover around, both helping and hindering, while they unload duffels, packs, boxes, and try to get everything stowed in the tiny sleeping quarters. They are hemmed in by cases of expedition food, the table we wash dishes on, the radio-phone and its car battery. But they manage, and we end up around our eating table as daylight bleeds away.

Marypat and I begin telling the story of our trip so far. The big water on the Smoky, the flood wreckage in train trestles, Vermilion Falls and the windstorm, our German friends. In some detail we relive the trauma of crossing Lake Athabasca, the conflict between us, the sense of butting up against that line of danger, and of crossing it more than once. Pregnancy is never brought up by any of us.

We talk right through dinner and the dishes. They relate

their epic journey. Mom pulls out Christmas ornaments and a jigsaw puzzle she brought along. Marypat goes over the cabin routine, tells them that if they need to pee during the night not to be shy about using the slop bucket instead of the outhouse. They are dubious.

Bitter cold swoops in again, like an owl settling on its prey, and won't lift until after my parents leave. Forty below (–40°C) or colder every night. Daytime highs of minus twenty-five or thirty (–32 to –35°C).

The rigours of thirty or forty below (–35 to –40°C) are dramatically different from minus fifteen or twenty (–26 to –29°C), a quantum leap in harshness. At forty below (–40°C), metal sears our fingers, camera viewers stick to our faces, our eyelids freeze together momentarily when we blink. Marypat's camera shutter, set at 1/60 of a second, freezes open. When we strip off gloves to adjust our snowshoe bindings, it takes half a mile of brisk movement before our hands are warm again.

Our harvesting of a Christmas tree may be the quickest on record. It is minus thirty (–35°C) outside, and we select a spruce from a crowded grove not twenty yards from the cabin, anchor it in a pail full of rocks, set it inside by the window.

Trees that live in this frigid land – jack pine, black spruce, tamarack, poplar, birch – have adapted accordingly. During winter the sap is ejected from cells, into the spaces between them. When the sap freezes, at minus forty (–40°C) and colder, it does no harm. More southerly trees don't have this capability, and temperatures beyond minus forty will kill them. Our Christmas spruce must be in shock, suddenly thrust into eighty-degree (27°C) warmth.

This holiday time is a throwback to the days of pioneering homesteaders. We read in bed by candlelight, play Scrabble with an oil lamp on the board. Each day the four of us trail down to the water hole, pound it open, and haul back buckets. The radio brings us news of mounting tensions in the Persian Gulf, political upheaval in the Soviet dis-Union, but from our porch we watch the undulating rivers of light flowing through the night sky, and the silence of the wilderness wraps around us, heavy as the deep, muffling snow.

"I feel so incredibly safe here," Mom says, from her bed. "It's like a little burrow so far away that the anxieties of life can't reach me."

It strikes me that I know so very little about these people, my parents. I have known them longer and more intimately than anyone else on earth, yet there are huge gaps in my knowledge. For nearly twenty years we shared a home, ate meals together, fought, played, travelled. But I don't know who their lovers were, who bullied them. What were their triumphs and defeats? Why did they fall in love? What turned their choices in life?

As a youngster I was too self-absorbed to care about the details of my parents' history. After I left home, life was too busy, our time together too short. Now we have time.

Big chunks of the cold days are spent inside, talking. A montage of images shapes up, and I glimpse them as lovers in college, see my father as he hears of the bomb on Hiroshima, appreciate the adventurous choices they made as young parents. Again and again, the things I don't know amaze me.

Several times every day we bundle into layers of clothing, strap on snowshoes, venture into the pristine, brittle beauty. One afternoon we follow fresh moose tracks up the river, through the thickets where it stripped bark from willows, along river ice, into the deeply drifted forest, where the animal's chest made a wide groove through the snow.

Our guests are entranced by the low, golden light, by the serenity. Noise travels a great distance in this cold. A flock of ptarmigan is scared up in front of us, and they fly into a stand of poplar. From one hundred yards we can hear the clicking of their beaks, the sounds they make eating buds. The birds are soft pink, rosy, in the afternoon light.

On Christmas morning it is minus forty-five degrees (−43 °C).

We are up in the pre-dawn greyness, and the air outside is still, hazy with frost, the cold miles thick. Twelve or fifteen ptarmigan adorn the branches of a small poplar in front of the cabin. There is a bird on almost every small branch, and they sit there, plump and soft, exactly like Christmas ornaments.

These birds, somehow, are a benediction. We all feel it, watching them in the milky light as if something more than chance has brought them here this morning. Then, one or two at a time, they flurry off, quickly lost against the snow.

We have a turkey, which we were able to order through the fishing camp in the fall. Marypat makes loaves of Christmas bread, the bird is stuffed, the cabin warms up with evocative smells. Our gift to each other is this time together. What else could possibly be required?

The radio-phone sounds during the day, greetings are transmitted across thousands of miles, but I feel none of the sentimental longing I might have expected. I feel, instead, that we are the ones who are home.

On Boxing Day a contingent from Fond-du-Lac comes over for a party. Brian and Jackie, with one of Brian's sons, and the family that manages the Northern Store, Darcy and Lezlie, with their young daughter and infant son. The baby is swaddled up in quilts and snowsuit, making a bundle like a pillow.

"I had to ask Lezlie which end was up when I handed the baby into the toboggan," Darcy says. "Then, when we were halfway here, we stopped to see how he was doing. He'd been upside-down the whole time!"

Coats and suits, mitts and hats, nearly fill the already overstuffed cabin. Cigarette smoke clouds the air. Coffee is consumed in great quantity. A blizzard of conversation rages while we serve soup and biscuits.

Darcy and Lezlie have been moved six times in thirteen months by their employer. The Northern Stores have taken over from the old Hudson's Bay Company in the far North. The

Bay has largely given up the territory responsible for its early fur-trade fortunes. It has evolved into a huge department-store chain and diversified into niches like real estate and finance, abandoning its northern legacy when it became unprofitable.

Besides being a mother, Lezlie works as a substitute teacher at the new school, while Darcy manages the store. His job includes being the local banker – balancing the Native ways with modern practices of commerce – and handling a score of local employees. And he stocks the necessary food, hardware, and clothing for a town of a thousand people. The merchandise comes, fitfully, by barge and plane.

Brian's son goes off on a snowmobile to tour one of our trails. He doesn't return for a long time, then appears on foot, labouring through the drifts. His machine has slipped off the trail and is mired in deep snow.

It reaffirms my basic distrust of travel by snowmobile. They are terrific machines as long as they run well and don't get stuck. But what happens when it's forty below (−40 °C) and the engine won't start, or you bog down in a pool of slush and get your feet soaked? Then you're suddenly a long way from anywhere. More than a few people die this way each year, caught in blizzards, breaking through ice. There is no towing service along the northern trails, and the wonderful sensation of power and mobility that a snowmobile gives is a pale, heartbreaking memory when it is gone.

This is nothing so serious. He and Brian work up a sweat heaving the machine around, but are back at twilight, just as everyone is dressing to go home.

Soon we have the cabin to ourselves again. Only a puddle or two of melting snow and the lingering pall of cigarette smoke give away the little party.

The ten-day visit is up before we are ready. In preparation for their departure, Dad braves a minus-twenty-six-degree (−33 °C) shower while Mom opts for a sponge bath. Nothing needs to be said about what a good visit it has been. We all know it. We haul the diminished pile of luggage out to the snow runway, then walk laps to ward off frostbite. The plane they came in, it turns out, has been put out of service by the cold. When a replacement finally does come the pilot can't turn off the engine.

"Battery froze up," he shouts. "Don't want to chance turning her off. But stay clear of the prop!"

We load the plane in the chilling prop wash, numbed, beaten with sound. Our embraces are hurried, sentimentality overwhelmed by the elements. But Marypat and I stand, listening, until the sound of the droning plane is utterly blotted out, before we turn for home.

We are alone, and feel alone, once again. The fact that it is our choice makes no difference. The silence that our Christmas gathering had beaten back now seeps around us, swallows us.

On New Year's Day Marypat goes off on her own for an afternoon walk. I watch her from the cabin window, then go out onto the porch. She moves down the water trail to the lake, on toward the mouth of the river. She is brightly clothed, her snowshoes fit quietly in front of each other, she moves gracefully. As she turns up along the river ice and passes from sight, I am stricken by the thought of her falling through. I imagine waiting, while the long night deepens, for her to return.

27

PROLONGED COLD AND all our socializing have depleted the wood supply. What I had hoped would last nearly until spring will be gone in a few weeks. Temperatures rise, up near zero (−18°C), and we take the opportunity to work in the forest.

Cutting wood in January in four feet of snow is an entirely different matter from cutting it in the fall. For one thing, we have cumbersome snowshoes on our feet and wear constricting layers of clothing. The snow has to be dug out from around a tree's base, and wielding the axe in this deep pit is awkward. Huge clods of snow drop down on our heads.

We cross the mouth of the river to reach a stand of dead wood. The water is shallow there, but fast, and we shuffle as quickly as we can across the danger.

One large tree surprises me by falling the wrong way, and I elude it at the last with a headlong dive into the snow. When a good stack has been cut and limbed, we begin ferrying the logs to the cabin. Marypat sets off with a heavy load bearing down on her shoulder, while I bend to pick up another. When I turn around, my partner is sprawled out on the snow, pinned under her log. A twig of underbrush caught in her snowshoe and tripped her up. She hadn't made a sound and is helpless as an overturned tortoise.

The firewood operation goes on until twilight and leaves us with a reassuring stock of logs to cut at our leisure.

After several days' work, the easily reached dead wood has been cleaned out and our fuel replenished, for the time being. The next morning we find water running where we had walked, carrying logs, half a day earlier.

"I think our timber cruising over there is finished," Marypat says as she looks soberly at the slush and open water. I don't ask what she is imagining.

Philip comes alone that afternoon with some mail, and we chat over tea.

When we tell him about crossing the river he shakes his head. "I think, danger," he says.

He tells us that a Fond-du-Lac man has already killed three

wolves this winter, and that the caribou are wintering north of town, near the Northwest Territories border. It is a half-day trip by snowmobile, one way, but people are going hunting all the time.

When he leaves we hitch a ride for a mile or two, then walk home on the hardened trail. The sun is huge and orange, falling into the trees, but the cold has returned. By the time we get back, my face is frostbitten.

In the past month we have had above-zero highs (above −18°C) on only three days. Marypat has a little thermometer hanging on the zipper of her coat, which we often refer to in the cabin. It is commonly eighty or ninety degrees (27 to 32°C) at head level, and thirty or forty (around 0°C) near the floor. When it is my turn to get up and start the fire, I sing out the rising temperatures to Marypat, who stays burrowed under warm blankets.

Some mornings when it is minus forty or fifty degrees (−40 to −46°C), the propane won't flow at all, and we have to cook on top of the wood stove. The trees outside, even the logs of the cabin, pop and crack during the dark hours, startling us out of sleep.

Even so, it is amazing how acclimatized we have become. At minus fifteen (−26°C), I do the outside chores in shirtsleeves and moccasins, bareheaded. Anything near zero (−18°C) feels like Tucson, Arizona. We go skiing in blue jeans, light gloves, and windbreakers. Even the deep cold isn't so bad any more. As long as we dress for it and keep moving, we can stay out for hours on end.

"Do you think it's even *possible* for me to get pregnant?" Marypat asks, out of the blue.

"No, I don't." My voice carries a weariness, a finality.

"I'm going to try the fertility drug one more time."

She has had a friend from home get another prescription

through her doctor. It arrived with the last mail. All I can think of is miscarriage, crippling pains, blood, the same outcomes as last time, but I nod.

Time slides by, another moon wanes. We switch sides on the bed, a monthly ritual, and reassert our routine of projects, wood cutting, ski outings, watching the quiet world.

Suddenly, the world we listen to on the radio is at war. It is rivetting, despite, or maybe because of, the contrast. I stay up late by flickering candlelight, doing nothing, while the story breaks.

Hour by hour the tensions mount. In Israel people learn how to seal rooms against chemical attacks, struggle into suits and gas masks. Huge air raids hit Baghdad in so-called surgical strikes. There is talk of massive moats of oil that might be set ablaze, oilfields torched, an environmental catastrophe in the Persian Gulf.

A madman is loose, a madman with power. It is the same madman who was, just a short time ago, our friend. We sent him money and arms, helped him fight an earlier war.

All winter the radio has brought us disturbing news. We listened to an anniversary memorial for victims of the Montreal Massacre, when a gunman on a college campus sprayed a class-room of women with automatic-weapon fire.

Somewhere on this same earth there are air-raid sirens, exploding bombs, people's bodies flying apart. Here, it is deeply quiet, a quiet within which one can hear the blood rush through the heart. Tree sap waits for warmth, water waits for release, bears wait for spring.

As I try to sleep it occurs to me that when people want to accuse someone of really heinous behaviour, they call him an animal. I think of the animals we have seen all winter. They do certainly kill each other to survive. But it is pure and uncompli-cated, without obscenity.

The next group from Fond-du-Lac arrives in late January. We have had more snow, with wind, and they have to bust through drifts to make it into the bay. It is the usual happy mob scene. Darcy and Lezlie try a new path to our cabin and their machine is engulfed. Lezlie is barely five feet tall, and when she dismounts she's in up to her neck. She swims to the trail. Four snow machines are now parked out front, eight guests crowding inside, the two of us scrambling to serve food and hot drinks. Talk bounces around the walls, from war to football to fur prices.

Marypat is in deep conversation with two nurses we haven't met before. She craves female contact. I take Brian and several others out to see our water hole and the mouth of the river. The water hole is an ice well, now three feet deep, with a huge mound of snow around it. They are aghast when I tell them we were carrying logs across the river. I mention that we want to ski in to town, perhaps within the week.

"This is going to blow your socks off," Marypat announces, when we're cleaning up after their departure. "We might be able to adopt a Chipewyan baby."

"There go my socks. What are you talking about?"

"I was talking to the nurses. They say it's not uncommon for Native women to have babies that they don't want to keep. Apparently some of the nurses at the hospital in Uranium City have adopted. There is even an agency down south that helps people arrange it all."

"Food for thought," I say.

"There's more. They know a Fond-du-Lac woman, right now, who isn't sure she wants to keep the baby she's carrying."

"What did you tell them?"

"Well, that I was interested," she says, turning to put dishes away, "and that I'd talk to you. They said they'd keep their ears open, keep us posted."

"Jesus." I am trying to see the whole picture. "This could complicate things."

"Yeah," MP agrees. "But in terms of adoption, if that's what we want, it might be incredibly simple."

That night neither of us sleeps well.

"No fantasizing," I say, in the darkness.

"How did you know?" Marypat is wide awake.

I hear a rasping noise on the porch, something gnawing. I rise, stark naked, flashlight in hand. At the window I turn it on and am staring into the red eyes of a snowshoe hare. It is on the chair where we leave leftovers for the grey jays, busily working over some frozen oatmeal. When I turn the light off, the gnawing resumes.

The animals around us seem, more and more, to accept us into their pattern. There are often several rabbits in view. When we come outside they hardly pay any attention. We see fox crossing the stage several times a week. Ptarmigan move through the exposed tips of willow bushes out front, even waddle beneath the porch. Once, as we were coming back from a ski, a group of the plump birds scurried across the path within two feet of my ski tips.

Willow ptarmigan are the true northerners here. Our location, just below the sixtieth parallel, is about as far south as they ever come. At night they excavate snow burrows, little clusters of plump holes. They are perfectly white, camouflaged for winter. Only their dark eyes and beaks and their red eyebrows give them away. We are often within yards of one before we see it.

As soon as the thaw starts, even before the snow melts, they are gone north, into the Arctic tundra, where they assume the mottled plumage that blends with lichen and rock and moss, and where they raise their young. This distant winter remove is, actually, highly populated compared to their summer home.

We have announced our intention to ski to town, even set a date. Expect us on the last day of January, we told our friends. Darcy and Lezlie have a dinner planned. We haven't been more than a few miles from our cabin since early October, but four months of confinement have encouraged our ambition. Our itch to travel, the need for an adventure, has us more than ready when the time comes.

We plan an early departure, organize our gear the night before. When I check the temperature before bedtime, it is already minus forty-eight degrees (−45 °C).

28

WE ARE UP at first light, peering through the frost at the thermometer. It is fifty below (−46 °C), maybe even a degree or two lower.

"We've gotta give it time to warm up," I grumble, coming back to bed.

Too antsy to sleep, we get up and eat, keep checking the temperature, plan our strategy.

Ski boots are our weakest link. They are substantial leather boots, but not insulated. Even with all our clothes on, working hard, it will be difficult to keep our feet warm.

"Look," I suggest, "we'll take the down booties. If our feet are too cold, we can put them on and walk. The snowmobile trail is hard enough to walk on."

The mercury creeps upward. At noon it is minus thirty-eight (−39 °C). If we were to go any later we would risk losing daylight before reaching town. Impulsively, we decide to leave. I am amazed at our decision, even as I close the door and snap on my skis.

"Let's reassess at the snowmobile trail. We can easily come back from there."

We both wear every conceivable layer of clothing. Long underwear, heavy shirts, sweaters, wool pants, wind gear, coats, down mittens, face masks. It's remarkable that we can move. It's remarkable that, wearing all this stuff, we are barely warm! In a pack we carry a sleeping bag, some food, matches, a saw, and a compass. We could survive a night out – but *survive* is the right word.

Bundled up like astronauts, we follow each other down the trail. Nothing else moves. The air is brittle and the light flat. I listen to my breath, keep wiggling my toes.

"Doing okay?" I shout.

Marypat turns. All I can see of her is her blue eyes.

"So far." Her voice is muffled. "But I'm not even tempted to take off any layers."

At the snowmobile trail we stop again, look each other over.

"Bit of an east wind," I say. "But at least it's at our backs."

Marypat nods. "Only problem is, once we start, I don't think we could turn back against it."

"Are your feet warm?"

"Amazingly, I think they are."

"Well, let's go."

The snowmobile road is hard as ice, ridged with tread marks, and the skiing is a monotony, like slipping along a flat glacier. Landmarks go by at a painfully slow rate. We say nothing, still have no desire to remove any clothing; we just clatter along, stride after stride.

The sky is grey, hazy with frost. Wind has scoured and sculpted the lake ice. Little permanent waves march across its surface. Mile after mile it is the same.

"If this is what skiing to the North Pole is like," I call out, "then no thanks!"

Marypat's stride is methodical and steady. She looks fifty pounds overweight, as if she'd have trouble tying her shoe.

"I need water," she says, after what seems a long time.

We huddle together like forlorn penguins on a vast ice floe. The water is bitterly cold and delicious. I gobble two bites of a sandwich, a hunk of chocolate.

In minutes we are cold again. "Let's go!" Marypat is stomping her skis. The east wind has risen. When I turn that way it is like a blade of ice cutting at exposed skin. I have to strip down to light gloves to secure the pack, and my fingers are utterly numb by the time we start.

I have to repeatedly clench my hands for two miles before I can feel them again. To entertain myself, I think about how to survive the night outside. Ski to the forest, dig out a pit in the snow, build a fire. Without fire it would be a desolate, desperate time. I wonder if we could gather enough wood to last a night.

When we break again it is only to guzzle water from the bottle I keep inside my coat. It is too damned cold, the wind too biting, to stop more than a minute.

"I think I have a bad spot on one heel," I say. But it isn't too painful and there's no way I'm about to pull a boot off here.

A bleak outline of buildings finally looms ahead. It is still miles off, and comes closer with excruciating slowness. The last hour is an endurance test, focussing on putting one ski ahead of the other. All this way, the only adjustment I've made is to pull back the hood of one jacket. Marypat hasn't changed a thing.

When we trudge into the Northern Store little kids and even the adults gawk at us. We are plastered with snow, our faces masks of frost.

A local man we have met briefly before recognizes us. "Come from Otherside?" he asks. "Today?" We nod.

Darcy emerges from his office and directs us to his house, across the street. Their door is completely iced up. "You idiots!" Lezlie greets us. "Get in here. It's the coldest day of winter," she chides, as we fumble with our clothes.

I walk down the linoleum hallway to the bathroom and notice I leave red footprints. I'm wearing red socks, and I am amazed they would be wet enough to bleed colour. But it isn't my socks, it's real blood. The sore spot I had on one heel is actually a huge wound. My ski boot is full of blood.

"God, Al, there's no way you can ski back with that!" Marypat is horrified by the look of it.

Brian comes over later, Darcy returns from work. We hold kids in our laps, watch television. The windows are so frosted and the windswept snow so dense that we can't see outside at all. After dinner I can hardly keep my eyes open. The television news reports on the weather in Saudi Arabia, Saddam's latest outrage, the wonders of our weaponry.

Jackie has gone south for a training seminar, and Brian drives us up to his house, shows us to the bedroom.

"I can run you back on the snowmobile tomorrow," he offers. "It's supposed to warm up. You shouldn't ski, anyway. It'll be nice to get away."

Marypat goes over to visit some nurses, and I fall into bed, then can't sleep. It is too warm in the house, the bed huge and soft, and I am overtired. I find a big patch of blistered skin, like a burn, on the back of my neck. Apparently, when I lowered my hood, the cold wind found an exposed patch. I never felt a thing. Christ, what a wreck I am!

Overnight the temperature zooms up. From fifty below (−46°C) to above zero (−18°C) in twenty-four hours. If we had waited a day we could have picnicked along the way, skied without hats. "Let's go back this afternoon," Brian suggests.

The appeal of town quickly fades. After all, it was the adventure of getting here, of leaving our cabin, that was the real draw. Besides a few food treats – a dozen eggs that cost $3.50, some evaporated milk for coffee – there is nothing we need.

"The nurses said that the pregnant woman probably wants to keep her baby now," Marypat tells me. "Maybe it isn't as easy as I thought."

We stop at Eli and Angela Adams' home. Eli has been south for open-heart surgery, is still feeble and skinny, but feels much better. Some of his old humour and spark is back, and the nurses say he is flirting with them again. "Maybe live long time," he says.

The local clinic handles routine medical trouble, and a doctor visits one day each week, but for surgery, deliveries, major procedures, people are flown out. Eli says that he watched his heart on television after the surgery. When I see him later in the day, walking to the Band office, he shuffles along like an old man.

It is overcast and warm when we drive out of town, Marypat riding behind Brian, me standing shotgun on the toboggan. Within minutes Fond-du-Lac is a dim outline of buildings and rock ridges behind us. The toboggan leaps and slams across the wind-roughened ice, a terrific, exhilarating ride.

Part-way home Brian stops for a smoke. We point out our cut-line trail where it comes to the lake. Marypat and I switch places. I look back at her once or twice. She grins like a fool, riding like a water-skier. In our bay the snow is in deep drifts. At one point we fall off the trail, keel right over on our side.

"Have time for a drink before you head back?" I ask Brian. It seems the least we can offer.

After all the cold, it hardly feels like we need a fire inside. The water hole isn't frozen too badly. Our cabin is quickly functional.

"I think I would have had to walk all the way home in booties," I say, toasting Brian. "Thanks for the lift."

"Scholar!" He sips his whisky.

Before long we have another drink. We all loosen up.

Brian tells of a Fond-du-Lac Native who ran down a wolf with a snowmobile.

"When they catch one out in the open, that's what they do. Saves a bullet. He tired it out and ran right over it to kill it. But when he went back for it, the wolf jumped up and bit him on the arm, then ran off. Serves him right, eh?"

At some point I get out a book of Robert Service and start reading.

> The winter! the brightness that blinds you,
>   The white land locked tight as a drum,
> The cold fear that follows and finds you,
>   The silence that bludgeons you dumb.
> The snows that are older than history,
>   The woods where the weird shadows slant;
> The stillness, the moonlight, the mystery,
>   I've bade 'em good-by – but I can't.

"The first time I heard that stuff," Brian says, "I thought it was pretty strange. But now that I've been up here awhile, there's a lot of truth to it.

"I'd like to get stationed in the mountains," he goes on. "Maybe when this posting is up."

Brian hasn't eaten all day. When he goes out to pee he stumbles off the porch.

Then we hear a snowmobile. Another guest. We go months seeing no one, then are inundated. It's Blaine Anderson, our first visitor from Stony Rapids, nearly forty miles away. He is managing the hotel while Ed and Margy are south for the winter; we met him during the fall at their camp. He has come all this way to our serene outpost only to find a party in full swing.

But Brian has to leave, stumbles out to his machine.

"Be careful," we caution. "We'll call in to make sure you get home."

He waves and starts off erratically.

Blaine and Marypat decide to take a ski before dark. I'm crippled by my injury and volunteer to make dinner. The cabin is suddenly quiet again. Half an hour goes by. Spaghetti sauce is simmering on the stove. When I look outside, Brian is trudging dejectedly up the trail.

"Stuck," he announces. "I'm in a damned lake of slush!"

"Let's take Blaine's machine and pull you out," I suggest.

"I don't think it'll work, but we can try. You drive."

I see where Brian's tracks slide off the trail, veering away into a field of snow and coming to an abrupt end where the machine is sunk in a wet quagmire. We wade out to it and the slush is to our knees. Ice water pours into our boots. For a few minutes we heave and haul on the five-hundred-pound beast, the engine smokes and strains, but it's hopeless.

"Need more people," Brian pants, and we drive back.

Providing dinner seems the prudent thing for the moment, and by the time Blaine and Marypat return the noodles are boiling. Then we hear another snowmobile. It's Bernie, the other RCMP officer, coming to see why Brian hasn't returned.

By now it's dark. We eat spaghetti by shadowy candlelight, barely able to make out the food on our plates. Five people and two machines to pull with. By rights we should have enough power, but Brian and I have experienced the predicament first-hand and remain dubious.

"If we can't get it out, I'll go home with Bernie," Brian says. "Come back for it later. Of course, by then, it'll be frozen up solid. Have to chip the damned thing out."

It's still relatively warm when our rescue squad heads off. I hear Marypat giggling at the absurd turn of events.

Three of us are stationed by the stricken vehicle, ready to shove, lift, heave, and, conceivably, drive the quarter-ton machine out of the mess. Bernie and Blaine man the tow vehicles, hitched together by rope on the solid trail.

On the first pull Bernie misunderstands the signal and tears off at full-throttle, jerking Blaine, who is patiently waiting, off of his machine in a neat somersault. The second time the rope breaks. The third time all elements are co-ordinated, and the machine goes nowhere.

One more try. The engines strain and the three of us lift and grunt with all we've got. The machine lurches ahead a foot, then stops. We try again, and make a little more progress, but the slush is extensive. Then, miraculously, the snowmobile slowly climbs onto firmer snow. Brian leaps on board, gives some throttle, and is out.

Back on the trail there is a good deal of backslapping. We relive our strategy, suddenly rendered coherent and synchronized. Brian has sobered up amazingly. Our visitors head home, headlights wavering through the darkness. I realize that I'm shivering, wet to the waist.

29

WE HAVE THE wrong kind of gas for the lanterns, and they are forever clogging up, sputtering, going dim and useless, despite frequent dismantling and cleaning. Over time we employ candles and oil lamps almost exclusively. On really cold days the propane won't flow, and I think that a wood cookstove would be better. The radio-phone works intermittently, depending on the local towers, the weather, our battery. The little generator we use to charge the battery becomes more inconvenience than benefit. It's loud and intrusive, and the side benefit of a couple hours of bright light hardly seems sufficient reward.

All these appliances and tools are handy, even essential at times. But there is a kind of elegant appeal to doing without, setting ourselves up right and then being independent of it all. It is, in some measure, why I come here, to get free of the demands and complications of gadgets that are meant to liberate us.

Now the time is really flowing, almost too quickly. I begin figuring my writing tasks against the remaining months. Light is returning, adding big chunks of day. When the full moon climbs above the northern hills again it is hot orange, its light spilling out like a warm lake.

We have brought an exciting new element to the work of hauling firewood. Rather than trudge heavily by snowshoe, burdened with logs, we cruise back on our skis. Marypat initiated the practice, and it caught our fancy immediately. It is unquestionably faster, and a good deal more fun – positively heart-stopping at times. Such as when I zoom down an icy slope with a twenty-foot length of spruce balanced on my shoulder, adding half my body weight and all the awkwardness of a portaged canoe to the already tricky business of keeping my balance.

A straight shot is no problem, usually. Turns at the bottom of a hill, on the other hand, are decided challenges. I hobble my confidence by imagining the worst: slamming into a tree with my battering ram, slipping off the track into momentum-killing snow, being gored by a jagged branch. But damned if it isn't such fun that we get addicted to it, keep upping the stakes with bigger hills, more weight. Marypat tries two logs at once, giggling the whole while. Cabin fever produces some strange symptoms.

Suddenly a midwinter heat wave whirls through the country. It's too early, certainly, to think about spring, but we scent the air like dogs on a track, drink in the warmth. One day in February it actually rains – light, sleety drizzle that turns everything to heavy slop.

In the fleeting warmth things come quickly to life. Squirrel tracks sprout in the woods. I read that squirrels place plugs of earth in the entrances of their winter burrows, then check the temperature outside by touching a nose against these doorways. When the earth reaches some nose-tantalizing degree, they push on out to forage and chatter.

Birds are busy feeding, stocking up against the cold weather's certain return. Throughout winter they shiver almost constantly to stay warm. It must be wonderful to relax. Several times a quick mink, long and sleek, scurries under the cabin. A silver fox entertains us on the bay, digging furiously in the snow. When we slip outside, the click of the door latch at one hundred yards is enough to send it running. Upriver, otters mar the hummocky ice near their lairs with fish carcasses, scat, tunnels and slides. The river chuckles below in darkness, full of hidden life.

Along with the warmth comes wind. The spruce and pine come alive, bowing and waving like an animated crowd. The poplar clatter dry-bone branches together. Drifts mount up around the cabins. When I go out to shovel the roofs, I can stand on the snow beside each cabin to do it.

Out of the blue Darcy and Brian show up one warm day. They are on a jaunt and bring the usual pile of mail.

"Went up to hunt caribou last week," Brian announces.

"That trail is rough! Almost six hours of it," Darcy adds.

The caribou used to flood south from the tundra that is their summer home, all the way to Fond-du-Lac and well past. Hunting pressure and habitat destruction have forced them to winter farther north, staying in the fringe of boreal forest that borders the Barren Lands. It's been decades since they came to the shores of Lake Athabasca in any numbers.

The local Chipewyan have an unquenchable appetite for hunting the northern deer. In part it is motivated by their need for inexpensive meat. But more than that, it stems from something close to a cultural need to hunt, something built up over generations.

Caribou is easily the prey of choice. In the old days, only a generation or two past, the Chipewyan foraged widely after the deer, even well into the tundra lands, as far north as the lower Thelon River. Perhaps only the interior Inuit people, who lived full-time on the tundra, depended more heavily on caribou.

The Chipewyan word for caribou is *etthen*, meaning, simply, "meat." In traditional times, hunting could be extremely laborious. Caribou were run through deep snow until exhausted, then dispatched with bow and arrow. Antler rattles were used to attract bulls in rut. Herds were driven into primitive corrals made of brush, snares made of babiche, or caribou-hide cord. The variations in migration patterns were, the Natives believed, the result of wounded animals returning to the herd and spreading word of danger.

As is often the case with neighbouring cultures, an enmity built up between the Inuit and Chipewyan. Territorial skirmishes, prisoner-taking, fierce battles stoked the fires of tension and fear. The Chipewyan got guns before the Inuit, then used this advantage to push northward with relative impunity. The smallpox epidemic of 1781, which wiped out 90 per cent of the Chipewyan, made any territorial claims moot, however.

Tension is still evident today, in the form of political wrangling over the Inuit land claim just to the north, in the Northwest Territories. Chipewyan are afraid that the Nunavut land settlement being negotiated – an agreement that would turn control of essentially all of the Territories to Native groups – would limit or cut off their access to traditional hunting grounds north of the border. They argue that the sixtieth parallel has no bearing on caribou migration, or on their ancient hunting heritage.

Caribou, besides being a crucial source of food, provided clothing, shelter, and tools. Each individual required up to twenty caribou skins for clothing and other needs. A single large tent could demand as many as seventy skins. Even today, Chipewyan families routinely consume forty to fifty caribou each year.

"The Natives can butcher a caribou faster than you can believe," Darcy tells us. "They use these huge knives, eh? Zip, zip, and they're all quartered."

Samuel Hearne, in his travels through the North during the late 1700s, reported that the Chipewyan needed only a knife, file, ice chisel, and hatchet to exist.

"Some guys in town make that trip every week," Brian says. "Up one day, kill as many as they can carry back, then home the next. Two days later, off they go again."

After they leave Marypat and I ski onto the lake. It is mild and sunny, a winter reprieve, and we travel out to an island. In the summer this little bit of land is only a foot or two out of the water, a nondescript jumble of broken rock with a small grove of birch. In winter it is transformed. Wind-drifted snow gives it more relief, a sharp cleanliness. The half-buried trees seem beautiful, wind-bitten, too delicate to survive, like trees in a Japanese tea garden.

On the trail we meet two men from the Chipewyan town of Black Lake, some fifty miles to the east. They are travelling slowly, their toboggan bulging with caribou. The driver lights up a cigarette, takes off his gloves.

"We're still far from home," he says. "Don't want to break down."

Their hunt required four days of travel to earn one of hunting. The trail north, they report, is very bad.

The driver works at the Cigar Lake uranium mine and has to be back to work tomorrow. He makes sixteen dollars an hour, with good benefits, works two weeks on, then gets a week off. "I'll leave the meat with my family," he says.

His cigarette is done, thrown on the ice. "Well, see you, eh?" He pulls his gloves on. We never learn any names. The snowmobile drones slowly off, and as we start home I think of this merging of two worlds; a man hauling caribou meat home for his family, who will, the next morning, climb aboard a plane and go to work at his sixteen-dollar-an-hour job.

30

ON VALENTINE'S DAY I produce a silly limerick for Marypat, and she awards me with a bag of jerky she'd hidden away.

"I think I'm pregnant," she announces, flatly.

"No you're not!"

"My period's overdue, and I feel different."

"No you're not!" I repeat. "How many times does this have to happen? How many times have you gotten your hopes up?" I feel both frustrated and protective.

"I just feel it."

"Dammit, MP, what about your miscarriages? You were weeks overdue those times. You can't afford to think this way!"

Over the years we've become as superstitious as compulsive gamblers about pregnancy, as if some kind of magic is required, mysterious powers must be appeased. Logic and science have failed us.

After my outburst, nothing more is said. I try to ignore the possibility altogether, as if by looking the other way I won't spook our chances. But every time Marypat goes around the cabin to pee, I move to the side window to watch. Blood is the fear, and I notice that she always checks for it. When she returns I study her face, but keep my mouth shut.

Another day goes by, then a week. Although we continue our superstitious ban, I notice that bounce in her step, a deep warmth evident in her eyes. And each of us is busy with mental calculations.

What if it's true? Will we travel on regardless, or go home? What about check-ups? Emergencies?

Along one of our trails Marypat finds an impossibly early pussy willow budding out. She snips it and carries it home, puts it in water, an omen. Hope infects me as well. I can't resist it.

At the same time I'm ambushed in the dark night hours by

horrible visions. I see us on the tundra, on a landscape as desolate as it is beautiful, painfully alone, burying a premature baby.
More immediately, I imagine miscarriage. Marypat doubled
over with pain, haemorrhaging in our outhouse, with help cut
off by the thawing lake.

"My urge to go to town is pretty well gone," I confide to
Marypat. "Especially when people come here once in a while."

We have just bid goodbye to another onslaught of Stony Rapids visitors, some of whom spent the night.

"We'll have to go in for a check-up before too long," she
counters.

"It's too early for that kind of talk!"

I say it as a warning, but it breaks the silence. All the thoughts
we've kept to ourselves come out. We calculate the date of
conception.

"I'd be about six months when we start travelling again this
summer, seven by the end."

"If we go at all," I add. "If you're pregnant, I'm not into taking
chances. If anything's risky, if you don't feel up to it, there's no
question what's more important."

I don't share my dark visions, I'm sure Marypat has her own.

She nods in agreement. "I talk to it all the time," she says.
"Encourage it, tell it to hang on. I just wish I knew what
to expect, what I'm supposed to feel. And I *do* want to go on
this summer."

March arrives like a polar bear. On the first of the month we're
socked with minus-forty-six-degree (−44°C) cold. Northern lights fire up the sky. "They always make me think of waving ribbons," Marypat says. We crunch through the brittle
snow to the edge of the bay. The lights arc and weave and
swirl above, soundless, but we can't help making Fourth-of-
July noises.

"Wow! See that? Ooooh!"

By the time we return our hands are numb and our faces nipped, but we keep going out to the porch for encores.

The war in the Gulf is winding down. More than ever, from this vantage, it seems nothing more than organized insanity. On the radio a helicopter pilot talks about his recent mission, flying a craft armed with night vision, invisible to his victims. He is young, still as pumped up as an athlete, his voice wondrous as he tells of people scurrying blindly for cover while he picked them off, like targets on a video screen.

The great army of Iraq turns out to be old men and young boys, starved and shell-shocked, many of whom are so relieved to end their hell that they run to embrace the enemy, kiss their feet.

Despite the pathos, it is all unbelievably distant, like another radio drama. Here, the snowshoe hare has become a regular visitor, up on our porch to scavenge for food every day, gnawing on shrubs as we work nearby. A flock of white-winged crossbills throng around the small spruce out front. The winter holds on tightly, but these surprise appearances are another sign of seasonal flux.

I should know better, but I begin to get restless for spring. It manifests itself in a longing for sounds. After the months and months of muffled quiet, sound means life. I want the trickling of water, the drip of melting snow from the eaves, the chattering of birds. But the silence holds fast, deep as death. And above, at night, darkness is pricked only by the hard light of stars.

My heel is finally healthy enough to ski some distance. To assuage our restlessness we abandon our work schedule one day and set off upriver. The sun is high and bright now, and has a buoyant effect on our mood. Cold, white, and quiet it remains, but there are hopeful signs. Otter slides mark the steep riverbanks, sledding hills of the North. Ptarmigan have a languid, relaxed manner, as though only the true bitter darkness of midwinter is a worthy adversary. The river has eroded openings here and there, is more audible through the cracks in its armour.

Bend by bend the winter vistas unfurl, austere and pure. Earth bluffs frozen hard, small hills, little islands full of white birch, thick stands of spruce half-buried in snow. The dark knots of empty eagle nests in the gnarled arms of jack pine.

But the landscape is poised, patient, nearly through another winter. I ignore renewed pain in my heel, and the two of us push farther than ever before, always wanting to see around one more corner.

Again, like so many times in these lonely lands, I see us in the aerial view. Two shapes toiling slowly along the stark river course, two blots of colour in the slumbering white space.

The day Marypat has marked on the calendar with a red **X** arrives. It is the day of the next test, the day our hopes might yet be dashed. I watch her closely for signs of change, disappointment, but they never appear.

Already she is noticing some symptoms. Her belly has a tiny bulge, and her pants are snug. Now and again she complains of nausea and vague, distressing pains. And she has terrific, quirky appetites. She talks for days about doughnuts, then decides to make some. The process takes hours, and all the while she drools over the prospect of eating them, but when they are done she can barely manage one.

As long as I've known her she has been a cold sleeper, always snuggling close for warmth. Suddenly she's a veritable furnace, almost driving me from the bed with her heat.

I am more hopeful than I have ever allowed myself to be, find myself inwardly cheering on this human bud. At night I lay a hand across Marypat's belly, try to project my encouraging presence. Repeatedly, I ask how she feels, whether she wants to nap, if there are any symptoms.

"Geez, Al, everything's fine. Leave me alone," she finally bursts out.

Marypat raises the Fond-du-Lac clinic on the radio-phone. "I have some questions," she tells them. It is the first announcement we have made, and I am absurdly worried that by letting the secret out, we'll jinx the whole thing. By the time she's finished we have an appointment. When the doctor is next in town, we'll ski in to meet him.

31

THE EVENING IS well along, and we've already cleaned up the dishes, when we hear dogs. In two minutes we have jumped onto our skis and are gliding down the well-worn track to the lake.

Marypat sees them first. Two teams struggling through snow up to their chests, the drivers shouting encouragement. It takes them a long time to flounder in to us, but the dogs are big and healthy, still eager.

These meetings on the ice are a little reminiscent of Stanley and Livingstone, significant moments made insignificant by the engulfing space, the powerful quiet.

"Welcome to Otherside Bay," I begin. "Snow's a little deep in here."

"It's okay. The dogs can use a workout. I'm JP," the lean young man says and offers his hand. "This is Moose." He gestures to the driver of the other team, who is well over six feet tall. "We heard about you guys. Do you have room for us to stay over?"

In the trees near the cabin they quickly rig a wire cable to which they attach the dogs by short chains.

"This one first." JP hands Marypat a dog by its collar. "Down at the end."

Marypat is promptly pulled onto her face.

"Here. Hold their front legs up, then they can't lunge."

He hands me another of the furry, muscular animals.

"These two don't get along." He points to a snarling member of the team. "If we don't separate them they fight."

Meanwhile, Moose is chopping up dog food. It is brown, waxy-looking stuff, and each dog gets a big brick. "High-protein mix," he explains. "They're actually gaining weight on this trip!"

Sixteen hungry dogs are all howling and barking, clamouring for their once-a-day meal. The noise is deafening, so loud that we have to shout. Only when all are fed does the bedlam stop. Food disappears in great gulps, then they lap snow to slake their thirst, and promptly curl up.

We set about feeding JP and Moose, whose appetites rival their dogs'. We prepare at least twice the amount of food we would make for ourselves, and it is gone in minutes.

"Started in Ely, Minnesota, in mid-January," Moose tells us. "We're going to Snowdrift, on Great Slave Lake. Twenty-five hundred miles. Should be there by mid-April."

They talk of their trail life, their love of winter camps under the stars and northern lights. They are even a little disappointed that they are forever being put up in the villages through which they pass, having to sleep in warm, stuffy houses full of cigarette smoke.

"People are really nice, but we like being out, making miles."

It disrupts the rhythm, they say.

"That's why we're really looking forward to this next leg, going up north."

"And we had to stop calling our girl friends. We just got so damned depressed and lonely every time. Now we just send letters."

Compared to the local dogs, theirs are huge and robust. Too big, they say.

"We thought we'd be breaking trail the whole way, but

between these Native towns there's always a snowmobile track. Small, fast dogs would be better.

"Every place we stop, the first thing people say is, 'Big dogs!'"

We share our expedition adventures, compare modes of transport, discuss the northern wilderness. We find that in the small circle of northern adventurers we have friends in common. But they have had a long day and want an early start in the morning, so we wind up before midnight. Later, in the quiet, I hear a moaning outside and think sleepily of wolves, before I remember the dogs.

At dawn JP and Moose each dispatch a formidable stack of pancakes, and their departure is delayed by more good talk. Then they wrestle the dogs into harness and lash in their loads, barely restraining the teams as we say goodbye.

"Maybe we'll see you in Fond-du-Lac," Marypat says. "We're skiing there in a few days."

"Probably not. We want to get north. But you never know." Then they tear off, dogs yipping and shitting, the sleds trailing a long length of rope behind, so that the driver has something to grab onto in case he falls off.

Our own departure, two mornings later, takes place in cheerful sunshine and moderate temperatures. To avoid the monotony of the lake trail, we aim down the cut-line through woods as far as we can. Compared to the first epic trek to Fond-du-Lac, this is a Sunday stroll. Coats and hats come off, photos are taken, animal tracks studied.

Even out on the lake I can take my boot off and tape up my heel, change the wax on the skis. We recline on the ice to eat lunch like heavily clad sunbathers. Closer to town there are black dots in the distance sprinkled over the lake surface. Dozens of people are out ice fishing, setting nets.

At one gathering we stop to chat. An entire family waits around a hole drilled through two feet of ice. A hundred yards off I see the flag at the other end of the net. We mention the dog teams. Everyone knows about them. "Big dogs!" they say. "Already go north."

They are just starting to pull up the net. Limp mesh slithers out of the black water, empty for long stretches. There are a few trout, some whitefish, nothing very big. The fish are thrown in the toboggan where they quickly freeze. We ski on.

The doctor has been delayed, and it is afternoon, the next day, before Marypat is able to see him. The clinic is full of children, pregnant women. Posters on the walls remind families to brush their teeth, eat right, vaccinate their babies. The facility is small, but tidy and well-stocked. A file cabinet displays the dominant names in town. The Adamses, Mercredis, and McDonalds each require nearly an entire drawer.

Down in the bottom right-hand corner, a single drawer is labelled "Non-Treaty." Non-treaty Natives are the second-class citizens of the North. They belong, but they don't, and since they aren't covered by the original treaties, they don't receive the same benefits and civil rights as treaty-status residents.

"Yup, you're pregnant," the doctor says, as he probes Marypat's belly. "Eight, nine weeks, I'd guess."

He tells us to watch for blood, having no idea how unnecessary his counsel is. MP is reassured that her aches are normal. He answers our barrage of questions patiently, seems mildly amused by us. Our ski to town, our circumstances, the questions we have about paddling on next summer, are far from ordinary, even here.

"You should have an ultrasound," he tells us. "The fertility drug increases the chance of twins tenfold. We should know about that."

The ultrasound machine comes to the hospital in Uranium City only once every six weeks. The next time is just a week away. A month and a half later is too late, we'll be isolated by the thawing lake.

"It's a little early," he says. "But we'll be able to tell. You can go over on the charter with all the pregnant Native women."

As we leave, he says to Marypat, "You're in good physical shape. That's half the battle."

The doctor's quiet certainty, the paper-covered examination table, the little wheel that tells you your due date, all make the pregnancy suddenly seem very real. At home in the cabin I could never fully believe it. Now it's official.

We all go to Darcy and Lezlie's for a caribou-steak dinner. I study the way they handle their kids with strong interest. Halfway through a Robert Mitchum war movie, the television channel goes out. Everyone groans and starts bitching about the local man in charge of the satellite dish. "All he wants to watch is wrestling!"

On the way home, Brian stops a kid on a snowmobile.

"Get that light fixed, Jimmy," he warns. "They have headlights at the store."

"I don't have any money," the teenager complains.

"Then don't drive until you save up. I see you again with no light, I'm taking the machine."

"All night the snowmobiles cruise," Brian says. "Drives everybody nuts."

He's been thinking about our extra trip into town for the plane to Uranium City.

"Look," he says, "I've got two machines. Take one and use it to come back for the flight. Leave your skis here, then ski home after that. It's ridiculous to ski thirty miles twice in a week, especially pregnant!"

Brian has no idea what utter neophytes he's handing his machine over to. Next morning he gives us a short lesson and walks off with a nonchalant wave. If we had grown up in the North, we would have been driving these things for years. But we are of the human-powered school of technology. Give us snowshoes, paddles, skis, and off we'll go. If this thing broke down, we'd stand around wiggling wires, pounding on it, then start walking.

But what the hell. I take the controls and creep out of town at about six miles an hour. Farther along I gain some confidence, push the speed up. The machine defeats the stillness, distracts me from the surroundings, jars over the hard ridges. But it is fast and easy, even at our timid pace.

Fair's fair, and halfway home we switch, just as we do every other day in the canoe. Marypat is even slower at the helm. But it's fun, in its own obnoxious way. We feel like escaped convicts making their getaway in a stolen cop car.

The machine sits garishly out in front of the cabin, never once used until we need to return. When we go back, we run into some difficulty in the bay. The packed trail is quite narrow in places, so that we repeatedly slip off, keeling over ignobly on our side. Half a dozen times we right the damned thing, dust ourselves off, drive back onto the trail, only to get dumped off thirty feet along. Finally I get up speed, crash into the deep snow, and just keep the momentum up until we gain the hardened lake.

"How'd it go?" Brian asks, when we reach town.

"Fine," I say, casual. "No problem."

Marypat is soon on the flight full of pregnant women, and won't be back until late in the day.

I wander through town. Every so often the report of a small-calibre rifle sounds in the distance. It is the day when strays are killed. Periodically the town becomes overrun with loose dogs that no one will claim. An announcement is posted: "Chain up your dogs tomorrow. Loose dogs will be shot." As I head toward the lakeshore a snowmobile comes over a drift, a dead dog flopping behind at the end of a rope. It leaves a ragged bloody trail on the snowy road that leads to the dump.

On impulse I stop at the church to see if the local priest, Father Brault, is in. The building is large and cool, quite dark inside. The door shuts heavily. My steps on the wooden floor echo cavernously. When my eyes adjust I see that Father Brault is in his office, sitting at a large desk.

He has a head of thick, greying hair and looks solid and fit when he stands up. We shake hands and a large cross swings against the front of his shirt.

He is curious about us, wants to hear about our journey. Geography interests him.

"This is our diocese," he says, spreading his hand across a map on the wall. The area covers a thousand-mile swatch of country from Lake Athabasca to the Arctic Ocean.

He enjoys skiing and, in his time off, has taken extensive bicycle trips.

"I want to bike from Thunder Bay to Montreal," he says. "I've already gone from Montreal to Halifax. Got hit by a car in Quebec City and had to take some time off. Broke ribs and punctured my lung."

"Do you ever get lonely?" I ask him.

"Never lonely," he says, shaking his head emphatically. "My problem is the opposite: not enough time."

He decided at the age of eighteen that he would be a priest, and that he wanted to work with Natives.

"I came to Uranium City in 1955," he says. "I was twenty-six."

A young woman comes to the doorway and stands there shyly, barely in view.

"Excuse me." Father Brault rises and starts out. "I'll take confession and be back."

A priest becomes part of a town in a way other white people almost never do. They are actually supported by the contributions of residents. RCMP officers, store managers, nurses, teachers, all come for their stint, then move on. It is rare for anyone to stay more than two or three years. But priests sometimes spend decades in one community, their entire adult lives. They learn the local dialect, know the people intimately.

The Catholic Church holds complete sway over Fond-du-Lac. Literally everyone is Catholic, and a priest is invested with the power to apply discipline and direction. He can ban people from church for drunkenness, or, quite commonly, for living together out of wedlock. Birth control is not discussed. To speak of "the flock," here, is not idle symbolism.

There are vestiges of the old spiritual beliefs among Natives. They don't bat an eye on hearing of a person who is able to assume the shape of an animal, for instance. One senses that a spirit world full of ravens and Windigo, ancient creation myths, still glimmers dimly in the cultural memory, but that it is fading.

I have heard it said that Native people throughout the North took so readily to European religion because it offered hope of salvation from a grim and brutal life. A life in which starvation, disease, grinding hardship, was the common lot. I have also heard that when Europeans first came upon them, Native people were remarkable in the degree of happiness and contentment they exhibited.

Father Brault returns. "The people here are very fervent in their devotion and beliefs," he says.

"After Uranium," he continues, picking up our conversation, "I was stationed south of Fort McMurray, then at Fort Smith and Fort Resolution. I came here in 1986. That was the year the barge sank in a storm. I lost all my belongings, including a canoe.

"Fond-du-Lac used to be the centre for this whole area. People from Stony Rapids, even Black Lake, all came here. Our history goes back to the mid-1800s."

In fact, I've read that the Hudson's Bay Company set up Garrison House here, across the narrows, in 1819-20, but that it languished for several decades. In 1853 Father Grollier arrived and built a chapel. The building, which included his residence, measured twenty-seven by seventeen feet, just a

Our winter home under its weighty
quilt of snow. (Photo: Marypat Zitzer)

Top left: For the most part, dog teams in the North have gone the way of the canoe, replaced by snowmobile and powerboat. These dogs are spending a night tethered outside our cabin en route from Ely, Minnesota, to Snowdrift, Northwest Territories, a marathon 2,500- mile run.

Bottom left: The weekly outdoor shower is certainly bracing, as long as our bodies can stand the shock when the warm water shuts off, leaving us naked and wet in temperatures as cold as -30° (-35° C)!

Top: After the thaw, and we are underway once more, windbound delays are often a welcome break, providing time for journal entries, explorations inland, and rounds of hot drinks.

(Photos: Marypat Zitzer)

Top: Clouds march across the wide
tundra sky. Protected with rain gear
and a fabric deck, we can paddle in
surprising comfort. The biggest enemy
of canoe-travel on the Barren Lands is
not rain but the winds that can blow
unabated for a week at a time.

Top right: Summer dips in frigid sub-
arctic water are almost always hurried
affairs. This sun-warmed pool is a rare
treat and allows for a more leisurely
immersion while surrounded by the
din of rapids.

Bottom right: These thunderous rapids
along the Kazan River are the first
obstacle in an arduous series of three
portages. Marypat, six months pregnant, insists on carrying her share of
the load. Fabric mesh "bug jackets" are
essential on the insect-infested tundra.

(Photos: Marypat Zitzer)

Rock cairns known as inukshuk were traditional markers on the treeless and generally featureless tundra. Visible from miles away, they identified trails, caribou crossings, gravesites, and camps used by the Caribou (or Inland) Inuit. (Photo: Marypat Zitzer)

Barren Land herds of caribou are among the few remaining species left on earth that are relatively unaffected by humans. Hunted by wolf, grizzly, and, to a limited extent, by Native residents, they roam across thousands of tundra miles, much as they always have. (Photo: Marypat Zitzer)

This Inuit gravesite, where a skull rests alongside a chipped enamel cup, lies open to the harsh northern elements. Permafrost and rocky ground prevented burial below ground, so the dead were covered with mounds of rock. The Caribou Inuit lived an almost Stone Age existence on the interior Barren Lands until as recently as 1955. (Photo: Marypat Zitzer)

Musk oxen are truly at home in the Far North. Although they move significant distances in search of forage, they never leave the Arctic lands, relying on their incredibly insulating hair and specialized feeding techniques to survive in an unimaginably harsh environment. (Photo: Marypat Zitzer)

Weather-beaten and renewed by
more than a year of unbroken wilderness living, we gird ourselves up for
our return to society, and for the final
chapter of our epic adventure, the
birth of our child.
(Photo: Marypat Zitzer)

little larger than our cabin on Otherside Bay. Here he held ser-
vices, lived, ministered to the people, who were scattered
across hundreds of miles.

Once more during our talk Father Brault breaks off to take
confession. While he is gone I look out his windows at the white
lake, across the bay where we fought headwinds on the last day
of August. I try to put myself in his place, this man who has,
already, spent thirty-five years with the Native people. But it is a
leap too great, to an identity too foreign. It is easier to put myself
in the place of an early fur trapper, a Hudson's Bay trader, an
explorer, than in that of this religious man. The dust motes he
stirred as he left the room still waft through shafts of sunlight,
but I am unable to grasp the essence of what drives him, understand the conviction that brings him contentment in places like
this, decade after decade.

When I return to Brian's house Marypat is already back.

"Well?" I ask.

She holds up one finger. "It's real, and there's only one."

"How'd it look?"

"Not like much," she admits. "The picture was grainy. Just
this peanut-shaped little thing with its tiny heart beating."

"Incredible." I hold her. "It's real."

"Strange, too," Marypat says. "On the plane I sat next to the
woman who had talked about giving her baby up. She's going to
keep it now."

For days, once we've returned to the cabin, Marypat immerses
herself in a nursing text on pregnancy and childbirth. It is a
thick, hefty tome, hundreds of pages long. She pipes up now and
again with another miracle that takes place in the pregnant
body, or explains some symptom she's experienced.

"God," she says. "It makes me nervous. How can so many

complicated things be going on in there all the time, and not one thing go wrong? It seems impossible!"

She takes a nap nearly every day and complains periodically of queasiness. I still watch her closely when she comes back from outside. Usually she ignores me, but sometimes she'll smile and shake her head.

For the first time in two months we make love. It has been another of our superstitious prohibitions, another jinx. And there is something profound and serious this time, as though there are three of us sharing in the intimacy. Inside Marypat, the cells of a two-and-a-half-inch body are quickly multiplying, and its heart, the size of a bird's, is softly beating.

One morning near the end of March I hear the clear, two-note call of a chickadee. Not once, all winter, have we heard it. It is a spring noise, a song that claims a territory, beckons to a mate, welcomes warmth and sunlight and the ease of summer. I hear it again. Just two drawn-out notes, always the same – but after the long haul through winter, it is a sound of indescribable beauty, a spring concerto.

"Up for a ski today?" I ask. "Who knows how much longer we'll be able to go up the river any distance."

A fresh skim of snow crystals lies on some new overflow ice, a good surface for our skis, even allowing us to skate for long distances. Recent winds have raised waves in the open fields of snow, a white seascape frozen in place. The afternoon sunlight plays on the waves with a rosy glow.

For more than two miles the trail of three companionable otters runs alongside ours. Their tracks are sharp and fresh in the new snow, showing the *gallop-gallop-whoosh* of the otters' progress. The belly-slides are eight, ten, fifteen feet long. *Gallop-gallop-whoosh!* No detours, no time for play. Three otters with a purpose, going mile on mile downriver on a promising day.

Pussy willows are budding out. Steep banks that face south

have lost their snow cover. Bits of rock and rubble trickle onto the river ice, or into patches of opening river. There are pine grosbeak in the trees, squirrels chattering. The water is a slowly rising torrent, full of itself, even at this early date. In the fast current blocks of ice are tipped up and ride against each other. We keep grinning, giddy with the surging hopefulness of spring and the two-note promise of the chickadee.

VI

THAW

32

PATIENCE IS REQUIRED. The tireless, unflagging patience of wildlife waiting out the season. Bears turn and stir in their caves, otters begin their spring migration in search of dens and open river, the snowshoe hare is tinged slightly grey. But the wide lake is solid and implacable. It will be months before it opens up. Snow lies deep in the forest, and it is cold at night, but I find myself repressing the urge to get going, move on. Anywhere.

The Otherside River is eating a narrow channel into the bay. One morning an otter hauls up on the ice to eat a fish. I slip out with binoculars to watch. Crystalline snow sparkles in the tree branches. The sun is high up, coming back north, warming the air. Overhead a pair of ravens barrel-roll around each other, wheel and play, their calls rasping. The birds' shadows pass near the otter, and it slides into the dark current. Ptarmigan fill the poplar grove, already talking their guttural summer language, making travel plans.

I stay outside a long time, until I am numb with cold. The river sings, the twitter of birds comes and goes, snow crystals wink in the sunlight. It's still winter, I repeat, as I return.

The final weekend in March is a social orgy. A Stony Rapids crowd roars in on Friday night, narrowly escaping whiteout conditions on the lake. Karl, the resource officer for the district, shakes my hand and asks, "How have you wintered?" I like the sound of the phrase, the quiet way he says it, like a farmer asking how the crops look, a New Englander inquiring after the state of sugar-maple sap. It implies a stretch of time, a process subject to various perils, a thing with weight.

And I think of the old Native practice of approaching each other warily after a winter's separation, judging whether the dark, starving time has brought on a certain craziness, infection by opportunistic spirits.

"We've wintered well," I answer. "But there's still the thaw to wait out."

Karl is lean, soft-spoken, without apparent vices. He doesn't smoke or drink, refuses even coffee, says he jogs every morning, much to the wonderment of the local population. He has an ample humour, a love of adventure, seems a steady man.

The province of Saskatchewan is broken into vast administrative blocks over which a few resource officers hold sway. But in practice the trapping permits and quotas are overseen by self-regulating regional committees of trappers.

"Sort of an old-boy organization," Karl admits. "But they aren't too bad. It's in their interest to manage game for the long term. We can try to keep an eye on things like fish-net size, wasteful hunting practices, but enforcement is spotty, to say the least."

When we tell of all the otter activity recently, Scott, the owner of a store in Stony, remembers his first experience of tracking otter in spring snow. "For the life of me," he says, "I couldn't figure why somebody was rolling a tire across the lake!"

Around midnight, everyone except Blaine sets off through light snow for the run home. The moon sheds its eerie glow through a gauze of cloud and the noise of the snowmobiles quickly fades.

Besides my parents, Blaine is the only winter visitor to stay over more than one night. The solitude of our place agrees with him, and he is good to have around. We break the news of the pregnancy, but he has already heard a rumour from the pilot of the ultrasound charter.

Blaine grew up in southern Saskatchewan. For years he's guided at fishing camps in the North. Every summer he putts around lakes and rivers in motorboats with all manner of fish-hungry clients from Minneapolis or Denver or Saskatoon. Last summer, at the end of the season, he and a fellow guide decided on a whim to canoe down the Fond-du-Lac River to Black Lake.

They took off after a day or two of preparation, carrying hardly any food. "Figured we'd fish," he says. They had borrowed a beat-up fibreglass canoe. Neither of them knew anything about paddling.

"Had some exciting moments," Blaine admits. Exciting moments like going backwards down rapids, half-full of water.

At Black Lake they ran into Ed and Margy and picked up work at the camp. Then Blaine agreed to manage the White Water Inn for the winter.

"Probably guide again next summer," he guesses. "After that, who knows?"

Within hours of Blaine's Saturday-morning departure, a Fond-du-Lac bunch piles in. Jackie, back from her nursing classes, Brian, and half a dozen other friends out for a weekend break.

"Hard to say how much longer we can travel on the lake," Brian tells us.

We coax them into staying for pizza dinner. Marypat corners the nursing bunch and bombards them with her questions. We leave the door open and sunlight pours in, bringing the smell of pine and earth, the sound of the nearby river.

It is a boisterous gathering, all of us buoyed up by the season. Groups head off for walks, snowmobile jaunts, picture-taking excursions. By the time they leave it is almost eight o'clock, but plenty of daylight remains for the drive home.

The excitement is over as abruptly as it began. It is as if we've been clattering along on a fast train, then are suddenly let off at midnight in a silent town.

It is April Fool's Day when I hear the first Canada goose of spring. We are still cutting wood, the winter drudgery. I am slogging through two feet of snow with a heavy log on my shoulder, lost in thought, when the sound stops me dead. A lone bird, flying swiftly, low over the lake. Its long neck swings back and forth, snakelike, searching. The call has a forlorn, anxious quality.

"Hear that goose?" I ask, when I get to the cabin. "Maybe we have enough wood to last us after all." There are some mornings, now, when we don't even start a fire first thing, but instead let the sun warm our den.

It is also on April Fool's Day that my parents call in with family news. My sister in Boston has had a miscarriage.

"How far along?" Marypat asks.

"Oh, it was very early," my mother says. "I think she was only about ten weeks."

Ten weeks is exactly how pregnant Marypat is, almost to the day. We haven't yet broken the news to our families, and my folks have no idea what cold dread they have brought us. My sister had been feeling fine, no warning. *Very early*, the words keep echoing. It is still very early, and our confidence melts away.

After the call Marypat lies on the bed, looking worried.

"Nothing we can do," I say. "Just keep on like we have been, take it easy, and don't fret over it."

But when we are in bed I lay my hand protectively over her slightly curved belly.

33

THE COMING SPRING won't allow any lasting melancholy. It clamours everywhere. Rains patter on the roof, water runs and drips and trickles off the land. The first pair of bald eagles returns to the river, huge dark shapes wheeling in sunlight over the bay.

We follow them upriver, walking on the thick, shore-fast blocks of decaying ice. On a hillside from which the snow has already melted, we recline under a large jack pine. The river is eroding big channels, brimming, running loud. A pair of squirrels chase each other up the scaly tree bark. Pine sap hangs in the air like incense. The sun is warm and strong, and we bare our pale, light-starved skin to it. The eagles come and go, always near the river, soaring in immense lazy circles then landing in the top clump of a spruce where breezes make them sway and bob.

We can't resist brainstorming names for our baby. Then I remember a day in Montana when Marypat's period was overdue and we fell prey to the same temptation, only to discover blood within hours.

"It's too soon for this," I say.

"Right," Marypat agrees, and the conversation ends.

It is bright until nine o'clock at night, and then northern lights continue the spring celebration. Once, waking up in the night, I dress and spend half an hour out under the light-show. Green spirals wheel through the Milky Way, curtains tinged with pink pulse and fade. A fist of light punches slowly from one horizon to the other, finally flaming out in the silhouettes of trees. It is still going strong when I go back to bed.

We can hardly concentrate on our projects. Every few minutes another bird draws us to the porch with binoculars, the otter pops up in the water, or the snowshoe hare, now decidedly grey, hops slowly past.

Marypat takes her camera and goes off for a walk while I try to finish a short story I'm working on. She is gone, it seems to me, a very long time. I begin to worry, inventing bear encounters, icy mishaps, miscarriage in the woods. I have no idea, I realize, which way she went. My writing is forgotten, I can't even read, end up pacing the floor.

When she returns she is exuberant over her pictures, the loveliness of the afternoon, the new buds on the trees. I am almost sputtering with anxiety and relief, even as I realize how stupid it is, and I can't help being testy for a while, as if to pay her back for all the worry she unwittingly caused.

For diversion we sleep outside on the porch. It is cool and fresh, the forest immediate. I wake several times during the night, to lights in the sky, an owl calling out, and, in the pale morning, the drumming of a woodpecker. It is well below freezing, but it is pleasantly comfortable, lying there, waiting for the sun.

"Well, should we get up and paddle?" I suggest.

Marypat laughs. "It is calm."

But for the snow on the ground and the solid ice on the lake, it could be a day for water travel, and I long for the constant dipping of blades, the smooth glide of the canoe hull, the summer air in my face.

Restlessness grows in us like a disease. It is impossible to ski, but too snowy to walk easily, and there is not enough open water to paddle. Our winter routine has grown old. We wash out underwear and socks in the basin, struggle through soft snow with the daily water buckets, try to apply ourselves, day after day.

I feel like a schoolboy in math class, with spring washing in through an open window, sounds from a baseball diamond, knowing I still have two interminable classes left before I'm out.

My urgency makes me think about bears. They may already be emerging, foraging hungrily. I clean and load the shotgun for the first time all winter, then prop the weapon in a corner.

Marypat has developed pregnancy mannerisms. Her belly just barely shows, only a slight roundness, but she often rubs it thoughtfully. I am reminded of a basketball player at the free-throw line, turning and wiping the ball out of ritualistic habit. And she has that concentrated, far-off look. I see her in that universal posture of fatigue, hand resting on her lower back, down where her bones are already softening, beginning to spread. She is always searching her body for change, hefting her breasts, staying tuned.

Her face has rounded out, warmed. She moves, always, in the knowledge of what she carries, charged by its heat, communing with it. There is a contentment that emanates from her like an aura, a fullness of purpose that leaves me a bystander.

When we make it through the third month, it is time to tell family. Marypat wants to reach my sister first. Ann Noel, still grieving at her own loss, says that she had a feeling we were pregnant. Her due date would have been within a day of ours.

"Now we've done it!" I say, when Marypat is off the phone. "Do you think everyone will help us decide whether to go on with the trip?"

"Ann Noel asked, but I told her we just had to wait and see, that we wouldn't take chances."

Once the word is out, it travels with a vengeance. The radio-phone sounds daily for a time, and everyone asks when we're coming back.

My mom bursts out, "I hope you'll come home!" but doesn't push further.

"I could feel the worry in her voice," I say to Marypat. "It gave me a flash of parenthood."

"I know. Right now we're concerned about the pregnancy.

Then it's whether the birth goes well. After that you worry about all the potential problems in infancy. It never ends."

Larger wildlife is scarce for a time. Days pass without any sign, and I assume that they are preoccupied with denning, caring for young, staying close to home. The ptarmigan population is already thinning out, pushing north, where it is still winter. Avoiding the crowds.

The river has reclaimed most of its summer channel. Only the thick slabs of ice along the banks and the quiet backwaters hold out. Ski tracks from our many sojourns over the winter stand up like hardened rails after the surrounding snow melts away. Old otter slides and familiar animal trails mark the blocks of ice that are now broken up and tilted at crazy angles. What were once landmarks to us are now melting away. No other human knows these tracks, these features of our quiet neighbourhood. It is somehow fitting that they should disappear in the warmth, that we, like the other residents, carry them in our memories.

Half a mile behind the camp we find the jack pine the eagles are using for their nest. One or other of them is always circling over it, or carrying grass to line the large platform of sticks. Sometimes one will be sitting there as we approach, that fierce eye watching us.

When an animal appears, it is always so sudden. On the bay one afternoon, a wolf is abruptly there, wearing a saddle of dark fur in a coat otherwise creamy white. It works along the margin of the open current, perhaps scenting for dead fish, maybe drawn by the sound and motion of glittering water. It goes out of sight behind the willow point, but later I hear a moaning howl. We go quietly to the willows, sneak through them, and there it is, lapping water from a pool on the ice. It senses us, looks sharply, then lopes off with fluid strength.

The next morning I notice two dark blots on the ice: the otter and one of the eagles. The bird is intently watching the otter, scavenging for scraps of fish, but having no luck. The majestic eagle seems diminished, waddling around heavily like a hungry, sheepish panhandler. The otter pays it no mind. A raven swoops in, hops boldly up to the eagle, then to the otter, finds nothing of interest, and flies off in search of more promising fare.

Three brown snowshoe hares chase each other playfully across patches of bare ground near the cabin. It is that time of year, and they are, after all, rabbits.

34

IT HAS BEEN drizzling and misty all day. The cabin is cozy, full of stove warmth and the smell of peppermint tea, and we have been quietly productive. At one point, Marypat looks up from her drawing. An otter is staring at her from six feet away. Huge liquid eyes, whiskers quivering. It stands at the bottom of our porch steps, one paw lifted up, its neck stretched inquiringly. Then it humps off across the snow and slides under another cabin.

"I was so shocked I didn't even think of taking photos," Marypat says. "It was such direct contact, eye to eye. So curious and close."

"She must be giving birth under that cabin."

For days we have watched a pair of otters in the bay. They nuzzle each other, roll in the snow, swim and dive playfully. And we have stalked them, hoping for pictures, without success. Now this, right at our door. This startling, straightforward connection made between an otter and a human who, it would seem, are both to be mothers. Too much could be made of this, and we don't even talk about it. The coincidence is incredible enough.

And there are small noises from beneath our own cabin. A chocolate-brown mink with a white star on its chest has been coming and going for some time. But until now we had thought nothing of it.

We begin Operation Otter Watch, but she almost always eludes us. Suddenly she'll appear out on the bay, eating fish, swimming vigorously. Then, when our attention has wandered, here she'll come, galumphing steadily, with surprising speed, up the slope and under the cabin.

There are other signs of new life. One or another of the eagles is now on the nest all the time. When we tiptoe up the trail, they invariably take flight, huge wings clattering through the branches. Mallards land in the growing pool of water, pairs of Canada geese glide in briefly. We see several dozen of them in some quiet weedy shallows along the Otherside River.

There is an excessive exuberance in the animals we see, behaviour unique to spring. All winter long survival is every-thing – finding the next meal, living through the night. But now that it is light and warm, there is a margin for play.

A mink cavorts on the ice with pointless energy. Up and down it scampers, sometimes standing on its hind legs, sliding repeatedly into the nearby water. Then it pops up again, out onto the ice, and runs in circles.

For a long time it spars with a raven that lands close by. At first I assume there is menace in their antics, but it becomes clear that it is no more sinister than kids playing tag. They sidle inno-cently toward one another, feigning nonchalance, until one of them makes an offensive dash.

The mink, when chased, makes for the safety of water, only to climb out again almost immediately to start another round. The raven, under duress, takes heavily to the air for a few wingbeats, but drops right back into the fray.

Several times the mink tempts its opponent by running

almost to the trees. I can imagine the gleam of triumph in the raven's eye, thinking it has the mink cut off from the water. But when the bird hops in determined pursuit, sunlight iridescent in its wings, the mink is always quicker.

We can't stay sedentary much longer. One night Marypat brings out the bag of maps to begin studying our options for the summer. We are thinking of several routes, and run the map wheel along various circuitous lines across the paper, adding up distance. As it travels, I see the sandy esker ridges, hear the throaty rapids, smell wood smoke and the damp tundra mosses. They are almost too much, these visions. I feel like a prisoner looking through bars at people walking in a park. But it is also a delicious indulgence.

Inevitably, we discuss whether we should go at all.

"It is so tempting when I look at the maps," I say. "But it also seems selfish and shortsighted. I mean, really, what's a summer trip compared to the safety of the baby?"

"I know. But everything seems so good. I keep thinking of Native people who gave birth and raised children up there. I want to think of it as just a normal part of life, something we can handle."

"Sure. But they lived there all the time. They had no choice. And plenty of their babies died, or the women died, because of the conditions. Don't you have nightmarish visions of what could happen?" I ask.

Marypat nods. "Of course I do. But I don't want to give in to them."

"Me neither. But let's not be stupid."

"It would be so easy to go home." Marypat is standing now, pacing. "Everyone wants us to, and they'd all be happy if we gave it up. But let's wait."

"Okay," I agree. "But don't get all competitive with yourself and try to do it for the wrong reasons. We'll use our paddle into Stony Rapids as a test run."

The map-reading session creates an irresistible urge in both of us to hold paddles in our hands again. Only a short lane into the bay has been opened up through the ice, but it is enough. To begin, we set the red boat on a high drift and toboggan down toward the bay, paddles flailing on the snow. Across the flat ice we haul the boat by its rope, as though taking it out for exercise.

Then, for the first time since September, we are on the water again. Feeling the motion beneath the hull, the first strokes with the companionable paddle, the silent forward glide, sends a shiver through me.

We soon exhaust the limits of the open water. There is another stretch of current farther out, on the far side of a short expanse of elastic ice. We ram against it, but the ice bends and holds under the boat. It is too slick to push across with the paddles.

"It's only about ten feet across," I say. "I'll bet it will hold us for a few steps."

Marypat looks dubiously around her as I step out. I put one foot gingerly on the ice, let it bear some weight, then the other, and I'm standing.

"Okay, Marypat, just stay in and I'll . . ."

The ice breaks with the suddenness of a trapdoor, and I plunge to my armpits before catching hold of the canoe gunwale. Marypat hasn't even turned around before I'm back in the boat, dripping wet, sputtering.

"Now that's cold!" I chatter. "On second thought, let's go home and wait for the ice to melt!"

Marypat is laughing hysterically all the way back.

By the first days of May we can taste summer. On warm afternoons insects buzz in the air, groups of butterflies make mosaics on bare ground. Birds are coming through in great groups, new species every day.

Still we haven't seen a bear, and we make bets on the first sighting. The forest is tinged with a vernal haze, a green suggestion of leaves unfolding. The paths have become muddy quagmires, soggy with water the colour of well-steeped tea.

Every day we paddle the lap of open water, now a mile or more long, out to the thick lid of ice still weighing on the lake. Gulls call raucously overhead, geese stand on the grey edge of ice, snow buntings hurry across the shrinking patches of white.

Just when we are convinced we are finally cut off from visitors, one of Eli's sons shows up. He introduces himself as Lawrence, and has brought along a young boy. They want to set a net in the open water, camp out for a day or two along the bay. "Bears are out," he tells us. "I saw one just east of here."

The next afternoon, at the end of our canoe lap, we stop to visit. At the edge of the willows, Lawrence's snowmobile and toboggan rest in the dirty, granular snow. A four-wheeler with a rifle strapped behind the seat is parked nearby; another man and his wife are in the camp.

"Did you see lots of geese out there?" Lawrence asks, jutting his chin toward the lake.

"Yes."

"Why didn't you shoot one?"

"We don't want to shoot any."

"You could have shot it for me. I'd eat it right now."

The four-wheeler couple guess that ice travel is nearly over, that the ice will be gone by the first week of June. They fell through in some shallows and had to rescue their machine.

Their wall tent stands in a little clearing, sides rolled up to let in the spring air. The two Chipewyan men hunker close to a smouldering fire. Lawrence drinks occasionally from a saucepan of cold tea. Part of a fish burns in the coals. Another fire smokes under a small rack draped with whitefish fillets and covered with a thatch of fresh spruce boughs.

They tell us there has been an election in Fond-du-Lac, and the band has a new chief. Elected officials are another product of western influence. In the time before missionaries and treaties, chiefs, as we know them now, didn't exist. Respected elders and warriors, yes. And temporary leaders for warfare or migration or hunts. But our bureaucratic politics was an utterly foreign concept.

We learn Chipewyan names for the birds we've seen recently – pintail, mallard, goose – and provide some amusement trying to pronounce them. Lawrence says he'll take a last batch of letters to the post office for us.

The Chipewyan are good at visiting. It is often what they choose to do if given free time. A day lounging in camp, drinking tea, snacking on roasted fish, perhaps setting a net or two, is their idea of time well spent. It seems to me a particularly sane point of view.

35

THE FIRST BEAR of spring turns out to be a bookworm. It announces itself with a muffled thud that breaks the evening quiet.

"What's that?" Marypat peers out the front window. She sees nothing, goes across to the side window. Just then a large black bear lumbers off the porch of the neighbouring cabin and stands a few yards away, looking us over. "Bear!" she hisses, and I am up, going for the gun, opening the door.

The bear is close enough for us to see the brown, liquid eyes and to hear the intake of breath through scenting nostrils. Only when we move forward and give a sharp yell does the dark visitor trot off, melting into the woods.

What was it doing? The two of us walk to the open door of the other cabin. Large wet prints lead right inside the building, over to a box of books we had stored there.

The thud we heard was the sound of a hardcover copy of William Shirer's *Berlin Diary* being dropped unceremoniously on the floor. "Now that's sinking your teeth into a book," I say. A blunt, tapered puncture penetrates seventy-five pages.

The bear sighting is only one episode in a day-long wildlife saga. Since morning the birds have been washing in, a wave of life. Till now they have trickled up one species at a time, but this has been a flood. At dawn, the polite sneeze of a phoebe from the top of a tamarack, then shrill calls of killdeer ricocheting across the clearing. Kinglets and warblers fill the woods with their outsized songs. Flickers undulate through the air.

All the coves on the bay are crammed with aquatic and shore birds. Rafts of green-winged teal, pintail, widgeon, mallard, goldeneye. All preening, feeding, quacking, taking off with bursts of wings. Along the shore, yellowlegs wade in the shallows, pipits scurry across the mossy rocks, red-winged blackbirds call from the rushes. An explosion of horned grebes with their gold-red necks and head tufts, surf scoters, red-throated loons, Bonaparte's gulls.

For hours we paddle among the quickening spring floodtide. After a while we don't even bother with binoculars; it is too close a focus. I want the whole panorama at once, all the noise, the beating wings, the smell of mud and weed, sunlight glinting off feathers. It is a sensory glut, and my appetite for it is boundless.

The high point is the tundra swans, which coast sedately, like white ships, dwarfing the other birds. They thunder off at our approach, wings like heavy sheets of canvas snapping in a wind.

At dinner time a wolf trots across our stage, the same colour as the greying snow, and makes its way into the thick spruce.

"The only way to stop seeing new wildlife," I say, finally, "is to go to bed!"

After the first sighting, bears appear constantly. There are fresh tracks along the moist trails, toe prints as big as ripe cherries. Almost every day another one wanders through camp. When we go to fetch water we look carefully between cabins, check behind us.

One morning I am wakened by a sound on the porch. A small black yearling is on its hind legs, looking at me through the window. The latch on our door is weak, requires only a push to break it open. I think of a bear leaning against it, suddenly inside with us.

I watch another bear eating willow buds across the bay one evening. It is a methodical, patient process. Up on its hind legs, the heavy animal waddles into the tall, flexible shrubs and gathers a bunch in an embrace, then pins it to the ground. With binoculars I can see the pink, mobile tongue stripping buds, licking them up. It prunes armful after armful in the lingering golden sunlight. I'm amazed that such a beast can fuel itself with these small morsels – buds, ants, grubs, seeds.

I have no idea how many bears are in the vicinity, but it seems a great number. Only once am I provoked enough to fire a warning blast. The trespasser is a full-grown adult with a distinctive blaze of white on its chest. It plods unconcernedly past the cabin, paying no attention to my shouts. I follow it, gun in hand, across camp to the row of toolsheds. There it begins to meander among the buildings, paw at things, ignoring me completely. The boom of my twelve-gauge shatters the bucolic spring scene. The bear finally reacts, running with stunning speed into the greening stand of poplars.

Halfway through May, Marypat suggests a long upriver walk. The weather is almost hot. Water runs in sheets toward the river. The only snow lies in small, bedraggled patches. My four-months-pregnant partner insists on climbing through the prickly branches of a spruce to take eagle pictures. The tree top affords a good angle across to their nest. Before long she is swaying up there at the spindly pinnacle, legs clamped around the trunk, scratched and bruised, clicking triumphantly away.

At the farthest point of our walk we reach a ridge that has been a favourite viewpoint all winter. The river is high and thick with silt. It may be the last time I'll ever stand here, I think. Flashes of winter scenes superimpose themselves on the green, watery warmth below – bony trees, tortured ice, wolf trails, face-biting cold. It is not melancholy, this thought. Our time here is nearly at an end, and I am ready to move. I know that this view, these sounds and smells are etched truly and deeply in my memory.

All morning I have done nothing. The snowshoe hare is grazing out front, its eyes and ears twitching constantly, reacting to sounds, assessing threats. Yellow-rumped warblers are busy in the tamarack, flashing colour. Mallards and widgeons cruise the shallows where the snowmobile trail started up to the cabin. Farther out a loon dives where we saw the only lynx of winter.

An osprey hovers above the moving current, crooked wings beating in place, eyes searching the water. One of the eagles circles the mouth of the Otherside, then flies on.

All morning I have watched this view, hardly moving. Doing nothing. And as I watch, images from books, ideas for writing, faces of friends, vague premonitions of life with a child, expectations for the summer, come to mind. Like fish moving through murky water.

It is amazing how little time I've allowed myself for this, and how profoundly refreshing it is, like a good, satisfying sleep. Supposedly, to do nothing is to waste time. One should keep busy, keep active, do something. Anything. But why does it feel like wealth, this peaceful time? Why does it seem anything but sloth to notice the small, miraculous events around me, and to allow the currents of thought to flow unrestricted?

We make preparations for summer on the assumption that we'll go on. Travel gear is pulled out of packs, checked over, repaired. Lists are begun: reminders of menu improvements, fishing licences to buy, packages to send home. We clean and reorganize the cabin, ready it for summer visitors, until it feels empty and foreign, like we're putting in time in a motel room. Every night I pore over maps, weighing distances and challenges and risks.

Around camp we putter with the chores to help open up. One of the barrels under the floating dock has broken free. I find it bobbing in the bay, punctured and half-full of water. We herd it back, try to lift it onto the dock. It is heavy and awkward, and in the midst of our efforts Marypat groans with pain.

"Oh," she says, straightening up. "I don't think I should do this."

Immediately I think of all the heavy packs we'll have to lift, over and over, through the summer. The portages, the headwinds, the bad weather. I think how suddenly we could be in trouble.

"I'm okay." Marypat is rubbing her belly. "Something stretched, but it's all right. I just shouldn't try that kind of lifting."

Cliff and Stella are coming back any day. They call in periodically to report their progress north and ask about the weather and landing conditions in the bay. We put up the wind sock at the willow point.

As if it senses the impending crowds, the mink under our cabin moves her young. One morning she makes repeated trips toward the river, and each time she bounds off she is carefully holding another pink, hairless baby in her jaws. Devoted to her task, she disregards us completely. Half a dozen times she runs back, grabs a baby, then takes a straight line to the water.

When Cliff's plane circles in, takes the usual approach for the landing, taxis toward the dock, it feels like no time has passed at all. Ptarmigan on Christmas morning, slush traps on the ice, dog teams curled in the snow – the nine months of winter are, suddenly, in another time, almost seem to have happened to other people.

It is with both sadness and excitement that I catch the wing strut and pull the Beaver in against the dock, see our friends waving hello.

36

MORE THAN ANYTHING else, it is open water that really signals the end of winter. On the last day of May, the ice is completely off our end of Lake Athabasca. Foliage is thick, bird song is in the air, camp chores fill each day, but it is the expanse of blue reaching across the miles, leading my eyes into the northern ranges of rock hills, that marks the end.

Our impending decision overshadows everything. For weeks we have been able to put it off, distracted by spring. Our talks have been abstract, hypothetical, but now it is upon us. Marypat makes another prenatal appointment at the clinic. Cliff offers the use of a fishing boat for the trip, says we can pick up some propane bottles for him anyway.

It is grey and cool the morning we drive across the watery miles, out of the shallow bay, into the space that was so recently solid and wind-sculpted. The lake is the colour of slate, choppy, ice-cold, but calm enough for us to make a straight run for town. At full throttle, the miles drop away. The aluminum hull pounds dully against the waves, and we hunch deep into our clothes.

In town we gather the last mail, including a box from one of

Marypat's friends who has sent up maternity outfits for the summer. The clinic is quiet, and while Marypat readies herself in an examination room I wait in the empty office.

A Native man I have never met comes in. He is my age, perhaps younger, comes right up to me.

"What's your name?" he asks, bluntly.

When I tell him, he continues in the same tone.

"You wrote that book, didn't you?"

I assume that he means *Water and Sky*, the book about our first northern winter, five years earlier, and I nod.

"I want you out of town."

"What are you talking about?" I am flabbergasted. It is like some Old West drama, this confrontation, and I am half-tempted to treat it as a joke.

"Who are you?" I ask, angry now as well as surprised.

"I'm the new chief. You have thirty minutes to leave." And he walks back out the door before I can respond.

"Jesus Christ!" I start to follow him, then stop.

The Native receptionist is smirking as I make my way down the hall, and I feel, for the first time in this place, very much the minority.

"What's wrong?" Marypat asks, when she sees my face. Jackie is with her, and the doctor has just begun his examination.

"We've been kicked out of town."

I tell them what happened, and see the same confused surprise on Marypat's face.

"Oh, for Christ's sake," Jackie explodes. "It's that new chief."

But we have other concerns. My anger and shock subside as the exam proceeds. Measurements, a urine test, Marypat's weight; it doesn't take long.

"Let's see if we can find that heartbeat," the doctor says, applying an instrument to Marypat's belly. He searches for it, finds only gurglings and static, then focusses. It is fast and steady, a fluid, gushing sound. We are all silent, listening to the sure signal of that tireless muscle.

I could listen a long time. It raises the hair on my neck, feels like a communication.

Marypat is smiling, eyes closed.

"Sounds good." The doctor steps back. "Everything looks good, in fact. You're obviously healthy."

"Okay," I take a breath, "what about this summer?"

And we tell him our plans, impress upon him the nature of our travel, the remoteness of the Barren Lands.

"If something happens out on the tundra, we're on our own," I conclude.

"Pregnancy is a normal part of life," he says. "You've come through the first trimester with no problem. You'll be back before premature birth is a worry. If what you want to do is within the realm of your normal activity, you should be able to do it."

"What do we watch for?" Marypat asks.

"Blood. If you start bleeding, you have to rest, move as little as possible until it stops. Same for any kind of bad cramping or severe contractions. I would try to avoid heavy lifting, like picking up packs. You can carry them, but don't try to get them up off the ground. You should be fine. In many ways it seems like a pretty healthy way to spend your pregnancy. But I can't tell you there's no risk."

It is our decision. He has given us a fair idea of what to expect, is even pretty encouraging, but I am left as undecided as ever. Easy enough to sit in an office and talk about resting until the bleeding stops, but I picture a tundra camp, food running low, the weather foul, no fuel for fires. Or sudden cramping halfway across a portage, Marypat falling with a weight on her back. The scenarios are endless.

But Marypat is sanguine, still glowing from the sound of the little heart. "Wasn't that heartbeat something?" she says with a grin, and I am brought out of the turmoil of sobering visions.

"I've never heard anything like it."

Brian has heard about my confrontation with the new chief and meets us out front.

"What's going on?" I ask him.

"Who knows? He wants to throw his weight around. Now he's chief, he thinks he's a big deal. He hasn't read the book, doesn't even know the title."

We had hoped to visit Eli and Angela, have a meal with friends, but now I want nothing more than to get out of this place. I keep running over responses I could have made, consider trying to find this guy, talk with him, but realize the folly of it.

"Look," Brian says. "I read the book, eh? Everything you said is right on, and maybe the truth hurts. I could see things in there that they might not like, especially when an outsider points them out, but everything is true."

Brian helps us gather up the propane bottles, load them in the boat. We shake hands, perhaps for the last time. He hugs Marypat.

"You've been a really good friend, this winter," I tell him. "I hope we can return the favour."

"Just take care of the little one," he says, as he casts us off.

"Salman Rushdie of the North," I mutter, bitterly, as I yank the starter cord.

I have no idea what gave offence, but I can't leave Fond-du-Lac quickly enough, and don't look back once.

Fishing clients begin to trickle into camp, several at a time. The first big bunch will arrive within a week. Every bed will be filled. By then we want to be on our way.

Stella gives us our first haircuts in a year, and Marypat has a foot or more of her waist-length hair chopped off. My partner makes a final trip to the eagle nest and sees two gawky, fluff-covered young tottering around in the high clump of sticks. It is another kind of closure, a full cycle, like the round of seasons, the coming and going of birds, bears returning. The time is right to move on.

The last night in camp Philip approaches me. He knows about our trouble in town.

"I'm your friend," he says simply. "It's bullshit, what the chief did." His words are angry. "I'm your friend," he repeats, and offers his hand.

It is mid-morning by the time we're organized and have said goodbye to everyone. The air is warm, almost sultry. The guides are off with the fishermen. Cliff is on a flying errand. The black flies are thick.

The loaded canoe, covered with decking, sits in the shallows we know so well. I climb to the stern, then Marypat shoves us off and hops onto the bow plate. She is dressed in a pair of green, loose overalls. It is a new shape to get used to up in the bow. Already her back is filling out, she moves more heavily.

It is just like any of the dozens of laps we have made in this bay, heading for the point, then turning north. Except that we are loaded up for the long haul. And that it may be the last time we will ever see the gap where the Otherside River tumbles into the bay; the rough line of spruce on the southern horizon; the little cabin hunkered against the woods that has been, for so many months, home.

VII

DISCOVERIES AND DECISIONS

37

WE STOP AT a small island after a few miles, hungry for lunch. The rock we sit on slopes gently into the clear water. It is full of tortured bands, whorls, wavy lines. The surface is warm and polished, and when Marypat finishes eating she curls up on her side for a nap.

It's remarkable how quickly it is all comfortable again. Hermit thrush call in the distance, a spotted sandpiper runs up the shore. Marypat has her head on a life vest, is asleep almost immediately. I can feel tightness in my back, know my paddling tone has gone soft, but it is a pleasant soreness.

The worn map lies open on my knees. We hardly need charts to finish Lake Athabasca, it is home ground, but map-gazing is a habit of mine, and no matter how familiar the landscape, there is no end to the curiosities. Besides, maps help my thoughts travel. I follow the blue line of the Grease River up through rock country, past falls and rapids, in and out of small lakes, north against the current, and I am off somewhere, absorbed, while the little waves buff the rock at my feet and our canoe pulls quietly at the end of its rope.

The hectic chores and preparations at the fishing camp feel distant now. My encounter in Fond-du-Lac no longer preoccupies me. After living on a short leash all winter, it is an overwhelming relief to paddle off into this welcoming realm of solitude, to know that horizon after horizon waits ahead.

It is remarkable, too, how soon I felt that we should continue with our journey. We were hardly out of the bay, hadn't spoken a word, when the challenges of the summer seemed completely within our capabilities. I said nothing to Marypat. It felt ridiculous, after all the talk of our trial run, my nervous caution, to be so sure all of a sudden. But that is exactly the way I felt. We embrace this wilderness so readily, fall so easily each time into the rhythm.

I expect Marypat feels the same. She has already exclaimed at how comfortable the paddling is. She has become, over the last months, more and more settled, calm, happily enduring. She stirs, stretches languidly, sits up. "This is nice," she says. "Really nice."

Our pace along the rocky north shore is sauntering. In and out through the scattered islands, back along the deep bays where the big jackfish sun themselves in weedy shallows and the warm afternoon stillness has almost tropical weight. The thick woods are silent, potent with the scent of black bear, the trails and burrows and nests of another neighbourhood full of its careful, vital life.

"The paddling feels really good," Marypat says again. "It isn't hard at all."

When I first wake the next morning rain is pattering on the tent. I turn over and sleep some more. Later, between showers, we kindle our fire, have breakfast and coffee, try to read the leaden sky.

Marypat is sterning today. "I don't want to give up my turn if I can help it," she tells me. Almost as soon as we start out it begins to rain again. Steady, cold drizzle with a gusty wind.

A pair of bald eagles circle above their high nest as we paddle past. The rock cliffs of Robillard Bay are black and sharp, the forest dark, uninviting. I keep asking Marypat how she's holding up against the winds, but she is unwavering.

"Last night I thought I felt the baby move," she says. "I couldn't be sure. It was like a little fluttering inside." Our canoe conversation has expanded to include bladder infections, baby names, and crib decorations.

In Pine Channel the lake narrows. The first current of the Fond-du-Lac River pushes gently against us, and the skies clear, although winds funnel into our faces. Far ahead I see where the power line crosses the water, punctuated with large orange balls.

It is only a thin strip taken out of this huge wild country, hardly worth mentioning, but it changes everything, knowing it is there, supplying power to televisions and toasters and CD players, humming insistently. I will, of course, return to my electrified town at the end of all this. And the local inhabitants are no doubt quite happy to enjoy the conveniences I take for granted. Yet it is an ominous presence. There is talk of a road coming up to Stony Rapids. First the line of poles strung with wire, then the road. The frontier of the wilderness beaten back, pushed north, and the human invasion swooping in.

It doesn't help that the beach at which we stop is full of trash: plastic bags, rusted tin, pop cans. Trees are hacked up, their limbs cut off. There are big spikes driven through the scaly bark of the pines. We camp at the water's edge to avoid these signs of aimless destruction.

In the evening, the wind attacks with sudden fury. We have just gone to the tent when it shifts 180 degrees and comes roaring up the channel from the west. Whitecaps are driven down on the beach, our tent is half flattened in the gale, and we have to lean against the door to hold it upright.

"Nothing this sudden and strong can last very long," I say. But it does last.

Marypat is hunched over with the tent pressing against her back. "I'll hold down the tent if you want to go out and check our gear," she says.

Outside, I am blinded by sand if I face the wind, so I back my way to our pile of packs and weigh down the flapping tarp with large rocks. The canoe has been picked up and hurled into a thick stand of willows. Without that vegetation the boat would have been carried right across the point of sand, and might be halfway to town by now. As I lash the boat, I promise fervently never to leave a canoe untied again.

"I don't know if we can do it, but we need to move the tent." I am standing at the door, looking at a likely spot amidst the litter in the trees.

"Okay, we can't keep doing this." Marypat starts to come out while I cling to the tent.

Together we grab the corners, grip tight, and start shuffling through the sand. Our light home bobs and tugs like a huge, awkward kite trying to break free, but once it is staked down in a sheltered hollow and we have piled inside, the winds can't attack as effectively. I lie there listening to the arms of trees whipping above us and the more distant crashing of waves on the beach.

Marypat is awake, too. "Do you find yourself getting excited about going north?" she asks.

I turn to her, reach out to touch her face. "It's just like you to get jazzed up right after some hair-raising episode. But yeah, I do. It's hard to resist."

"Maybe we shouldn't. Resist, I mean."

Well into the next morning the winds continue stiff and strong, so that we don't leave camp until quite late, and only then because we give in to the temptation of a tailwind. It is hardly necessary to paddle. We use our blades more to keep our balance on the surging wave fronts than to provide forward momentum. The wind does all the rest.

Every so often we pull in behind an island for a break. It is exactly like turning into an eddy part way through a rapid. That same sudden calm, that surprising relaxation in the midst of the action. We stretch, talk a bit, catch our breath, then go on, surf-ing each heaving wave, balancing on each cresting whitecap.

Skeins of Canada geese cross overhead. They angle into the wind, using it to ferry them north. Their formations break, string out, regroup, and snatches of their talk whip by in gusts of air. The first barge of summer passes us, outbound from Stony Rapids. Waves crash against the blunt, steel hull, sending spray high in the air.

All the way in to Stony Rapids the west winds push us. Even the current of the Fond-du-Lac River is no match for it. For miles we chase a pair of geese up the river, their laboured honking leading us along until the squat gas tanks on the waterfront come into view and the air is suddenly loud and busy with float planes.

Within hours we hitch a ride out to Ed and Margy's camp. Ice still lies heavily on the lakes farther north. It will be weeks before we can hope to push on. But already we both understand that we have made our decision.

38

MARGY IS TWO months ahead of us in her pregnancy, so we get a rough idea of what Marypat will be like by the end of the summer.

She is large, and needs more rest than usual, but is able to work pretty normally. With one helper she cooks elaborate meals for as many as thirty people every day, supervises the cabin-cleaning and laundry, takes care of her two daughters, helps with other odd chores that come up. Life in the wilderness is radically simple and calm compared to her camp routine.

Only, as Ed has reminded me, unlike here there won't be a clinic nearby. We will carry our complete first-aid kit, our medical books, and the emergency beacon, which theoretically can alert overflying satellites with a distress call. We are confident of our skills, our stamina and judgement, but Marypat's pregnancy has shaved down the margin for error. Events that might normally make our trip only a little more gruelling, a greater challenge, could turn life-threatening and grim this time.

Our families try hard to be supportive, but their worry is palpable when we speak on the phone. Marypat's father is more forceful about it than anyone else, keeps reminding us not to lose sight of our priorities. I imagine the agonizing guilt I would feel if something actually did go wrong, how devastating a tragedy would be.

But Marypat is cheerfully confident, ready to go, and I've come to respect her instincts. There are no indications of trouble, nothing amiss. What is going on inside her is hidden away, a mystery. We can only watch the gradual growth, the changes in Marypat's body, feel for the faint movements, and hope all is well.

We hear through the northern grapevine that some friends of ours from Wyoming are paddling the Cree River into Black Lake, and that they hope to see us before we leave. Dodie and Stearnie are in their seventies, have made northern forays for decades, and show no sign of quitting any time soon. They built a cabin on a small lake north of La Ronge and come up every year as soon as the ice is off, staying until the snow blows in the fall.

They call from Black Lake, and we tell them to paddle on to camp, that we'll canoe out to meet them. It feels good to paddle our light boat along the boreal shoreline. Halfway to town the two boats meet. We see each other a long way off, each team paddling steadily, efficiently. Then the boats coast smoothly together and we lean across the gunwales to shake hands and embrace. It is hard to imagine a better way to meet good friends.

The canoes drift side by side on the still water while we tell our stories. All the way to camp we blab at each other about the winter, their trip down the Cree, our plans for the summer, news from the States. Ed and Margy welcome them into camp and give them a cabin to stay in for a few days. Doug, the camp pilot, agrees to fly them back home after he takes us up to Kasba Lake. Making these plans brings our departure suddenly very close.

Much of the idle talk in camp is about flying. Flying and fishing. Stearnie is a pilot, as are both Ed and Doug, and there are often pilots among the fishing clientele. Evenings in the lodge are the usual forum, when the stories come tumbling out, full of the wry humour of hindsight.

This is bush flying, not the tame stuff of commercial airlines far above the clouds. This is flying with a topographic map open on your knee, looking out the window for landmarks in the wilderness, skirting thunderheads in a craft that can be tossed about wildly in the turbulent thermals.

When pilots talk, the sky has a kind of landscape, is a terrain full of mountainous clouds, calm valleys, violent rivers of air. Every pilot, it seems, has a tale. Wings icing up in a cloud, losing your bearings and running low on fuel, flying just above the hills to avoid being blind in a fog. And the mind working it all out – fuel and wind and alternative landing sites. Always, when these stories are told, there is great laughter and commiseration, the jovial relief of survivors.

The lesson, over and over, is to keep your head, remain patient, calculating. Even as panic comes in nauseating waves and your frantic questions have no answers, keep your head until something comes clear.

Our own flight is imminent. We have looked over the load with Doug. He has figured the distance, fuel weight, a safety margin, and says it's doable.

On June 23 we both wake up early, hours before anyone else. We take the last shower of the summer, make the final checks through our gear, put on our expedition clothes, clean for the last time.

Margy makes a big pancake breakfast after the fishing crowd has gone off for the day, but I hardly taste the food. It is always the same, these first mornings. Emotion-numbing preoccupation, a sense of an impending, irrevocable threshold to cross. And this time it is especially strong, with our little Stowaway along for the ride.

At the waterfront the blackflies are incredible. Demonic swarms of them smother us while we lash the canoe to the plane, stuff the packs inside, watch the floats sink lower and lower in the water.

There are final hugs. Dodie passes Marypat a package for her birthday, two days off, and we dive into the shelter of the plane. While Doug taxis in circles to warm up, I smash black-flies against the Plexiglas. Our friends stay on shore for a while, waving their arms in a farewell bug frenzy, then trot back to the lodge.

Doug opens the throttle and begins his takeoff. I watch a float plough heavily through the water, almost submerged. The plane is sluggish, as if the water is syrup, despite the all-out roar of the engine. I wonder if we'll just tear along on the surface until we have to turn around, but finally we're free, begin the slow, laboured climb into the warm sky.

"We're heavy all right," Doug says, looking over after he fin-ishes adjusting the flaps, setting his course. "I was beginning to wonder if she would lift off. And we aren't climbing any too fast, either."

Our course is north and east, a bearing we will follow all sum-mer long: north beyond the trees, where we will paddle toward the Arctic Circle, and east, following the slope of land toward Hudson Bay.

The plane hop allows us to avoid an arduous traverse full of portages, over the height of land. The packs are the heaviest they'll be all summer, and to saddle ourselves with that extra exertion, with Marypat's condition, seems like a foolish test of our luck. It will be challenge enough as it is.

Big popcorn cumulus float in the distance. The tapestry below is lush and sparkling. The view from a bush plane does map-reading a giant step better. I am looking down over the real thing, seeing the fast streams flecked with white, the snakelike esker ridges left by glaciers, the connections between lake and river and portage. Of course, when route-planning from the air, there are no blackflies to combat, no boot-sucking muskeg through which to portage. It all looks fresh and untouched and full of potential.

Within fifteen minutes I hear Marypat rustling a plastic bag in the back. She is notorious for airsickness, but we had hoped the smooth weather would give us a break. I look back at her and she manages a sick, rueful smile. The plastic bread-bag is open on her lap. We have more than an hour to go.

Doug and I are on the lookout for ice, but all is green and blue below us. We tick off the landmarks on the map, point things out. Somewhere we cross the Northwest Territories border. Marypat is lost in her misery, quietly retching behind us. I squeeze her knee, wish I could do something. These flights are the worst part of northern trips for her.

Then Kasba Lake spreads below us, fifty miles long, a vast watery plain. It is open and calm. Rafts of ice are piled up around some islands, stuck on shoals, but the water is free, and there are no frozen lakes in view. The ground seems to be just this side of tundra, an ice-heaved landscape with stubbly clumps of dark spruce holding their own on the permafrost frontier.

We are aiming for the outlet of the Kazan River, almost at its source, and Doug is bang on, flies directly to it. I see the riffle of current below, the first few quiet bends, and can barely contain my excitement.

"There it is, MP. The first current of summer."

She pukes in response.

Doug circles, looking for a landing beach. He finds one, but there are boulders in the water, and it is hard to tell how far below the surface they are. He shrugs, circles again, lines up for his approach.

He lands smoothly, hardly bumps against the lake, and we are soon beached on the white sand. As soon as we free the canoe Marypat wobbles to shore and collapses thankfully. There are wolf tracks where we pile our packs. The air is still and warm, smells indefinably of the North. Indefinable, but unmistakable.

Doug checks the sky. Thunderheads are building and he is anxious to be off. As soon as we are unloaded he turns the plane, climbs along the float, ready to sever our link. Marypat rouses herself to say goodbye, apologizes unnecessarily, as though she could help her sickness.

The engine coughs, catches. I give the tail a shove and Doug goes into his takeoff run without prelude, is in the air before I have walked to the packs. His wings waggle once, then he is a spot in the sky, aiming between thunderheads, and then he's gone.

A cold gust of wind ripples the water. I look up at the grey base of towering cloud. It looks like we'll have thunderheads of our own to dodge.

39

AT THE BOTTOM of my rubberized clothes-bag, crammed in a pack, lies a plastic baggie with my other life in it. Some traveller's cheques, a phone card, money, my wallet – things I have already stopped thinking about, that I will unearth at the end of our travels like an archaeologist uncovering artifacts. None of it has currency here, with distant storms flashing, wolf tracks in the sand, the wind freshening.

"How are you, MP?"

"Not great, but I'd rather get going than be rained on here with everything scattered all over."

The water is so cold and eerily clear, it seems almost sterile. When I look into it I get vertigo. The rocks Doug worried about hitting are five feet down. I can't even reach them with my paddle.

The monotonous song of Harris sparrows hangs over the tundra, a pair of swans swim around the end of a point, mergansers fly past just above the water. I think what a relief it must be for these birds to arrive here. Over thousands of miles they run the gauntlet of electrical wires, radio towers, highway traffic, polluted water, not to mention the rigours of headwinds and storms. Here they can live undistracted and focus on the furious need to mate and make nests and prepare young for the flight south only a few months off.

It is a relief for us, too. It always seems as though my chest expands two sizes when I arrive in the wilderness, that I breath big, that my eyes take in more and my observations are keener. But our Stowaway never leaves my thoughts, tempers the usual uninhibited exhilaration.

"Here we go, Little Grebe," Marypat says. She talks to the baby out loud now, makes up new endearments every day. As we reach the outlet of the lake, feel the beginning pull of this great river, she seems over her airsickness.

The channel is tight and narrow, with surprises on every turn, and the water is high. Willows along the shore are submerged. We sweep around a bend and into our first rapid. Marypat stands briefly, but there isn't enough time to scout and she drops to her knees.

"I don't know, Al. We'll just have to take it as we go."

I follow her strokes as best I can. The water is loud, surprisingly strong. We rush around the outside of the curve, almost in the overhanging willows, clumsily avoiding rocks, slapping through waves. At the bottom there is a boulder dam that we can't avoid. The boat hangs up and we shove hard to get over, bump down to the end.

"Damn, not the smoothest run ever," I mutter. But it feels like we've begun, now. The plane flight, our friends in camp, events that took place just hours earlier, seem unimaginably distant.

Then we see a group of people on shore downstream. There is a fishing camp on Kasba Lake, and this must be their clients having shore lunch. They are likely to be the last humans we'll see all summer, but I resent the intrusion.

They make a disgruntled group, standing there in the drizzle, batting at mosquitoes. Three aluminum boats are tied in the shallows, a bunch of men with a few boys along, everyone in rain gear. We are almost upon them before anyone notices us. I see one youngster windmilling his arms in a bug-induced panic while he fixes a man I take to be his dad with a withering look. Inexplicably, somebody lights a firecracker.

Then they all turn to watch us go by, stricken dumb at the sight of us, here, out of nowhere.

"Where ya goin?" one finally calls out.

"Hudson Bay."

"Far out!"

"Hey, look out for those shallows," somebody yells, as if we have a propeller to watch. We glide silently by and then they are behind us in the drizzle.

The quick little river uncoils over the miles. Rains come and go, an otter pops up nearby, winds fight or help us, depending on the river bend.

When we find a place to camp, another rain is just starting. The air is humid and dense, sultry, and the mosquitoes are as bad as I've ever seen them.

"Should we set up or wait out the rain?" I ask.

"Let's move. These bugs are incredible!"

Once in a while I look down at my exposed hand as I heft the packs. Mosquitoes are crowded seven or eight to the square inch, all industriously pumping my blood. I swipe at them now and then, but it's a waste of energy. As I tote the packs, Marypat gets the tent up and starts tying a cooking tarp. By the time we're set, the rain is falling in earnest and our gear is damp.

"I'm not into struggling with a fire tonight. Let's cook on the stove." I begin pulling stuff out of packs.

But then I fill the pot too full and it takes forever to boil. When it does, it overflows and snuffs out the flame. We eat a lukewarm dinner, stash everything away, and run for the tent. Even there it's gritty and damp, and mosquitoes by the score find their way in with us.

"Wow," I sigh, when we're under control. "A little rusty at this, aren't we?"

"If it hadn't been for the bugs, it would've been okay."

I don't fall asleep right away. Rain keeps plopping against the tent and my thoughts crash drunkenly into each other. I finally find sleep, but wake abruptly to the call of a tundra swan. Then its wings beat past, close overhead. In the darkness the sound is so immediate I can feel those powerful muscles, those broad wings, pulling through the damp air. Perhaps it is one of the swans that stopped to rest in Otherside Bay this spring. Perhaps I've heard those same strong wings before.

A long channel at the southern end of Ennadai Lake is bordered by a high sandy esker that points north for eight or ten miles, finally ending in an elongated island. Trees and tundra mix together here. Islands are fringed with spruce, but bald on top. Hills are bare, the lowlands coated with tree growth. It is the transition from boreal forest to naked tundra, from protection to exposure.

When we stop for lunch we find the ruins of some old buildings. The logs are rough-hewn, notched crudely, and the structures tiny, with barely enough room inside for a person to turn around. These are, likely, old trappers' quarters. The sod roofs are caved in. A small birch grows in the centre of one. Weathered caribou bones lie half buried among rusted tin cans. There is enough wood here to build with, to heat with, but tundra lies just down the lake.

This transition zone also served as the boundary between the Inuit and Chipewyan peoples. Inuit were, truly, people of the deer, their culture wedded to the Barrens and the caribou. The Chipewyan made forays onto the tundra to hunt, but their true home remained the sheltering forest.

Thierry Mallet traded with the Natives for their furs during the 1920s, and travelled these lands extensively at all times of the year. He is one of the few of his breed who kept a journal, often eloquently describing the scenes he witnessed.

In this very spot he recorded his thoughts one fall day.

Just before sunset we went through the last narrows and entered the southern bay into which the Kazan River flows. And then suddenly the first trees since we had entered the Barren Lands two months before . . . the first spruces and tamaracks of the Canadian forest seemed to welcome us home . . .

A mile away from us, on the extreme southern point of a ridge of rocks, four human figures stood motionless, silhouetted black against the crimson of the sky – the last Eskimos of the Barren Lands, watching us go south toward the unknown country of plenty. . . .

There they were, at the edge of their native land, but looking south, as if straining for something which was not theirs to have.

Paddling on, into the spacious wilds, I feel a similar welcome, but mine is in the line of blue sky in the north. One of the last bald eagles we will see circles over the water. It is that very "country of plenty" to the south from which we seek a reprieve. It has become a country of excess, in every sense imaginable, and it is with mounting exuberance that we strip ourselves free of it, mile by mile, month by month, with every fluid stroke of our paddles.

The human silhouettes are long gone, but the Barrens themselves have hardly changed over the millennia through which Stone Age cultures hunted and fished, danced and wrestled, gave birth and buried their dead.

We have arrived, and when we make camp on a smooth bare knoll, the winds die. The lake is sparkling and still. Our small fire crackles under the grill with its smokeless flame. Both of us are quiet with a kind of reverence for this rare sanctuary, and with what feels like the beginning of the final chapter of our journey.

The next morning is Marypat's thirty-sixth birthday. I serve scrambled eggs and refried beans to her in the tent, with a fresh sprig of bog laurel on the side. She opens her few gifts. Among other things, Stearnie and Dodie have sent along a bag of firestarter – dry wood chips and curls of birchbark.

It is fitting, then, to be awarded a slight tailwind to speed us down the lake. By lunch time we are ready to make a crossing through a cluster of islands to begin our exploration of an unknown river. The Kazan flows out of the eastern leg of Ennadai Lake, but we have decided to follow the western outlet, a tiny, blue, unnamed squiggle on the map. For a week or more we will navigate this mystery trail, this string of lakes connected by a small river. Farther down, at Angikuni Lake, we will rejoin the Kazan.

My first glimpse of this new territory is discouraging. We have eaten our lunch on the naked crown of an island. Marypat is curled up in the small stones, taking her daily nap among the egg-filled nests of the Lapland longspur. When I explore another high point I see what looks very much like an expanse of ice blocking our way.

I'm not overly surprised. It isn't even the end of June. Ice on these lakes is common well into July. But I had hoped to avoid the extra challenge, the toil and delay. But there it is, a bank of grey-white covering the entire lake surface.

"It does look like ice," Marypat agrees, when I share the news. "But who knows. We've been fooled before. Maybe it's just fog."

40

IT ISN'T ICE that stops us, but wind. At first I hardly notice it, preoccupied as I am. But the whiteness recedes before us, finally disappearing altogether as wind roughens the water.

"It must be a kind of fog that lies on the cold water," I guess. "But it sure as hell looks like ice."

"What about pulling in at that point," Marypat says, and I realize that I've been paddling as hard as I can and we're pretty well staying in the same spot. The waves are big, too, rolling at us in choppy swells, spray flying from our paddles.

On the map this point is on the very edge of green. Beyond is solid white. And even here, the tundra is dominant. What trees there are stand only a few feet tall. Gnarled, twisted clumps of spruce grow in tight groups, as if to physically support each other.

We make our first windbound camp in a slight hollow below a ridge. There is enough driftwood for a fire, and a tiny stand of spruce offers a windbreak to huddle behind. We keep putting on more clothes as the temperature drops. Marypat sits next to the small fire, holding a cup of hot tea in both hands.

"Sometimes I feel guilty," she says, suddenly. "Like I'm doing this trip, taking risks, out of my selfish desire. We could have just gone home, chosen the safe route."

"It's a little late for that, Marypat. If you really felt that way, you should have said so before the flight."

"But I didn't feel it then. I knew I wanted to keep going, and I still do. Just once in a while I get these pangs of doubt." She rubs her belly in one of her pregnancy mannerisms, then changes the subject. "At least the bugs are gone for a while."

Bad weather keeps moving in on us. By morning a sleety rain is falling intermittently, surf roars against the point. The spruce wave stiffly in the gusts. In our sheltered spot, backed right against the wall of little trees, the rain blows right over our heads, missing us completely.

A loon swims in the quiet water behind the point, parading back and forth twenty feet out. There is something deeply satisfying about being in such a spot, on such a day. It is as if we have made a comfortable living room, complete with fireplace, in the midst of a storm. Shrouded in greyness, the swells of empty tundra roll away in the distance.

In the afternoon we try a walk inland. A mile or two over hummocky ground sit several shallow lakes on a higher ridge. The weather is like November, and the moss is grooved with caribou trails. Antlers lie around like discarded bits of clothing.

Near the lakes a broad, flat stone has been pulled out of the earth and then propped upright with smaller rocks. It looks exactly like a backrest.

Tentacles of forest reach gingerly into the open space, sticking to low spots, drainages, sheltered hollows. Boulders dropped by glaciers litter the ground. Two parasitic jaegers stroke against the wind, dark strong birds with eyes like hawks'. On the way back I pick up whitened scraps of wood, light and bleached, skinny branches of twisted wood that might be a hundred years old. We are the only things moving, the only living shapes in sight.

"You're pretty relaxed about being windbound," Marypat observes. "It's nice."

"I've been thinking about it a lot, and I don't want to get anxious. The baby changes things in a way I can't put my finger on. I should probably be more nervous, but instead I'm more patient. I don't want to fall into that combative style, especially so early. I never like being that way, but it seems like a dangerous tendency, now."

I am, however, distracted by thoughts of the route we are to take. I have exhausted the map, gleaning every bit of information. There are half a dozen tight spots in the early going that might require portages. There is no obvious height of land to cross, but I'm suspicious just the same. It wouldn't surprise me if a small land bridge escaped the attention of map makers on such a little drainage.

The next day, when winds drop enough for us to proceed, our course takes us toward a narrows in Ennadai Lake. We should be able to discern some current there. If it is with us, there is certainly no height of land to cross.

Big, jumbled rafts of ice are jammed up on rocky points – dazzling, exhaling coolness. I see the narrows far ahead, with bits of white denoting a small rapid, but I can't tell which way it's flowing until we are closer.

It is against us. "So much for an easy passage," I grumble. It is our first portage, a short wet carry across ankle-twisting tufts of grass. Marypat is determined to take her share, although she lets me lift the packs for her and leaves the canoe to me. Near the top of the rapid the current slackens, and by paddling hard and using eddies we can overcome it.

"I'm hungry," Marypat says, out of the blue. These needs of hers, now that she's pregnant, are immediate and inflexible. When she says she has to pee, or wants to eat, it means right now. But why not? There is no reason not to stop to eat. I am antsy about this strange drainage system, but the answers will come soon enough.

After lunch, the longer we paddle, the more calm the day becomes. The lake is a placid sheet and the sun warm. I half-nap as I stroke steadily along, absently watching the shimmering reflection of canoe in the water. The carcass of a winter-killed moose lies washed up on a narrow island, bloated and brown as a wooden barrel. White gull shit ignobly streaks its side. The hindquarters are gone. Victim of old age, a wolf pack, an accident? I imagine winter up here, and the shortage of shelter, the scattered and meagre islands of refuge on this windswept plain.

Marypat agitates for a campsite before I'm ready, but, again, why not? We are in striking distance of the blue squiggle on the map that begins the unknown, and twenty miles or more are behind us for the day.

Later, eating our evening meal with blackflies flying in our faces, I ask Marypat if she is happy to be here, just the two of us. "Yes," she says, without hesitation.

The tundra moss is soft under our tent. When I wake in the night, a cold moon hangs above a bare hill, in a sky never quite dark. There are moments, like this one, as I kneel naked at the tent door, when the beauty and stillness fill my chest with an urgency of emotion. When I lie down again, that cold moon lingers on the backs of my eyelids.

Winds stir in the morning, then grow into a whipping, broadside gale. The lake is shallow, rocky, the waves rough. In the stern I have to draw or J-stroke almost constantly. Despite a blue sky and warm temperatures, there is this bludgeoning foe holding us back. We are determined to battle on and discover whether this route will work, to discover our fate, but it is a long morning by the time we get there.

"I don't see anything at all," I shout. "You sure this is the right bay?"

"It's gotta be in here somewhere." Marypat is studying the map. "I'd say it's right there." She points to an unpromising spot on the far bank.

It isn't visible until we're twenty yards away: a narrow gap in the bank, a modest trickle of water flowing toward us. We nose into it, hold ourselves there with lazy strokes like trout waiting for food.

"Well, dammit, where *is* the height of land?"

We could turn back, here, and follow the known course of the Kazan. To retrace our steps at this point would lose us only a day or two. Ahead lie certain difficulties, mysteries both worrisome and enticing, beginning with the riddle of water-flow. The drainage could be so low that we have to wade or portage for miles. The maps might be off in critical ways. Yet neither of us suggests turning around.

Marypat takes a stronger paddle stroke. I keep pace. The canoe edges forward, breasting the current. We enter the gap, begin paddling in earnest, and leave one more option behind.

41

THE FIRST STREAM is short and shallow. Wading and poling up it, we reach a narrow lake full of shoals and decide to have lunch. I squint at the map, trying to find something I might have missed. There is no break in the waterway. Each lake in the chain is connected by a small blue line, and the elevation clearly descends. But if that is so, the water must be flowing uphill!

On this smaller lake winds are only a nuisance, so we push on after a distracted lunch. As much as I am concerned with our route, there is another feeling mounting in me. In the matter of a few hundred yards my outlook has changed dramatically. Nothing is different about our surroundings. The same wind punches us, the same rocky hills shoulder out of the tundra, the sky is still full of the same fast clouds. It is within me that the change has occurred.

We are off the beaten path. There is no trip report to follow, no name given to this river, no indication of previous travellers. I have no doubt this route has been taken before, even in modern times, but from our perspective we might as well be the first. Every new vista is an undescribed discovery. These Barrens are, as a whole, a remarkable fastness, a wilderness free of signs and fences and bureaucratic management. And within that fastness this is a very quiet corner. That knowledge heightens the clarity of our time here. As soon as we entered the inauspicious stream, another layer of mundanity fell away.

I am not in the least tempted to turn back from this exploration.

Again, the way into the next length of river, on the far side of this short lake, is obscured to the last. With map in hand, we approach a low, unbroken mass of willows, trusting that the connection is where it's supposed to be. Then I look down in the water and see weeds pulled our way by a slight current.

"I think it's going with us now," I call to Marypat. "That height of land was in the middle of this little lake. Can you believe it?"

"I'll bet it was that really shallow spot where it seemed like an esker crossed under the water. But this sure isn't much of a river."

The link is barely more than a canoe's width across, only a few inches deep, but we bump down it fairly easily, into the next pond.

"First mystery solved," I say. "Now we'll find out if there's enough water to float us."

The next link is an undifferentiated sheet of runoff pouring through willows. Portaging would be a nightmare, but hauling and pushing the loaded canoe through is little better. Even with pants rolled up to our thighs we get soaked. A good deal of red paint is left behind on the rocks, and the whole while hoards of tiny mosquitoes, devoted to their work, bore into our skin.

Again, at the other side of the next lake, an unportageable, unrunnable maze confronts us. The bugs are just as fierce. The bottom of the canoe gets a second round of abuse. We get ever more wet. Ahead on the map there are a great many more tight spots. But now we are really committed. No way are we about to haul back up through this stuff.

Our passage is not without moments of humour. In the first real rapid the next day, a hatch of insects is so dense that it literally curtains off our view. Bugs bat against our eyes, hang off our faces, soft wings tickle our skin. Partly because of this distraction we get trapped in a dead-end jumble of rock. I hop out of the canoe, shove it through a narrow gap into better current, impressed by my own presence of mind and agility, but then have to make a sprawling dive for the boat before it is whisked away.

"Like a cat!" I yell, when I've reorganized myself. Marypat is laughing so hard that we ram another rock, and I have to step out again to manoeuvre us past.

"You wouldn't be laughing so much if I was still standing on that rock back there while you went on alone."

"No, but it would almost be worth it for the picture," she says.

There is not a sign of humanity anywhere. No inukshuk cairns left by the Inuit, no scraps of trash, footprints, fire scars. Rough-legged hawks hunt over the tundra, their wings panting in the pale air as they hover. Marypat catches a glimpse of an arctic fox in a ridge of rocks.

Unwittingly, we choose one campsite that is near the ground nest of an arctic tern. This has happened before. Usually, if we are quiet and careful, the tern will settle down and tolerate us. This bird, however, is exceptionally protective. If there were another nearby campsite we would move, but everything in view is either broken rock or wet bog.

The tern screams shrilly above us, dives within inches of our heads. We take to walking stooped over, hands up, as though we're surrendering. This is a bird nonchalantly at home in the air. I watch it scratch its neck with a foot while in flight.

Arctic terns migrate an unbelievable distance. Each year their round-trip marathon covers as much as twenty-two thousand miles. After nesting and raising her young, the angry bird above us will cross the North Atlantic, then fly along the coasts of Europe and Africa to its winter home in the Antarctic Ocean. They are, by virtue of their extraordinary efforts, the beneficiaries of more sunlight than any other creature on earth. On the southern oceans, as on the northern tundra, the summer sun hardly sets.

Given these frequent-flyer habits, it's astonishing that they can manage any of life's necessities. Where do they find time to eat and sleep, much less to court mates and raise their young?

We mean the tern no harm, resist the temptation to look at her eggs, but she finally wins the battle of wills and drives us to our tent. The bugs are so bad that our retreat is a relief anyway.

We shed our clothes in the tent, but it is still too warm to be in sleeping bags. Any blackflies that came in with us have been puréed against the tent walls.

"Check this out," Marypat swings her feet toward me. Her ankles are covered with bites, welts, scabbed-over sores.

"Wow!" is all I can say. Even for blackfly country her wounds are impressive.

"It's those damn overalls," she tells me. "When I pee I have to take them completely off. Then when I pull them up, all the blackflies go right down to the ankle cuffs."

When it finally cools we lie belly to back in our sleeping bag liners. I can feel that warm bulge in Marypat's stomach against me as I start to drift off. Then it elbows me sharply.

"That was the Little Grebe, wasn't it?"

"Yup, it's really moving."

And it keeps moving, kneading my back with soft punches. There really are three of us here, I think. It is not a frightening or sobering thought. I am glad to be in touch, to be reminded. It is the same way I felt the first time we heard the fast, gushing heartbeat.

Outside, the tern has settled down. A ptarmigan gargles loudly, somewhere nearby.

More rapids, another lake, more insect hatches to paddle through. The bugs don't bite, but are maddening, like having spider webs constantly breaking across your face. From miles away we can see a striking sand esker. On the map this glacial legacy snakes across twenty-five miles. It very nearly cuts the lake in two. Only a narrow channel of water breaches the ridge.

The opportunity for an easy walk and a view is too much to resist. On the gravelly crest a steady breeze keeps the bugs down. We walk along it for a bit, then find we can't stop. A northern shrike perches in a lone, half-dead tree. Wolf scat marks the trail. I keep watching for the brown shape of grizzly in the willow bottoms, the dark opening of a wolf den in the sand, caribou antlers moving against skyline.

When I turn to look back our canoe is a tiny red speck at the waterfront. More sand ridges lead off invitingly, erratic boulders the size of cars lie around like furniture set down randomly on the tundra floor. Thunderheads build in the afternoon sky, the view is mottled with lakes and streams, seamed by eskers.

The indescribable vastness is made real by the knowledge that there is no fence to climb over in another mile, that no village lurks beyond the hill, no road or train track penetrates here. It is unlikely, in fact, that any other human being is within one hundred miles of us.

When we are almost back to the canoe Marypat spots a large piece of wood in the moss by the water. Wood of that size is a rarity, here, and we scramble down for a look. Half-buried in the soft mosses lies the better part of an old weathered paddle.

The bleached piece of wood has lain on the ground a long time, long enough to embed itself in the spongy tundra. The shaft is broken and warped, so we can't tell if it was half of a kayak paddle or most of a canoe paddle. The tip of the blade is snapped, but still attached, as if a wandering caribou stepped on it.

I hold it in my hands. The dried, weathered wood weighs nothing, like a husk. What other hands closed around that shaft of wood? Where did it take its owner? Had it been held by an Inuit, Chipewyan, white man? Was it left at a grave, next to a kayak stand? Had it been washed down by floods after a capsize?

Marypat puts the paddle back in its perfect mossy mould, and we take up our new paddles, smooth and finished. But my callused palms hold a lingering memory of the cracked, lichen-encrusted wood, long after the esker is out of sight.

42

ACROSS OUR ROUTE lies a band of islands, peppering the lake. It looks, on the 1:250,000-scale map, like a swath of the Milky Way thrown over the water, just that dense. It is my day to navigate.

The air is still, but sultry. Huge thunderheads have been building up since the early morning. Hard showers force us into rain gear, and force me to hide the map under the decking. There are times when the map-reading is so challenging that we don't even paddle while it's raining, because I'll lose my concentration. If we pass one point without consulting the map, a tiny bay, slip around an island, I'll lose our position completely. There is no end to the blind alleys and convoluted detours we could spend the day exploring in search of the outlet.

Four miles are represented by each inch on the topographic sheet, so it doesn't take long to go badly wrong. Some substantial islands show up as tiny dots, and smaller islands may not be there at all. My strategy is to ignore the islands altogether, and to keep track of mainland points and bays instead. This is tricky enough, and there are spots in which islands are the only thing to go by, but I keep track pretty well for about two-thirds of the way through the maze. Then I become confused.

All of a sudden a point appears where it shouldn't, then a pair of islands instead of three. The rain squalls are growing more intense, harder to ignore, all the time.

"I know roughly where we are, I think, but if we can find a current, we should just follow that."

The lake splits around a point and there is current heading down both sides. I have no idea which is better, pick the one that seems to have the most water.

"See," I try to explain my confusion, "there's supposed to be a long skinny island right there, not three little ones. And I have no idea why the current goes that way too. It should be a dead-end bay."

Thunder booms overhead, and the rain comes down in distinct pellets.

"I think we better just go to shore, wherever we are, and wait this one out," Marypat says.

I look over and can see the wind rushing toward us across the water, raising waves. We get to a sharp, rocky shoreline just as the storm hits. Waves are whipped up instantly. The thunder claps hard and close, like a physical blow. Rain falls like hail. The boat is going wild, and it is all I can do to keep us off the rocks while waves crash one after another over the side.

"Al!" Marypat shouts. "Let's get in those willows." She points a little way off to a section of willows growing in shallow water. "We're gonna wreck the boat if we stay here."

The willows are, indeed, much better, once we fight our way into them. The water is only a few inches deep, and the vegetation calms the waves. But platinum forks of lightning light up the black sky. The thunder is so loud it hurts our ears. Every minute or two I dump another gallon of rainwater out of my spray skirt.

Humility is the only conceivable response. Even our posture is humble – heads bowed, hands tucked in our pockets. We can't talk, can only wait for it to end. This kind of awe hardly ever confronts us in society. We just close the windows, nudge up the thermostat, and go back to making dinner. But there is an exhilaration that flowers in these exposed moments, a fierceness, an affirmation, along with the acceptance of powerlessness.

When the storm moves on, still booming in the distance, we gather ourselves and resume our difficult navigation.

"Do you think the Stowaway was awake, listening to all that?" Marypat asks.

"If it wasn't, it can't hear anything. I wonder if it was scared."

For a time we paddle blindly, following the current where we can find it, trying to make sense of landforms.

"Sometimes a map is more trouble than help," I say. "You get so sucked in to this tiny focus and forget the big picture. Then, when you lose it, you're really confused."

Eventually the topography resembles something I think I can match on the map. The lake narrows to a wide channel, the branches of the watercourse come together. We are out of the thicket of islands. Black storms keep rolling through, none as strong as the big one, but respectable all the same, and we eat a hurried lunch on a mid-stream rock, with the bowline tied off to my ankle.

In camp, lighting a fire is difficult enough to warrant a curl of birchbark from Marypat's gift bag, and we have to sprint for the tent with our pot of macaroni and cheese, *al dente*, to avoid another deluge.

There are times when I see Marypat's potbellied profile and wonder what the hell we are doing here – hundreds of miles from anywhere, running rapids, sitting unprotected under torrential rains, heaving packs around. Marypat has her occasional pangs of doubt, and I have these bad moments. It doesn't help that she admits to muscle spasms in her back, greater fatigue than she expected. Yet she is stubborn about taking her days in the stern, doing her share of work.

The thunderstorms are followed by a spate of what I think of as classic Barren Lands weather. Cool, grey, windy – conditions that accentuate the desolation of the land, remind me that winter is just momentarily offstage. We wear jackets and wool hats.

Progress is possible only because the lakes are narrow and we can hug the lee shore. Even there, three-quarters of my effort in the stern is spent hewing to a straight course.

I keep trying to pin down what it is that makes the Barrens such stunning wilderness. Words don't do it, pictures don't do it. It is being there, weeks from seeing humans, with chapped hands and wind in the face, the glacially bulldozed hills rolling away, waves torqueing the canoe. Mile after mile after mile.

For the first time an inukshuk cairn marks a hillside. Below it, a bench of land offers what appears to be a likely summer camp for former residents of the region, but there are no tent rings, nothing to indicate the ancient, yet recent, people.

Later in the day it is Marypat's turn to be confused. More islands speck the lake surface, and she heads us confidently to the end of a blind bay before she realizes her mistake.

"Let's camp here," I suggest, referring to a bald glacial knoll. There is plenty of travel time left in the day, but I am holding back, savouring our exploration. This system of little rivers and lakes that began so unspectacularly is coming to an end too soon.

When we are set up Marypat climbs into the tent. It has become her pattern, this summer. She escapes the bugs, strips off her clothes, doodles in her journal, naps. We understand without discussion that this is her daily sanctuary, her private space. Mine is by the fire. I am a chronic fire-fiddler, poking at it, shifting wood, studying the patterns of flame and wood grain. A cup of coffee in hand, sitting on an ammo can that holds the camera, maps, journals, insect repellent, hanging out as if I were on a front porch on a lazy summer afternoon.

If it is my map day, I mark our progress, our campsite location, tot up the mileage. I might write some notes. More often than not I simply sit, stir the flames, stay quiet. It is the biggest luxury of our journey, this stillness.

This river has never become very big, but now it is full and fresh. The rapids are respectable and fun. They carry us down with increasing speed toward better-known country. From the final fast stretch the big lake that marks the end is visible, spreading below us.

The river current slowly dissipates until we are ploughing through the dead-flat lake. The weather has turned suddenly hot and heavy. The bugs are bad again, even far from land. Strangely, neither of us wants to lose sight of the river outlet. We need to say goodbye to that flowage we now know from its first weedy trickle that is more land than river, to this strong, heady finish.

The heat motivates us to brave the numbing water and voracious mosquitoes long enough to bathe. We are pink, juicy morsels for the insect world until our clothes are back on, and the water is only a couple of degrees free of ice. I discover blackfly bites all around my hat-line, at my ankles, covering the back of my neck like a warning in Braille.

It doesn't take a meteorologist to know a weather change is coming, it is unmistakably in the heavy, baited air. By evening it is raining gently. Inside the tent I retrace our route on the maps. It is somehow very important that I remember this backwater place.

Rain is a comforting, soft sound against the roof. The air is calm. Birds don't even bother to curtail their loud busyness with territory and nests and foraging for food. There are, in fact, only a few grey-light hours in the night when it is truly quiet. When I wake in those hours it takes a while to place what is missing, as if my eyes have opened in a strange room.

By morning it is winter again.

VIII

ACROSS THE BARRENS

43

AFTER A GOOD string of travelling days, some time spent in camp, even trapped inside a tent, is a vacation – rest well earned, a break in the routine.

"On days like today," Marypat says, "our tent feels like a little womb, a protective skin."

"Funny you should choose that image," I say, although it fits exactly.

A laundry line hangs above our sleeping bags, draped with socks, underwear, shorts. Wet snow splats against the roof and sticks to the ground. The birds are quieted by the storm, keeping eggs warm in nests that are little more than scraped depressions, huddled against the penetrating damp.

Our sleeping bags are warm cocoons in which we read books, jot down notes, study maps. The peaty mattress beneath us is comfortable and soft. Crouched in the tent door I boil water on the stove outside, and we sip our morning coffee. Back home I'd shudder at the thought of being out, being exposed, on such a day. But it is decidedly cozy, actually pleasant.

By the second day, our vacation begins to feel a good deal

more like detention. Squalls keep racing through, dropping rain and sleet. The wind hasn't lulled once, and we can watch the boiling lake through our front door. The waves have that dangerous, cold look – blue-grey, snarling with white, smashing the shore.

It is cold and wet enough that we curtail our forays outside. Birds flush up underfoot, fly a few yards, and disappear again into the shag of moss. The tent that was so snug and comfortable the first day is more and more confining, dank, littered with gear.

"I keep reminding myself," Marypat says, "how wonderful it was the day we finished the river and came riding down those last rapids to the calm lake. How great I felt."

On the third morning, overly rested and fed up with the sedentary life, we are up very early, preparing to leave. The clouds are more scattered, the rains have stopped, and the wind is down enough that whitecaps are rare.

Our tent is packed up and we're hurrying through breakfast when I notice the breeze rising again. I ignore it, but in a matter of minutes it is undeniable; the lake is again alive with froth and watery hills.

"Look at it!" I explode.

"It's not the lake's fault," Marypat says, trying to calm me. "We'll just go on in the evening lull, if we're even still here."

We *are* still here in the evening, and there is no calm. We have taken strolls around the large island, watched birds, made elaborate wind screens behind which to cook meals. As prisons go, this is a pretty attractive one, but it's still a prison.

Much of the day my thoughts have been on the Inuit who peopled this tundra until the 1950s. I imagine a summer camp set in a place like this: people in caribou-skin tents sharing gossip and stories, eating dried fish and caribou, making love, enjoying the respite from bugs. Or, perhaps, getting on with their work. Clothed to keep out the weather, busy with hunting or fishing, or engaged in the endless gathering of scarce fuel for fires. They were, certainly, less cowed by bad weather, although I doubt they'd have gone out on the lake in a wind like this.

Marypat must be thinking along similar lines, because suddenly she suggests making an offering.

I'm sceptical, curmudgeonly, but go along for the diversion. Then, as we actually start to perform this spontaneous, unrehearsed ceremony, it gathers a kind of solemnity and power.

We take dried caribou meat given to us by a Chipewyan woman from Black Lake. Standing at the water's edge, in the spray of breaking waves, I strip pieces of meat, hold them high, then let the wind snatch them away. I find myself talking.

"We ask for safe passage through this land. We offer meat that has come from here. We ask this with respect and with humility."

Marypat does the same, saying, "Help guide us the true way. Remind us who we are and where we are. Accept our gift."

What I had considered, at the start, as a silly exercise, seems, when we finish, to have weight and a calming meaningfulness. I don't try to analyze it further, but it feels like we've done something right.

Offering or no, another day dawns with unabated winds. By this time I have grown philosophical. While wind tugs at the tent I nest against Marypat's back, placing my hand on her belly, and feel the movements of the Stowaway answering my touch.

The sound of air tearing over unsheltered ground, driving the water against shore, has become so constant and unceasing that I have forgotten what calm is like. The wind is as inexorable as gravity – streaming down the land.

On the fifth morning we escape, but it is a near thing. The gale has calmed, and the waves are reduced to small hills, without the snowy, dangerous crests. We only napped through the night and are up even before the sun. A crescent moon hangs like a cutout in the sky, a keyhole into distant brilliance. We have a

Dutch-oven coffeecake saved for breakfast, which we agree to eat later on.

Within half a mile the wind is building again. Whitecaps blink here and there, then multiply. It is very cold. I wear gloves, a wool hat, jacket and windbreaker, and am still barely warm. We paddle grimly up one side of a headland, each ignoring the impulse to stop again and get out of these waves. As we round the rocky promontory, our adversary pushes more and more from behind. Then, for a time, we are sheltered by a low ridge.

In that protected lull the first caribou of summer comes to view. A lone bull keeps pace with us along the shoreline. He is as curious as we are. As Marypat takes pictures he poses broadside, antlers limned against sky, prances closer, then jogs ahead. This is the first large animal of the trip, and its appearance makes me sanguine about being out in these conditions.

"Let's have breakfast," Marypat suggests.

It is too cold to sit down and relax. We gobble coffeecake with gloves on, pace to stay warm, then scurry back to the boat. There the wind greets us again, full on. A whimbrel shoots past downwind, its long bill like some prehistoric artifact. Seeing this other life abroad, today, is momentarily cheering.

"Al, this is ridiculous!"

We have inched ahead several miles, but it is brutal labour, slamming into wave after wave. The wind is unrelenting, like something solid and muscular, without remorse.

"I know. It's bad." The shoreline is all riven rock, broken hills. "But if we can get down this bay, then turn east, I think we'll get more of a tailwind."

Marypat just sits there, looking ahead. We are holding ourselves in place against a boulder. "Who knows what the wind will do," she says. "It could just whip around a hill and be in our face again."

"If it is, we'll stop. But if we can get a tailwind farther along, maybe we can get off this lake. It's kept up for five days without a break. If we can move at all, it seems like we should."

I almost give in once more before we turn the corner. Then we pause again to decide how to proceed. The best angle, with the wind behind us, will aim us at a point two miles away. Two miles of heaving, cold lake. The boat wallows under us, waiting.

"Are you game?" I ask.

"We've worked pretty damned hard to get here," Marypat says, still not committing.

I pry the stern more in line with the waves, feel them start to roll under us. Wind plasters my coat against my back, as if I am a sail. My face suddenly feels warm and tingling, sheltered. Then we just start paddling.

After the torturous pace, the boat seems to scream ahead. Wave after wave hurls us forward. The bow comes clear of water all the way back to where Marypat is sitting. Then, in the trough, we seem to stop altogether before the next ridge throws us on. But the point still takes forever to come near.

We are a mile from shore and I keep turning away from the seduction of fear. As long as the waves are lined up behind us, and roll uniformly, I am confident and in control. Once in a while, though, a rogue wave is uncommonly steep and violent with us. Sometimes our angle is wrong and water slaps us broadside. It is sickening to feel this offhanded power, these little slaps, chilling reminders of our insignificance.

I am tormented by a vision in which our boat is turtled over and we come thrashing free in the numbing water, where we are roughed up by waves, and swallow gulps of the lake. There are three of us. Marypat and me in our bright life vests, and, also, this tiny entity that has no say in our choices, but, like us, is dying.

To diffuse the dark image I think about what my response would be, how to survive. If I am quick enough, I might right the boat before the decking lets in much water. Then I would stabilize the canoe long enough for Marypat to climb in and bail. Perhaps, then, I could hoist myself right over the stern, while Marypat braces.

It is not a strategy I want to test. Better not to think, just concentrate rigidly on each wave that catches us. But the image returns with every bad moment, like a slide flashed starkly on a screen – the three of us floundering in the dark water, my eyes finding Marypat's, having no way to tell her what she means to me.

It is physical and emotional exhaustion that finally makes us stop. That and the unceasing wind. But we have reached the river outlet, come more than twenty miles, and the day has hardly started. As soon as the tent is up, we pile in for a nap. A cold rain drums overhead as I drift to sleep.

"I feel really bad about saying this," Marypat begins, "but there were times, yesterday, when I just wished we were home."

"It was the first time I was afraid since paddling Lake Atha-basca," I agree. "But it's *still* windy. If we had missed that little lull, we'd be stuck back there still, starting our sixth day!"

Even in the more sheltered narrows the wind is a tough adversary. It is warmer today, and the sun breaks through now and again, but every foot is a battle.

It is afternoon by the time we reach Angikuni Lake, near the spot where we would have arrived on the Kazan River if we had taken the other arm out of Ennadai Lake. Here the winds again have long open reaches to work with.

I distract myself from the work by thinking of Samuel Hearne. In the fall of 1770, six years before the American Declaration of Independence, he traipsed through here on his way back to Hudson Bay after a season of exploring with Indian guides. He was twenty-five years old.

He had been travelling since late February, often going days at a time without food, through every imaginable weather. His quest was the Coppermine River, and the rumoured wealth of ore said to be there. He got nowhere close to the Coppermine, but explored a huge circuit through Barren Lands country that was as yet unpenetrated by white men.

"Provisions still continued plentiful well into September," Hearne writes of this segment of his travels, "which was a singular piece of good fortune, and the only happy circumstance of that part of the journey, for the weather was remarkably bad, and severely cold. We were in a forlorn state as we continued to the south-east. . . ."

We are here in July, and the weather isn't exactly balmy. He was two months further into the season, had been living almost entirely off of the land, and had already been out seven months. I have read that there is a marker somewhere in this area, left by Hearne more than two hundred years ago. We pull in to explore in several spots, as much to escape the wind as anything. On a low rise there are several prominent inukshuk cairns and an old meat cache made of stone, but that is all.

Hearne reached Fort Prince of Wales (now Churchill, Manitoba) in winter conditions on November 25, "having been absent from it for eight months and twenty-two days upon a fruitless . . . journey."

Not two weeks later, on December 7, Hearne set off again for the Coppermine. This time he succeeded, although he would find no significant bodies of copper, and would be gone in the wilds more than a year and a half.

Before he was thirty Hearne had walked nearly five thousand miles of unexplored country, with no companions other than the Natives he met, some of whom he employed as guides. Much of the territory he saw wouldn't be travelled again by white men until the 1920s.

Modern adventures, aided by advanced communications, air support, all manner of fancy gear, seem contrived and insignificant compared to Hearne's. It is hard to find enough room to disappear for a month, let alone years at a time.

But the ancient land, the winds blocking our path, the deadly cold water, are all the same. We pitch our lonely camp on a point of smooth rock. It has been windy for a week, and another long lake is ahead.

44

I AWAKE KNOWING something's wrong, then I sit up and listen. No waves crashing, no airy roar. Nothing. I am dressed and outside in minutes. The lake is an undulating plain. Fog nestles in the hills. The bugs are back. I light the morning fire casually, with one match, without having to lie down next to it as a wind screen while cupping tinder in my hands to protect the first flame.

"Give me a hand, will ya?" Marypat calls from the tent.

Heaving herself around has become more of a chore. Sometimes she asks me to push her from behind so she can sit up in the tent. Before she settles down next to the fire she makes sure she has within reach everything she might possibly need. The endless bending and squatting involved in setting up camp, moving things, feeding the fire, has become the most difficult part of our wilderness life for her.

"I'm beginning to understand what pregnant women mean about bending over," she tells me. "It's like you have this ball attached in front of you that won't ever get out of the way. I don't know how obese people can stand it."

She is increasingly preoccupied with the portages coming up in a few days. There are three of them in a row around a series of rapids and falls, and she worries that she won't be able to cope.

As we begin paddling, we talk about her fear. Benign clouds float in the sky, reflected on the smooth lake. It is quickly warm, the fog burns off. A sandhill crane patrols along a ridgeline, a black sentinel against the pellucid sky.

"Look, MP, we just have to take our time. It'll be nice if you can carry things, but if you can't, I'll just make more trips. Big deal. It'll be good for me."

"I think I can carry my packs," she says. "I *want* to carry my packs. I'm not into hanging out while you take everything across like some Sherpa."

"Fine, but don't get competitive about it. Nobody's going to question your strength or stamina. It's already pretty amazing that you're doing the trip at all. Why push it?"

"I know. I know. I just would really like to do my share."

"Well, it isn't worth losing the baby to say you took your load, for Christ's sake. If you can't do it, you can walk back and forth with me, keep me company."

On the windy days we hardly talk, are absorbed by the battle, involved with our own thoughts. But the calm miles present their own challenges. Paddling is an endless, steady rhythm. There is nothing to fight against, no anxieties to overcome, nothing but the mirrored water and the miles of passing shoreline.

On these quiet days we exhaust every topic we can think of. All the while we gather the distance like wealth, gluttonous for the smooth going. Ice-scoured points, shallow bays, lovely islands, pass one after another. I keep waiting for the wind to rise again, but we are within a few miles of the river outlet before waves start building up. The lake crossing is essentially behind us by the time we set up camp below a series of ridgetop inukshuk markers.

There is a pool of sun-warmed water in the bedrock, where we bathe for the first time in a week. When I look at Marypat's body, framed in the rock bathtub, I see how she has been taken over by the life she is creating. Her belly is round and taut, and all her movements, even her expressions, are infused with the serious joy of growing a baby. She is made distant by it, as if always listening to an interior melody.

The bitterness of our trial years has evaporated, along with the rest of the encumbrances with which we began this journey. The grating sharpness in our arguments is gone. The wilderness, the months alone, the shared struggle, have absorbed all that.

Not with any program of therapy, not even with any clear intention. It has, simply, been washed away by this immersion.

"Let's walk the ridge," Marypat suggests after dinner.

These bedrock elevations are irresistible, especially when rock cairns built by the Inuit stand on them. The walking is easy along the smooth surface. Long corridors of low hills here and there lead my eyes into the distance, almost commanding the feet to follow.

An arctic ground squirrel scolds from its rocky burrow. The vast lake we have crossed today stretches away, mile after blue mile. On a knoll we stand next to the cairns built by another race, people from another existence altogether: a life of winter starvation and smoke-filled tents, of killing swimming caribou from kayaks and eating the raw meat.

And yet, we have things in common. Our eyes share this same scene. We both know the watery trails through this country, have hunched into the same implacable winds, perhaps felt the same satisfaction in putting miles behind us, finding a good camp, scavenging enough fuel for a fire.

"I like having them watch over us," Marypat says, nodding at the cairns when we are back in camp. The piles of rock stand mute, primitive, even crude. But unspeakably eloquent, unimpeachably appropriate.

By the next evening we are at the start of the three portages, camped in the mist of the first tremendous rapid. The winds have returned, but we have had the current of the Kazan as our ally and have come nearly forty miles in spite of them.

The river has grown huge since we paddled it near the source, since that first day when we passed the fishing expedition, the only people we've seen. It is broad and deep, now, a superhighway of current, running unchecked and formidable.

The only blemish on the day has been finding of a cache of empty gas drums on the riverbank. It was the first intrusion of twentieth-century trash, a garish and enduring pile of metal,

destined to rust away through the centuries, dregs of fuel drib-
bling off into the tundra.

Pilots flying to a remote place like this carry the extra barrels
of fuel necessary for their return trip. Then, once they've
pumped them dry, they leave them there on the ground, as if the
trouble of throwing the empties back on board is too much. Better to scar the landscape with their garbage for a lifetime or two.

I spend a long time hunting for firewood for the night. Driftwood is scarce and the dead willow branches are no thicker than
pencils. The rapid is a steady thunder, pulling my eyes toward it
again and again, that deadly plummet of fluid weight slamming
down the face of rock. Watching the endless stampede of river is
as mesmerizing as gazing into flames. Suddenly I realize that I've
been in a trance, ignoring my pot of lentil stew, hypnotized by
the elemental power.

Marypat is preparing for tomorrow. She fidgets with the
packs, tinkering with her loads, while I patch my canvas pants
by the tiny fire. She is more competitive with herself than is
good for her, I think, but saying anything will do no good.

The next morning, though, I speak my thoughts.

"Look, let's just take it slow, take as long as we need to."

The packs are huge, bulky things. I hoist Marypat's up for her,
and she shrugs it on, suddenly dwarfed.

"If anything hurts, if it feels like too much, drop it right away.
I don't care if I have to carry every blessed paddle across. Okay?"

She hasn't been listening, looks up from adjusting the straps
and nods vaguely. I watch her start off through the short willows
– this pregnant, stubborn, strong woman. And I think again
how alone we are.

The second portage is the long one, a mile or more around a
falls. I keep asking my partner how she's doing, and she keeps
nodding her head. From underneath the canoe I watch her feet
leading the way in front of me. Blackflies swarm in at my head. I
see wolf tracks in some mud, what looks like a grizzly print, and
the confusion of beaten caribou trails. Every time I carry a canoe

I am reminded that it is a craft meant for water, not land. It grinds down against my neck and shoulders, catches on bushes, torques sideways in the breeze.

On the return for more packs Marypat admits to some discomfort for the first time.

"I'm sure it's nothing," she says, "but I got kind of a stitch low down in my belly. It feels better now, but it was painful."

"Okay, I'll just carry the rest while you walk it off," I say, sounding adamant.

"We'll see."

Back at the packs Marypat goes right for her next load.

"Marypat, at least carry the little day pack this time. Let me get the big ones."

"I feel better." She is strapping a life vest on top. "I think it was the waist belt. I'll just leave it really loose."

"I'm not going to fight you. You know how you're doing. But I really don't mind the extra trip. In fact, it would make me feel a lot better if I took it."

"Help me up with it. If it starts again, I'll quit."

I mutter with frustration the whole time, but she ignores me, sets off at her slow pace while I scurry to load up and catch her.

At the third portage she is still insistent, determined, and I have given up my solicitations. Caribou hair lies along the shoreline like a furry bathtub ring. The carcass of one of the deer is washed up on shore, stinking up the place. It must have been dragged over the falls, unable to make the crossing.

Where the portage ends there is a big ledge of snow left in a shady spot. We set the canoe on it and walk to a spot overlooking the last rapid to have lunch. Marypat hobbles like an old woman, hands against her lower back.

"My bones feel all sloppy," she says. "Like the sockets can't hold them in. I think my hips have really spread apart." I just look at her, shake my head. She is clearly proud of herself, exhausted but proud.

"Let's just float this afternoon, camp early," I suggest.

The river continues its downhill canter. Another ten miles whip by while we do nothing but steer. I sing beer commercials and bird-watch while Marypat dozes. The island we camp on looks as if it is regularly bulldozed every spring. Our firewood consists of the dead willow bushes that have been ripped up by ploughs of ice.

"I just felt the Little Grebe moving," Marypat says, before we go to bed. "It's nice, after a strenuous day like today, to feel it move again."

I take a last look around before entering the tent, and notice that the shoreline is alive. Caribou, thousands of them, carpet the view. Now that I see them, I can hear them as well: faint wheezes and grunts from the milling herd.

There are a great many newborn calves among the adults, tiny spindly things mimicking the moves of their mothers. In the grey evening light we sit on the stony edge of the island, watching the spectacle. The deer keep coming over the horizon, antlers bobbing along like a leafless, marching forest. The herd pushes upriver, seems to be looking for a place to cross. If we had gone to bed a few minutes earlier we would have missed this. How many things *have* we missed?

Caribou travel constantly over thousands of miles – north to their calving grounds in the Arctic each spring, south to the shelter of boreal forests every winter. All summer they move and graze, swim rivers, outrun wolves and grizzly bears, across the trackless expanse. It is another of those unappreciated miracles that they pass on, from generation to generation, this knowledge of place, this mental map of river crossings, sheltered spots, safe places to bear young, in a home the size of Alaska.

45

THE KAZAN IS really charging now. Ice-wracked shoreline clicks past like a scene outside a train window. The river makes big-water sounds, even in calm stretches. Waves snarl over obstacles, eddies suck things into their vortex, and beneath the watery rush, the thudding of rocks being moved, one roll at a time, down to the sea.

In rapids the noise intensifies, focusses our attention on the dangers. Reefs of stone jut into the current like half-completed dams overwhelmed by the river. Big sets of waves slap the canoe around. We run them, scout them, line the boat past the edge of a big hole, work our way along, a tiny dot of red colour in an ocean of green and blue and brown. At the same time we are full of ourselves, big with confidence and assurance built up over weeks of self-sufficient travel.

A gyrfalcon rises off a bank of pushed-up rock, flies over us with fast wingbeats, strong and predatory. For miles the river is an amusement ride, a gigantic water slide in a tumult of noise and motion. We giggle out loud at the joy of it.

This is why we come. We are alive here. Alive and sharp and strong and alone in the stunning space, a space in which we count for no more than caribou or wolf or lemming.

Where we camp, overlooking a loud rapid, I find the fresh tracks of a grizzly in the sand. I go on collecting driftwood, but idly follow the big-tracked trail along the shore. The prints veer up the bank and are lost in the mosses. Claw marks rake the mud where the bear heaved itself up, over the edge.

I resist the fear that starts up in my chest, the response, ever since our deadly confrontation with a bear on the Athabasca River, that always rises up. It is there, simmering inside, but I resist it. The bear lives here. We are passing through, intending no harm. And anyway, in the din of the rapids we would never hear a grizzly come upon us, so why dwell on it? I don't mention it to Marypat.

The tracks are still on my mind as I sit quietly by the fire the next morning. Marypat is snoozing in the tent while I sip coffee and stir the flames, thinking of the day ahead. And the grizzly is the first thing that flashes into my mind when I turn my head and catch sight of a large brown animal not fifteen feet behind me.

Perhaps, on another day, when the tracks weren't fresh in my memory, I could be cool enough to turn quietly and calmly, to greet this visitor without agitation. Instead I leap up, turn 180 degrees in mid-air, and let out a startled shout. It is not a grizzly, but a lone adult caribou who is just as surprised as I am, and comes to a crashing, loose-kneed halt. It hesitates, no doubt still intent on the drink of river water it was absent-mindedly anticipating.

We stare at each other. Then it tosses its head and trots back the way it came, slipping, stopping frequently to look back at the strange, excitable apparition that erupted out of the peaceful tundra. I turn back to the dying fire, chuckling at myself, my heart galloping in my throat.

The bugs are bad again, and we opt for a floating lunch, lounging in the canoe. Black scoter and goldeneye swim alongside, another pair of tundra swans watch from a quiet cove.

"Check those rocks out with the binos," Marypat says, interrupting my siesta. Several times each day we are fooled by animal-shaped rocks. Downstream there are some dark blots on the shore, but when I lazily focus on them I discover they are in fact musk ox, the first herd of summer.

The river carries us closer. There are a good number of animals lying in the willows, and as the canoe approaches, a big adult heaves to its feet to stare at us. One or two more stand up. We are very close now, the head of the nearest bull filling the frame of the camera. All of us, human and musk ox, feel the tension build. The whole herd, twenty or more, is up and facing us, waiting for some signal, a sudden move. Some of the animals browse on willows, stripping leaves off the branches with sharp upward tugs of their heads.

Then the lead bull gives a loud snort and the whole band whirls and gallops away, with massive heads held high. Their short legs whicker through the willows, hooves thump across the ground, dark skirts of hair flow in the wind.

The herd runs a short distance, regroups, then charges away again. They disappear in depressions, rise up again on ridges, a swirl of brown motion in the green and grey space.

It isn't so much the sight of these tundra beasts that is invigorating. It is the idea that these animals live in an untainted, unfenced, unregulated land, a land that they have evolved around and thrive in, both winter and summer. And that we have taken nearly a month to penetrate to this remove.

It is the immediacy of it – that warning snort, the rush of legs through willows, the musty animal odour, the way they fade into the immensity of their home.

We watch the animals until they are distant specks. The willow branches they were feeding on are stripped of leaves, the bark shredded. Fresh, glistening droppings lie amongst the round hoof prints.

We arrive at the watery expanse of Yathkyed Lake. Yathkyed means "Where the snow lies," and Thierry Mallet was here one July when the ice was solid from shore to shore. To occupy his time he climbed a nearby hill, several miles inland.

> I reached the summit at last . . . and there I found an Eskimo grave . . . entirely made out of loose rocks which had been brought up there by hand, one by one, and neatly piled one on top of the other, over the dead. . . .
>
> At the head of it, a few feet away, a spear stood erect, stuck

deep in the ground and solidly wedged in at the base between heavy rocks. The point was of native copper. From it fluttered, in rags, the remains of a deerskin coat.

At the foot lay, side by side, a kayak with its paddle and harpoon and a twenty-foot sleigh with its set of dog harness and a snow knife. . . .

On the grave itself I found a rifle, a small kettle with a handful of tea leaves inside, a little wooden box containing ten cartridges, a pipe, a plug of tobacco, matches, a knife, a small telescope, and a neatly coiled rawhide belt. . . .

I tried to picture to myself the faithful companions of the deceased hunter struggling up that hill, bearing on their shoulders the rigid body of their dead; their search for those hundreds of rocks, and the work of piling them, one by one, for hours and hours, until the mound was able to defy the efforts of the wild animals and the incessant pressure of the years to come; finally the long descent to the camp, to bring up again, one by one, the precious belongings of the deceased.

To me, there alone, leaning on that grave on the top of that immense hill, the whole undertaking seemed incredible . . . not only to choose that almost inaccessible spot to lay their dead to rest, but to abandon unhesitatingly on his grave that wealth of articles which I knew represented an immense value to them, in their constant bitter struggle for mere existence.

Yathkyed Lake is ice-free for us, but the day has turned cold. The miles are a slow toil through choppy waves. By the time we stop for the day on a small island, Marypat is cranky with the effort of sterning and has been agitating to call it quits for some time.

Once the tent is up, Marypat disappears into her sanctuary while I roam the rocky coast looking for driftwood and willow and whatever else might be found. The sight of the galloping musk ox keeps coming back as I look out on the rough lake and the sweep of glacially scoured land.

Starvation is the most common cause of death for the musk ox, as it was for the traditional Inuit. Storms and cold have little effect on them. Their insulating coats shield them from the worst blizzards. Wolves aren't often successful in killing healthy animals. Human beings, who brought the species almost to extinction, slaughtering them for their hides, are now banned from hunting them. What kills them is thick ice crusted over their forage.

Musk ox move snow aside with their noses, or they paw through with their hooves. Sometimes they even use their chins to pound at hard snow. But a bad freezing rain or extended cold after a wet snow can defeat their most desperate efforts. Unless the armour softens the musk ox will rapidly waste away and die in great numbers.

Cold winds rise during the night, and by morning the small island is a rock breakwater battered by waves. Wool hats and gloves are sensible breakfast attire. Hot drinks cool as fast as we can gulp them down. Yathkyed is the second largest lake in the Barrens, next to Dubawnt, and there is no sense taking her on in a bad mood.

The passage between our island camp and the main shore is sheltered, so we take the empty canoe across to explore and hunt for firewood. It could as easily be October as mid-July, except for the dwarf wildflowers that nod and twist in the wind and, borne on the gusts, the guttural talk of sandhill cranes. Here and there the sticklike profiles of the tall birds stalk along the ridgelines.

The ground is a thin mantle of spongy moss and tufts of wiry grass insulating permafrost. In every hollow water lies atop this impermeable layer, so that cross-country walks inevitably mean wet feet. From a low ridge the rugged, serrated shoreline of this huge lake extends to grey horizons. Patches of snow linger in protected gullies, islands withstand the onslaught of waves. I have forgotten how far into the trip we are, and don't care.

The next morning we are let free, although the lake is still rough, the air still fresh. It is a day-long game of tactics with the wind, keeping to the lee side of islands, the best angle of canoe and wave. Our shoulders and wrists feel every one of the twenty miles we cross to another waterside camp on another bed of moss and lichen and dwarf willow. We find caribou trails, goose feathers, the skull of a weasel, and ptarmigan call out alarms or greetings.

And the next day there is more wind, a swampy portage across a neck of low land at the end of Yathkyed. The portage is so wet at the start that we take off our shoes and wade through the muck to get the gear to drier land.

At one point we stop because Marypat wants to try for crane pictures. She creeps up behind a boulder, fixes the birds in her lens, when they suddenly take flight. Then into her camera frame a wolverine comes running, crossing the rough ground. The huge, ungainly birds flap after the wolverine, that "skunk bear," as old-timers call it. The birds are, one would think, no match for a wolverine in a fight, but they harass it until it disappears over a hill.

"The Grebe's awake!" Marypat leans back in the canoe seat after a particularly strong movement. She seems, when I look at her now, a little Buddha-like, with her round, perfect belly.

"I think it's good we're coming out before too long," she says. "It isn't painful, but it sure can be uncomfortable."

The weather is still cool, the sky threatening, so when we make camp we hurry efficiently through the chores and start dinner.

"Yup, it's getting harder every day," Marypat says, straightening up from a tent stake.

But then the clouds break up. In the coolness the bugs are almost nonexistent. The evening light is a lambent glow, as if the land itself is radiant. Thunderheads sail in the sky, their shadows riding over the endless distance.

Much as we are together, much as we depend on each other, we are also often alone. As we paddle in concert, or sit next to each other by a fire, we are alone with our thoughts, communing with this wild place. Over this year we have attained the ability to be simultaneously separate and connected.

"This is what you can't get in a camera lens," I say, looking around. By her silence I know that Marypat agrees.

What else could I possibly need, I think.

46

THERE ARE CARIBOU on the skyline. Marypat sees them first, brown shapes trotting along the ridge, eating up the miles. More come into view, a denser stream of animals concentrated together, descending.

"I'll bet they're crossing," Marypat says, and we paddle hard to see.

The caribou press down from the ridge, straight to one site on the bank, as if this spot were the only possible crossing point. Perhaps, given their instinctive knowledge of the land, it is. They surge into the current and join the line of heads and antlers strung across the fast, blue river.

On the far side they heave up the cobble bank, shake spray, resume their trotting pace. They are powerful swimmers to hold their own in this flow. We park the canoe upstream and walk along the bank, well away from the river. Bands of caribou skirt us carefully, but without panic, simply detouring. We can hear them grunting as they run. There, in the willows, lies a freshly killed calf. Most of its head, neck, and hindquarters have been eaten, leaving a bedraggled, crimson corpse in the moss.

Caribou calves are a major source of food for both wolf and Barren Lands grizzly. Unless they are protected within a large herd, the little deer are easily separated and run down. Half a mile farther on, where we stop again to scout a rapid, there is another small carcass, also fresh, similarly devoured. Wolf tracks are embedded in the mud around it. In two stops we have encountered dead calves. How many more lie scattered over the Barrens?

Marypat has always been game for whitewater. She takes a rapid the way she takes a ski slope, grinning all the way down. But this summer she is uncharacteristically nervous.

"Maybe we should line or portage this," she says whenever we come upon bigger water – water she would normally take on without a second thought. "What do you think? Can we really do this?" As if the baby in her has overwhelmed her ability to judge.

And at the end of a rapid, normally I would get the distinct impression that if I suggested carrying the boat back up and doing it again, she wouldn't even hesitate. Now she heaves a sigh at the bottom of each run; another danger put behind us.

In a fast stretch of water we sneak up on a lone bull musk ox. The wind blows our scent back upstream, and we are only a few feet away, ghosting along, before he notices us. He is so startled that turning around he falls down. The shock must be equivalent to what we would feel coming home late at night to an alien leaping out of a closet. We'd fall down too.

He recovers, though, trots off a short distance, and stands majestically on a large flat boulder. Wind parts the hair above his nose, blows the long curtains that descend from his body. He glistens in the sun, exudes regal disdain. We see him for miles, a dark vibrant spot, later joined by another solitary animal.

Our days, our chores, the things we see, are more and more seamless, all of a piece. I sing all the time now, something I rarely do on the outside. My repertoire spans the musical spectrum, from Janis Joplin to the Kingston Trio, with a few commercial ditties thrown in. It is, in a strange way, an expression of my lust for this life, this place. It is too big to contain, so it explodes in these wacky snatches of song.

And the river bears us downhill, itself seamless. Caribou jog away, shaking their tattered summer coats like streamers. A yellow-billed loon dives in a cove where we stop for lunch. We climb a prominent rock hill for a view – and the land is all the same, rolling in every direction. At another place I lie in the middle of a tent ring, a circle of stones, now sunk into the ground, that once weighed down a caribou-skin shelter in a summer camp. The leg bones of caribou are scattered around me, cracked open so the marrow could be sucked out. Weathered remnants covered with lichen. An arctic fox hunts through the hummocks of moss, its movements erratic. Birds flush up, scolding, as it runs here and there. Then it stops, cocks its ears to listen, and pounces.

At an island campsite a herd of caribou spooks and stampedes past us, then takes to the water. I keep smelling their animal odour as I make a circuit of the island, coming up with a meagre armload of desiccated twigs, tiny dead roots, sticks that are consumed as fast as I feed them to the flames.

A huge thunderhead floats slowly toward us. It is towering, black-bottomed, and we speculate on the chances of its hitting us before we finish making our chili. Dinner and the storm come at the same time, and we sprint for the tent before it blows away. Winds buffet our shelter, but there is nowhere to hide. The two of us lean against the walls so it won't flatten on top of us. Outside there is a horizon-spanning rainbow. The evening light is golden, serene. But the winds are like a hurricane. It feels like we're in a dinghy being grazed by an ocean liner.

We are coming to the end of this odyssey. In a way it seems as if we've just arrived, that it's taken this long to really be here. We have been out for a full year, and then some, yet it's only a quick gulp of life, now that it is nearly over.

There is a funny discord in the artifacts we come across, a confluence of old and new, Stone Age and Industrial Age, that symbolizes the conflict we feel about finishing.

Jammed under a rock by the riverbank, near Forde Lake, I find the rusted remains of some old leg-hold fox traps. Forde Lake is named after a Hudson's Bay Company interpreter who was transferred to this region from northern Labrador in the early part of this century. His descendants are still prominent citizens of Baker Lake, where our trail will end.

Another jarring cache of gas barrels lies on shore. Then, an Inuit gravesite open to the elements. Human bones are mixed with caribou vertebrae. Next to the winter-beaten skull of one of my own species sits a white enamel cup with a blue rim.

Was the grave disturbed by animals, by modern people, or had it never been finished properly? Perhaps this camp was struck by smallpox, and bodies were buried hastily, in a panic, as the living fled the awful plague. We leave our own offering, more dried caribou meat, on an inukshuk overlooking Thirty Mile Lake.

At one stop we discover planks and boards strewn on the ground, fashioned to some purpose. It becomes clear that we are looking at the remains of a kayak. The long boards are remarkable enough in this treeless expanse. What journey was made to collect wood this size? More incredible still is the precise fit of the pieces, the long wooden pegs that go snugly into painstakingly drilled holes. Not a nail or screw in sight, everything fashioned simply but exactly.

Some paddler, a person possibly still alive, felt the same lift of waves on these lakes, the same twists and eddies of current through the skin of his wooden boat, worked slowly past the same shoreline.

'm getting more tired the closer we get," Marypat complains.

"No, you're more tired the more pregnant you get."

We have walked to the top of a high island, drawn by the profiles of inukshuk. Marypat is leaned over, hands on knees, catching her breath. There are spent cartridges on the ground from a .30-.30 rifle. One of the inukshuk cairns has tumbled down over the years. The heavy rocks lie at our feet.

"Maybe we should rebuild it," Marypat suggests.

But we hesitate. I have the same feeling I would at a Roman ruin if someone suggested reconstructing a broken column. There is something sacred, inviolate, about these markers. Yet we have developed a sense of kinship with the Native people, a feeling for the land, an appreciation for the rigours of their life. And I want to know what it feels like to make one.

We look over the island-filled lake, feel the strong wind that has again forced us to stop. Marypat recovers her breath. Then I heft one of the big boulders and set it up. The rock is sun-warmed and smooth, settles into place firmly. The next is almost as big, the same shade of pink granite, and it shifts unsteadily no matter how we turn it.

Marypat finds a flake of stone we can use as a stabilizing shim, and it slips neatly under one corner. The last rock is head-shaped, flat on the bottom. It grinds against the lower one, leans a little off centre, but sits firmly.

Camp is within sight of our construction. As the day ends I repeatedly look up at the rock profile. The weight of stone in my arms, the sounds of blocks grinding together, the perfect fit of the shim, are still fresh. The project elevates us from the status of museum-goers, spectators, and it feels like a thing we've earned.

Fall weather returns although it is early August. Dark, showery clouds race overhead. The familiar black water shoves us around. Near the end of Thirty Mile Lake we eat lunch at the base of a ridge of rounded cobbles, a pile of stones fifteen feet high, shoved up by ice. We are in full rain gear and have on most of our clothes.

"Another couple of weeks and these pants won't fit," Marypat says, looking down at herself. She is feeling the strain of separating bones, stretching tendons, walks more and more carefully over rough ground. Her pregnancy is the only thing pushing us to finish. In spite of that, we decide after lunch that we don't want to fight on. All afternoon and evening Marypat and I are quiet and watchful, drinking it all in as the clouds parade by and wind whips the lake.

At dawn it is another world, washed with warm sun, the water inviting. The canoe eats up the easy miles, our paddles enter the water at precisely the same instant. At one of our final portages I notice how slowly Marypat walks, how frequently she stops. But I trust her, know how much she has given already to this baby. She's just pacing herself, and I saunter alongside over the swampy ground, keeping her company.

When we are paddling again, we come upon a herd of caribou in the shallows, some distance away. They have become a common sight, almost not worth the effort of a detour, but we head over.

They stand their ground, just off shore, clustered together. The canoe glides closer and closer. I see bugs swarming around the deer, smell the dusty scent. There is hair in the water all around the boat.

The group is made up of cows and calves. As we come even closer, they pack densely together. They are all grunting. Little bleats from the calves amid the belly rumbles of the cows. It is as if they are all continuously saying, in their individual voices, "I'm here. I'm here. I'm here."

We have to backpaddle or we'd run into them. The deer are peeing and shitting in the water. Some of their insect cloud moves over to us. It is we who finally break away, paddling off when we've had enough.

The current picks up, pulls toward Kazan Falls. We both

want, for some reason, to reach them today. It is a threshold in the journey. Beyond it we enter the outside: water accessible to powerboats, hunters, air traffic.

Marypat is more nervous than ever in the rapids leading up to the falls.

"I don't mind a longer portage," she says. "Are you sure about this?"

"We can run them," I keep telling her.

But her concern makes us timid, and we cling to shore. The consequences of a mishap here are irrevocable, and the growing thunder of river powering over the brink won't let us forget it.

When we stop we are at the very lip. Mist from the concussion of water hangs around us. The noise is a drumroll of the giants, an incessant and exultant beating of careless power. I want to be in its midst, in the eye of it, close enough to feel it through the earth.

We embrace each other there, in the tumult, our boat still loaded and rocking in the wild river.

"I'll bet you're the first seven-months-pregnant woman ever to paddle to the brink of Kazan Falls," I say, in Marypat's ear.

47

I HAVE NO idea whether it's Sunday or not, and am not a churchgoer anyway, but today is sacred, a day of rest, at the cathedral of these falls. Lying next to Marypat in the morning I listen to the huge pounding weight while the Stowaway elbows and kicks my partner's belly. Is the baby churned up and excited by the muffled roar?

When we get up and begin to explore the gorge, the fir
people of summer appear over a rise. Four figures stride toward
us: an Inuit man and three boys, wearing the usual rubber boots
and armed with rifles, fishing rods, a fish spear.

"We brought you mosquitoes," the man says.

"Thanks, but we already have our own!"

He introduces himself with a formal air. "My name is John.
We're looking for caribou. The boys have never seen the falls, so
I brought them up."

"You're the first people we've seen since June," Marypat says.

The boys pay us little attention, wander off along the lip of
the cliffs. Half-a-mile wide, the river slides its gigantic bulk over
the jagged bedrock lip, froths past buttresses of rock, down into
the cliff-bound gorge. There it is a churning beast, held in a vice
of ancient, craggy bedrock. The water is green and full of upwel-
lings, steep waves, eddies like whirlpools.

A plaque commemorates the Kazan as a Heritage River, and
the message is written in both Inuit and English.

"Which are you reading?" I ask John, as we stand there.

"English," he says. "I can read both, but English is faster."

He tells us that his people came from the Garry Lake area,
along the Back River drainage. They lived in small nomadic
bands made up of several families. His history contains
inukshuk cairns like the ones we've seen, stone meat caches,
tent rings, weathered caribou bones. And the stark, open
graves. In the same life he has become a man who uses radios,
drives powerboats, eats frozen pizza, watches television.

"Maybe we'll see you in Baker Lake in a few days," I say, when
we split up.

"The ice just finished going off the lake a week ago," he says,
then saunters off after the boys.

There are more messages from the outside. In a coffee can
marked "The Brotherhood of Kazan Falls," there are notes from
trips extending back twenty years. "What about the Sister-
hood?" Marypat grumbles.

t is the familiar talk of ice and winds and portages, bad bugs nd bear problems. Some people we have heard of, some are even friends. We read both eagerly and reluctantly, because it is another sign that we are through, back in touch. We write our own story and leave it there.

The plaque, the notes, the local sightseers, make this an offi-cial beauty spot, a Niagara of the North. It is the most stupen-dous place on our year-long route, but it is the less impressive sights along the way that are in my thoughts all day – the places where we stood together and looked out over some lonely, unvisited, unremarkable scene. Memories of places that already make me yearn for them, like a man far from home.

And after we make love there, late in the afternoon, in our well-worn portable home, I remember the years of thwarted hopes, painful emotions, ugliness, that preceded our journey. It is like recalling a difficult adolescence, a distant time of suffocat-ing frustration.

Winds beat at the tent during the night and when I emerge in the morning my hat is snatched off and blown fifteen yards away. The final portage of the voyage, nearly two miles long, is ahead of us. Before that, though, it takes both of us to pin down and roll up the tent. The stove sputters for an age before water boils, and the whole time we're sprinting after escaping belongings.

When I try to swing the canoe over my head the wind catches it halfway up and rips it out of my grasp. I try again, manage to get under the boat, but am spun around like a weather vane.

"There's no way!" I shout, stumbling under the weight.

"Here, let me grab it," Marypat trots after me and takes hold of the stern loop.

"Hey! What are you doing?"

"Just holding the stern."

"Well, keep doing it! Now at least I can walk straight."

So we go all the way across like some strange pack train, Marypat leading from behind, carrying her pack. Without her steadying grip I am completely helpless. She steers me this way and that to avoid wet ground, rough rocks. Only the strongest gusts force us sideways. We move slowly, carefully, but eventually make it. By the time we have everything over the winds are stronger than ever.

Paddling, even with some helping current, is dangerous and exhausting, so we pull in for lunch not half a mile along. There we sit all day, our canoe packed and ready, while the sun circles and the winds rip past. We nap, nibble at lunch, play cribbage. I find a disgusting pile of used toilet paper on the ground.

"I hear a boat," Marypat says.

Wind brings us the sound of an engine for some time before we see the aluminum craft coming around a corner. When they spot us, they turn in to shore and half a dozen Inuit come piling over the side.

They are friendly and animated. We shake hands all round, and they sit comfortably on their haunches while we pass the usual information back and forth. Where are you from? How long have you been out? How's the weather been? Have you seen caribou? They don't comment on Marypat's gravid state.

Their clothes are stained with blood, covered with caribou hair. The deer they killed are just downstream, butchered and ready to be carried home. There is an air of energy in the group, that adrenaline that comes from killing things. It is an ancient joy for the Inuit, to hunt the deer, and to have meat laid up.

"What's it like?" Marypat asks when I get out of the tent the next morning.

"Yesterday the wind was damned strong. Today it's just pretty damned strong. I think we should give it a try."

Once we gain the main river channel, the current helps us combat the flow of air. The Kazan is on its final descent, all of its massive volume rushing to the end of the journey, and we ride it swiftly. The day turns warm, then scorching hot.

Along a side channel a pair of sandhill cranes display together. They ignore us as we quietly come to shore a few feet away. The birds spread their huge wings like sails, hunch over and stalk each other, their snakelike necks held in a deep bend. One stands tall on its long legs, red patch brilliant on its head, and spreads its wings in a posture of crucifixion. The birds call to each other in their guttural voices. It is another gift, this vision, another bit of grace we gather and lodge in our memories.

At lunch I dunk my sweaty head in the clear water. Then the Kazan takes us on, and it's as if we couldn't stop ourselves if we wanted to. The river is all jostling muscle in the final fall to Baker Lake, and we give ourselves to it. Rough-legged hawks perch on the jagged banks, huge blocks of ancient rock jut out of the velvet tundra. Another day full of sky and wind and soft empty space.

We camp where there is still current, the very last of it. Baker Lake lies to the north, but we stay, one last night, in the island-strewn delta of the Kazan. Filaments of river find the level of the lake, just eight feet above sea level. Grande Cache, where we put in on the Smoky River, sits 3,500 feet above the sea. We have not only paddled across the continent, not only spent more than a year in the wilds, but have fallen nearly three-quarters of a mile.

"It must be nearly one hundred degrees," I guess.

It is too hot even for bugs, so we lounge away the afternoon stark naked, taking dips in the ice water to cool off. Marypat is rotund, a healthy and potent cherub.

"The paddle hits my belly on every stroke, now," she says, looking at herself. "Much longer and I'd be really uncomfortable."

"You're awfully relaxed about finishing up," I remark. "I've never seen you so calm near the end."

"That's because it's not over," she says. "It won't be over till

the baby is born. And I've been thinking about making a plec_
to this river," she goes on. "I want Kazan for the baby's middl_
name, boy or girl."

"It's perfect," I agree.

We offer the last of the dried caribou meat to the last of the
river. Neither of us says anything. Instead we silently make
our pledges. I say some kind of goodbye to the wide land, a
thanks for our crossing, and, also, bury the pain we bore with
us at the start.

The last two days bring wind and calm, tremendous shimmering
heat, a wicked thunderstorm. But we paddle at a remove from it
all, as though we've hit the highway after a backcountry vacation. Trash and wooden shacks and gas barrels litter the shore.
The town of Baker Lake is visible on the horizon, fifteen miles
away. The drone of powerboats and distant roar of airplanes
hangs in the air.

Some trips end with fanfare and celebration, a glorious cre-
scendo, paddles flashing in the sun. Ours ends with a mile of
dragging our boat over sandbars to reach the airport. We haul
the canoe by its ropes, shoes off, pants rolled up, feet numb.
Marypat stops repeatedly to rest. If anyone notices us, they give
no sign. No one comes out. No one waves.

We land among discarded buoys, bits of plastic rope, pop
cans. We step out, like passing through a doorway. And when
we start toward the airport building, toward our other life,
Marypat takes my hand and holds it all the way there.

Epilogue

All day we have stayed close to each other. Marypat has been cramping off and on since early morning, leaking amniotic fluid. It is October 25, our due date, and the baby is stirring right on time. We stroll to a friend's house to share breakfast and the news. Marypat takes a driver's test to renew the licence that lapsed while we were gone.

I feel apart from this, as I have all along. Already Marypat is vaguely withdrawn, tuned to things only she can feel. I can see her collecting herself, gathering endurance, becoming solitary.

It is late at night before the cramping intensifies and grows more frequent. Our friend Ursula joins us. Marypat's sister, Nancy, comes over to help. Vicky, our midwife, arrives with her kit and a bottle of oxygen, sets up in the bedroom.

Hours drag on. Marypat moans quietly, rocking herself with each contraction. She lies on her back, then her side, spends much of the time on her knees. Vicky is quiet and composed, doesn't intrude unnecessarily. The rest of us do what we can to comfort Marypat and grow increasingly sleepy.

"Her body is in good tone," Vicky says. "It just takes time to stretch those muscles."

Outside it is cold. Snow begins to fall. For a moment I slip a year in time, back to the little cabin on Otherside Bay. The stillness of that wild place is vivid again, almost heart-stopping. But the distant noises of town intrude – passing cars, a siren, the hum of a populated place. Here we are with the people we missed. We have electric lights, plenty of space, can warm the room with a turn of the thermostat. The only thing unchanged is my sense of being on the edge of unknown territory, uncharted terrain.

Marypat's labour is slow. After hours of contractions she has dilated only a centimetre or two. Nancy goes home to her family for a few hours. The rest of us take turns to nap, listen for any change. I lie down but can't sleep. Very late at night Marypat gets up and takes a shower, brews a pot of coffee, walks around to get things moving. Still nothing happens.

When there is finally movement a problem develops. The baby's head is caught against a band of cervical tissue and can't get past. With every contraction Marypat cries out, moaning and writhing. There is nothing we can do to help her. She is far away, walled off inside this pain. Vicky tries to slip the band over the baby's head with her finger when Marypat pushes, and the moans escalate.

"I can't do this!" she gasps.

But she does, she has no choice. Vicky keeps working calmly, until the head is past and Marypat sinks back in exhausted relief.

Still, it is a long time coming. Marypat actually dozes between contractions. Once or twice she vomits weakly. The head inches down the birth canal. I keep asking Vicky to check the heartbeat. That steady, fast gush of life comes over the monitor.

"Sounds good," Vicky keeps saying. "Really steady."

All I can think of is claustrophobia. This little life clamped in a vise of flesh, hour after hour, squeezed and pushed, making the slow transition from a life in water, in darkness, with muffled sounds, to our bright, noisy, airy world. But the beating pulse is unvaried, calming.

Then the crown of the head is just visible, a tiny patch of hair. By now Marypat is on her feet, draped over the bed. With each contraction she pulls hard against Nancy and Ursula, who grip her arms from the far side. Vicky and an assistant crouch beneath her with warm compresses, coaching her to push. I help where I can, catch glimpses of the head, coming so slowly.

"Next time I want you to really push," Vicky says.

Almost immediately a contraction starts. Marypat's legs are shaking. Ursula and Nancy can hardly keep themselves from being hauled across the bed. But the head is finally there, really coming.

We help Marypat onto her back, cushion her with pillows. Vicky takes Marypat's hand and has her feel the head, connect with the life she has carried all these months, the baby she talked to across the tundra miles, who has already been rocked on the waves of northern waters.

"Now just breathe it out," Vicky says. "Slowly ease it out with each contraction."

She is busy massaging, trying to keep Marypat from tearing as this impossibly large head passes out.

Suddenly it is there. A human head. Slippery, with wetted hair, a vein pulsing under the skin. Vicky checks expertly for the cord, cleans off some mucus. All is well. She looks at me inquiringly, and I come over.

Then this tiny, warm, slippery head that is my child is in my hand, fits easily in my palm.

"Support the head," Vicky tells me. "The next contraction will do it."

And it does. The baby slithers abruptly into my hands, an entire human, whole and warm with life.

"I'm done!" Marypat sighs, and falls back.

Quickly the baby is wrapped in a towel, placed on Marypat's chest. There is quiet bedlam in the room – crying, garbled words, emotion like something we can swim in. It is some minutes before we even think to check the sex. I unwrap the towel to see.

"It's a boy, Marypat."

He hardly cries. A short wail is all, then he's unbelievably content. His eyes are open, calm and deep blue. His complexion is clear, unblemished, almost unwrinkled. He seems, after this extraordinary transition, completely ready, profoundly centred.

And Marypat is suddenly vibrant. Tired but vibrant. The baby is already nursing. His blue eyes are locked on his mother's blue eyes, twelve inches away, and they watch each other, steady and sober.

"Welcome to the world, my child of the North," she whispers.

Acknowledgements

Our expedition, and this rendering of it, are not simply our accomplishments alone. They are also the products of a small, co-operative society.

Our scattered northern friends have made what is an isolated and remote corner of human civilization feel like a second home. More than that, our stay would not have been possible without their support and assistance. Cliff and Stella, Ed and Margy, Brian and Jackie, Blaine, Darcy and Lezlie, Philip, Joe, Scott, Eli and Angela, and all the rest. Nurses, police officers, store managers, camp owners, pilots, full-time residents . . . friends.

Several sponsors provided the equipment we used for transport and shelter, and to carry our gear, cook our food, and keep ourselves warm over the full cycle of a boreal year. They include American Harvest, Bending Branches, Coleman, Dagger, Dana Design, JLM Visuals, Omega, Rome Industries, Schnee's Boots & Shoes, and Sierra Designs.

Sue Higgins and Scott Gill handled our affairs during the year we played hooky from "normal life." From insurance payments care packages, homemade jerky to bank withdrawals, they never failed us. The rest of our support crew was an informal collection of friends and family who brightened the months with mail, packages, and distant but palpable good will.

Thanks to Matthew and Sandy for the ride north to our put-in, and for the final wave from our life on the "outside"; and to Doug and Fred, for a welcoming retrieval at the other end.

Writing a book is a lonely, arduous, demanding enterprise. Without the encouragement, advice, and working space provided by Marypat, it could never have happened. More than a partner in these adventures, she is my partner for the long haul.

Thanks to Jeanne Hanson, a literary agent with energy, determination, and profound integrity, who never flagged in her efforts. And to Doug Gibson and Alex Schultz at McClelland & Stewart, sympathetic and astute editors who have the good sense to appreciate the unfathomable treasure that is the northern wilderness.